SOAR

The Breakthrough Treatment for Fear of Flying

Captain Tom Bunn, MSW, LCSW

LYONS PRESS
Guilford, Connecticut
An imprint of Rowman & Littlefield

Lyons Press is an imprint of Rowman & Littlefield.

Distributed by NATIONAL BOOK NETWORK

Library of Congress Cataloging-in-Publication Data

Bunn, Tom.
SOAR : the breakthrough treatment for fear of flying / Captain Tom Bunn, LCSW.
    pages cm
1. Fear of flying. 2. Fear of flying—Treatment—Popular works. 3. Relaxation—Study and teaching. I. Title.
RC1090.B86 2013
616.85'225—dc23

                                                    2013015033

ISBN 978-0-7627-8800-2

Printed in the United States of America

The health information expressed in this book is based solely on the personal experience of the author and is not intended as a medical manual. The information should not be used for diagnosis or treatment, or as a substitute for prefessional medical care.

To the many anxious flyers who persevered, doing whatever it took to overcome fear of flying—listening to you and learning from you helped me to develop the methods in this book.

We all encounter turbulence.
Engaging it, we cope.
Embracing it, we rise.
Dancing upon it, we soar!

Contents

Introduction

You are not alone. According to research, one person in three has difficulty flying. And, you are in good company. A lot of very accomplished people, some of them well-known, feel the same way you do about flying: prolific author Isaac Asimov, actress Whoopi Goldberg, comedian Jackie Gleason, former President of the United States Ronald Reagan, film director Stanley Kubrick, hockey star Wayne Gretzky, sportscaster John Madden—the list is long.

Some tried psychotherapy in an effort to overcome this phobia. And while the therapy may have been helpful in many areas of their lives, they found, to their great disappointment, it did not help them conquer their fear of flying. You may have tried this route yourself. Others have attended workshops for fear of flying led by pilots with vast experience in the air. They explain the mechanics of flight. They point out how safe flying is. Though the statistics show the chance of being on a doomed flight is incredibly low, this rarely works. I know, because that approach was tried in the original fear-of-flying course at Pan Am led by my colleague Captain Truman "Slim" Cummings. I worked as a volunteer with his course.

I had joined Pan Am after seven years of flying the first supersonic jet fighter, the F-100, and the F-105 at a United States Air Force base in Germany. I flew DC-8s, 707s, and 747s at Pan Am, and later I flew 727s, 747s, 757s, and 767s at United Airlines. In all, airlines and Air Force together, I spent thirty-eight years in the air.

Recognizing the limitations of the Pan Am course, in 1982 I founded SOAR, Seminars On Aeroanxiety Relief, to find a more effective way to help people overcome the fear of flying. The addition of techniques based on Cognitive Behavioral Therapy was a huge step forward. Though no other program could match our level of success, there were still some clients we could not help. Continuing the search for a way to help everyone fly comfortably and confidently, I earned a master's degree at Fordham University, became licensed as a therapist, and then went on for several years of postgraduate study at the Gestalt Center of Long Island, the New York Training Institute for Neurolinguistic Programming, The Masterson Institute, and seminars on neurological research.

Coupled with years as an airline pilot, this advanced training in psychology gave me a unique perspective on how to help people overcome their fear of flying. Since feelings of anxiety, claustrophobia, and panic develop unconsciously and automatically, any effective solution would also have to work unconsciously and automatically. This took years to find. But, as brain scan technology began to reveal the inner workings of the mind, I was able to find a way to control feelings automatically when flying. Now, almost ten thousand people who were afraid to fly have the whole world open to them! It is a great satisfaction to receive their e-mails and share their joy. Here is an example:

> *I just wanted to write to thank you for the tremendous resource you provide, and to let you know that SOAR helped change my life. I used to cry from anxiety every time I boarded a plane and have nightmares every night for a week before flying. Today I fly 3 to 4 times a week (!!) for business and am an international speaker flying more than I ever thought possible. I would never have had the courage to pursue these opportunities without your course. I want to especially thank you for the free materials you provide online, as I first took your course when I was a starving graduate student making only $1,000 a month. I was not able to afford more expensive counseling, and you really changed my life. Ten years later, I still recommend your content to anxious fliers I meet, and I think of your lessons often when I fly. I just wanted you to know how grateful I am for your service to all of us anxious fliers, and you show so much compassion, wisdom, and kindness in sharing this help with us.*

People all over the world have completed SOAR. There are clients in Australia, New Zealand, Japan, China, Thailand, India, Saudi Arabia, the United Arab Emirates, Poland, Greece, Italy, Germany, Switzerland, France, Brazil, the UK, Canada, and, of course, the United States. Available also in Spanish, SOAR has reached anxious fliers in Spain, Mexico, Argentina, Chile, Peru, and Ecuador, to mention a few countries. And now, for the first time, I am able to offer it to you in book form.

But why is flying such a problem? With the earth firmly beneath our feet, we can approach what attracts us, and withdraw from what unnerves us. If there is real danger, we can run. Mobility means security, both physically and emotionally. Flying takes away our most basic way of regulating feelings.

On the other hand, flight expands our mobility one-hundred fold! Rather than five mph on foot, we can cover five hundred mph when aloft. That's marvelous. But, expanded mobility requires commitment. It necessitates placing our destiny in someone else's hands. It things go wrong, there is no escape. How could we possibly not have concern?

Anxiety begins when faced with making reservations. It increases as the flight approaches. Claustrophobia—the feeling of being trapped—may set in once the plane door closes. Takeoff gives rise to doubts. Is the plane struggling? Will it get off the ground only to fall back? Amazingly, the plane finds its way upward, suspended by some invisible means. As the initial crisis passes, a bigger challenge awaits. Here is how one client expressed it:

> *I could manage the takeoff mostly because it doesn't last that long and I loved the landing because the flight was almost over. It was the time in the air and the turbulence that struck fear and terror in my heart. Even when there was no turbulence, I was afraid that there would be, and that kept me in a high state of terror for the duration of the flight.*

Physically, the safest part of the flight is cruise. Emotionally, it is the riskiest. Being high above the earth defies all reason. A car sits solidly on the road. If there is an accident, it is easy to imagine stepping out and walking away. But flying is different. First, there is no escape. Second, nothing seems to be holding up the plane. It only seems right that with nothing holding it up—nothing that can be seen—the plane should fall. Accidents prove they can; or so the anxious flier thinks while waiting for turbulence to make the plunge happen.

"So many things could go wrong. If anything breaks, the plane will fall like a rock. I have no control. There is no way out." Anxious fliers try to shut out these thoughts by staying occupied. But it also means praying for their only salvation—smooth air—for if turbulence strikes, dreadful thoughts will rush in. "What if the pilot loses control? What if the plane falls out of the sky?" Thoughts of disaster loom larger with each jolt, until finally, all is lost and sheer terror sets in.

Landing accounts for the majority of accidents. But, since the ordeal is almost over, there is little if any distress as the plane nears the ground. This paradox illuminates the psychological nature of this fear. Fear of flying is not just about crashing. It is not just about not being alive. It is about feelings. The anxious flier fears that feelings—far worse than he or she can endure—will arise. And, unable to escape, there will be nothing he or she can do about it. As one client said, "Yes, I know. Flying is a hundred times safer than driving. But if my car crashes, it doesn't fall thirty-thousand feet *first!*"

Those who suffer from this fear wonder how others fly with so little trouble. What is the difference? For an answer, we need to understand the systems that regulate emotion and how their operation differs in the anxious or fearful flier.

The Urge to Escape

Anxiety, fear, claustrophobia, or panic? Take your pick. All of these feelings are caused by high levels of stress hormones. Stress hormones are released when tiny parts of the brain, the amygdalae, sense anything unfamiliar. The hormones activate systems that determine what we feel, and how intensely we feel it. One of the systems, the Mobilization System, responds to stress hormones by producing an urge to escape. However, at the same time, a high-level thinking and decision-making system called Executive Function is activated. If this system is well-developed, it overrides the urge to run, assesses the situation, and, if called for, develops a plan of action. When Executive Function deals with the matter, by dismissing it as irrelevant or by committing to a plan of action, it signals the amygdalae to end the release of stress hormones. The urge to escape disappears.

If it were not for Executive Function, we, like some creatures, would bolt if a stranger were to appear, or if anything unexpected were to happen. Worse, imagination would rule us. Mere imagination that a stranger might appear would cause us to hide. We would speed away from any place where something unexpected *could* happen.

Indeed, there are individuals whose Executive Function is so poorly developed that their regulation is based primarily on mobilization. When a stranger appears or something non-routine takes place, the urge to escape overpowers them. If they cannot escape quickly enough, stress hormones build up and cause panic. In some cases, the very idea that escape might not be instantly available triggers panic. If so, these people may remain home where, by ruling out all possibility of encounters with strangers and situations they do not control, they hope to avoid imagination-based panic. This condition is called agoraphobia.

How Relationships Affect Emotional Regulation

If the release of stress hormones is due to encountering an unfamiliar person, yet another sophisticated system, the Social Engagement System (SES), is activated. According to researcher Stephen Porges,

Ph.D., this system unconsciously reads the person's facial expression, voice, and body language. If the reading indicates the person is trustworthy, this system produces a calming effect.

The Internal Replica System (IRS) serves as a database for the Social Engagement System. It records a person's relationships with others and with the environment, particularly those that took place early in life. When facing a challenge, replicas that represent supportive relationships stabilize the person emotionally. On the other hand, replicas of unsatisfactory relationships destabilize the person. Thus, the Social Engagement System stabilizes or destabilizes a person emotionally based on his or her personal history stored in the Internal Replica System.

For some individuals, this sophisticated system regulates stress hormones automatically, unconsciously, and reliably. At 30,000 feet, fully aware that others are in control and that mobilization is not an option, the person remains regulated and comfortable.

In other persons, automatic unconscious regulation is not well-developed. They rely on Executive Function to consciously control every situation. If unable to control the situation, they may become unable to control their emotions. Knowing control can be lost, they feel secure only when, the Mobilization System, with its immediate escape, is available as a backup.

When flying, Executive Function faces its most daunting challenges during takeoff and in turbulence. Every unfamiliar movement—and every unexpected noise—triggers a release of stress hormones. Each release demands Executive Function's full and undivided attention. With one stress hormone release after another, Executive Function is hard-pressed to keep up. If it is unable to promptly certify that each and every movement and noise is of no concern, stress hormone levels rise. If hormone levels rise too high, Executive Function collapses. It relinquishes control to the Mobilization System; its answer—escape—can't be acted upon. When neither the sophisticated Executive Function nor the primitive

Mobilization System can end the release of stress hormones, claustrophobia, high anxiety, and panic result. How can this be changed? How can emotion be controlled in flight?

The Pivotal Difference — Psychological Development

When flight attendants close the cabin door, the Mobilization System—our inborn way of regulating emotion—is blocked. Can sophisticated systems take over and regulate our emotions when stress hormones are released? Sophisticated systems are not innate. They require development. If their development is not adequate, when the door closes, the passenger feels—and indeed is—out of control. The difference between an anxious flier and a non-anxious flier is the neurological and the psychological development of systems that, if well-developed, regulate emotion automatically and unconsciously.

For the most part, development of these systems takes place—or fails to take place—within the first two years of life when the brain is growing rapidly. A child's neurological wiring is organized not only by its genetics but by its experiences. Full development of the child's emotional regulation systems depends upon interactions that take place between the child and its principal caregivers during that all-important period. In general, the more emotionally available, the more empathic, and the more attuned the caregiver, the more sophisticated the child's emotional regulation systems become. This is a serious matter; the most important studies a child will ever engage in take place during the two-year period of rapid brain growth.

The Internal Replica System

The mental replica of a steady relationship can steady a person emotionally. As the child's brain is developing, the Internal Replica

System needs to establish the most important replica it will ever possess; it records the essence of the child's relationship with its primary caregiver. If properly established, when the caregiver is not physically present, the replica keeps the caregiver psychologically present in the child's mind. In an emotionally secure relationship, the child senses there is a place exclusively reserved for a replica of itself in the caregiver's heart and mind. If so, it is never a case of "out of sight, out of mind." Profoundly valued, the child trusts the caregiver to return.

With adequate development, when facing a challenge, replicas provide emotional stability. Just as a replica of the primary caregiver—usually the mother—keeps her real psychologically when she is absent physically, a replica of Mother Earth keeps the earth real to us when flight removes us from it physically. For the fortunate child, when he or she becomes an adult, there are emotionally stabilizing replicas within. The child who intuitively used replicas of others to maintain psychological contact with them when they were away intuitively uses his replica of the earth for psychological security when in flight as an adult.

If the Internal Replica System is not well-developed, the person must rely on physical connections. When physically disconnected from the earth, it is—emotionally speaking—as if the earth has ceased to exist. This loss of physical connection profoundly undermines the person's ability to regulate his or her feelings in flight.

The Social Engagement System
If well-developed, the Social Engagement System automatically and unconsciously overrides the effect of stress hormones. This system senses the facial expression, body language, and voice quality of a person physically present. If the person is sensed as trustworthy, the Social Engagement System constrains heart rate and provides calming. Integrated with the Internal Replica System, the Social

Engagement System can override the influence of stress hormones based not only on a person's physical presence but also on a person's psychological presence as a replica.

Replicas include characteristic facial expression, body language, and voice quality—the kind of data the Social Engagement System uses when determining how much calming to apply. Depending upon the quality of the relationship it represents, a replica can be a source of emotional stability or of emotional instability. Replicas of emotionally secure relationships can provide the Social Engagement System all it needs to counteract the effect of stress hormones, override the Mobilization System, control the urge to escape, and provide a sense of calm.

The Executive Function System

Well-developed Executive Function has integrated pathways of communication between the conscious mind and the unconscious processes that regulate the release of stress hormones. Integrated development takes place in the first few years of the child's life if its relationship with caregivers is adequately supportive (discussed later in this book).

If not well integrated, Executive Function can regulate anxiety only when the person is in control of the situation. For example, highly competent people—doctors, lawyers, and CEOs—may thrive in stressful occupations. They regulate anxiety exquisitely when they are calling the shots. Yet, they become flooded with anxiety when control and escape become unavailable in the air.

Speaking of control, one of my clients was a New York City undercover cop whose career was so colorful that a television series was based on it. He said he had no fear on the streets, dealing with mobsters, or even in a gunfight, because he knew he was in control. Certainly, I would doubt that the level of control was as great as he felt it was. But, in any case, he could not fly. Without the idea—whether accurate or an illusion—that he was in control, he had no way to control anxiety. He was able to develop internal resources that allowed him to fly comfortably and confidently, as you will when you have completed the program prescribed in this book.

The Objective—Automatic Regulation of Flight Anxiety

If you are an anxious flier, or a non-flier, this book can provide the internal resources necessary to regulate anxiety by automatically regulating the release of stress hormones. The information and techniques offered here will help you to fly as others do. Feelings you have been unable to control consciously can be controlled unconsciously and automatically.

It will not take long. In fact, the shorter—and thus the more focused you are on this project—the better. A week to ten days is ideal. I'll show you step-by-step what you need to do.

Skeptical? Of course. How could you not be if you've tried everything without any success? Most of the people I have worked with had tried other things and failed. They believed, at least in their case, that nothing would work. Fortunately, since this isn't faith healing, it works whether you believe or not! So give it a whirl. Whether you want to help yourself, or you're a therapist trying to help a client, you will find here the tools needed to effectively treat flight phobia.

Motivation? I wish I could offer you motivation like Fred Melamed, an announcer for CBS Sports, was given. For twenty-five years, he didn't set foot on an airplane. But the opportunity to work at the 1998 Winter Olympics in Nagano, Japan, was too good to miss. "I had to do it," he said. "It was like a million dollars in a bag—I just had to pick it up." After SOAR, he made the thirteen-hour flight to Tokyo. He later flew to London and Paris. When the *Wall Street Journal* asked us to find someone to interview whose fear of flying had impacted their career, he bravely volunteered, and thus we can mention his name. As you continue, you will read quotes from other clients; their names, however, are withheld or changed to protect their privacy. Recently, I received this wonderful letter from Fred, who is not only doing well with flying, but has had great success as an actor.

I don't know if you remember me or not, but I took the SOAR program in late 1997 in order to fly to Japan to work as the Voice of CBS's coverage of the 1998 Olympic Winter Games. I was interviewed in an article in the Wall Street Journal *about the effect the course had on me, which was profound. My fear was so daunting that I had avoided flying entirely for over twenty years at the time I took the course in preparation for the non-stop flight to Tokyo. Since that time, I have not only thrived as a voice actor, but I have also had a resurgence in my career as a regular actor as well, having appeared in several Oscar-nominated films and many television programs. Since I took the course, I must have flown over a hundred times, and I can honestly say that in the majority of cases, I actually enjoy the experience. My work requires fairly frequent travel to locations or California (last year I flew to the Canary Islands off the coast of Africa for a Sacha Baron Cohen film called* The Dictator*), and none of this would have been possible if I had not started flying again. I am writing just to let you know about what has happened to me, and to express my gratitude once again.*

I could say that motivation is up to you. But since motivation can be suppressed by believing you cannot succeed, I need you to understand that, regardless of what has happened in the past and regardless of what you have tried, advances have been made that can allow you to fly comfortably and confidently. The problem is no longer how to successfully treat flight phobia. The problem is proving to those who doubt that the tools needed for success have been developed. They are here.

PART ONE:

PSYCHOLOGY

CHAPTER 1

The Breakthrough in Flight Phobia Treatment

I've tried everything. I've read two books. I went to a therapist. I tried hypnosis. My doctor said drugs would help, but they don't. I know these things work for other people. But they don't work for me.

Doubt seems to be an integral part of flight phobia. If you've tried to deal with fear of flying and not been successful, you didn't fail. Inadequate methods failed you! For example, fearful fliers are given statistics about the safety of air travel. Statistics don't help. They zero your thoughts in on flights that became statistics. Friends say, "Just keep it out of your mind." But how?

Pilots believe you just need to understand how safe flying is. They offer courses, sometimes with the help of a psychologist who offers relaxation exercises. The combination is far from satisfactory. When pilots say flying is safe, they mean accidents are rare. It doesn't matter how many millions of flights arrive safely. Planes do crash. That is a fact, and the anxious flier has no guarantee that his or her flight is not going to be the rare one that crashes. Though they work well on the ground, relaxation exercises produce no reduction of anxiety in the air.

Courses typically measure their success rate by the percentage of participants who take the graduation flight. But since most people who take these courses can fly, but do so with great difficulty, a 90 or 95 percent "success rate" means very little. What is telling is the number of course participants who are able to fly six months later: It is almost the same as the number who could fly before taking the course.

For example, Harold, a fifty-seven-year-old architect had not flown in the twenty-three years since he took the "graduation flight" of a course given by an airline:

> *They basically taught me how to relax, explained the mechanics of flying, and tried to desensitize me to being in an aircraft. I took the several-week course and made the graduation flight, but that was it. I really didn't learn any skills to deal with my fear of flying afterwards. After this, many years passed without attempting to fly.*
>
> *My recent motivation to fly again was one of my sons was doing what I had done in college; he was studying architecture in Florence, Italy. My wife—an avid flier—planned to visit him with or without me. I desperately wanted to make this trip happen.*
>
> *I bought the SOAR program and started watching the videos and practicing the Strengthening Exercise. I bought refundable tickets and scheduled a short flight with my wife. I made the decision to go to the airport. I would decide at the airport whether or not to fly.*
>
> *The airport was very quiet on a Saturday morning. We went through security and got to the boarding gate. I froze. I was devastated. Though I had done what I committed to—to go to the boarding gate and then decide—I was furious with myself that I had not taken the flight. Anger turned into commitment. I went home and was determined to fly on the following Monday no matter what. I went to the airport by myself and boarded a Southwest flight to Baltimore-Washington. I gave my SOAR letter of introduction to the flight attendant*

and he introduced me to the captain. The airline was great and I had my first flight on an airliner in twenty-three years.

Now I needed to prepare for my flight to Europe. I was extremely concerned about the flight overseas, first to Paris, and then on to Florence. I discussed my apprehension about such a long flight with Captain Tom. He said that most people prefer longer flights because after the initial maneuvering, you have a chance to relax while cruising. He said to bring a lot of things to do, and not to depend solely on the airline for entertainment. I continued with my Strengthening Exercises.

I was able to meet the pilots; they were fantastic. Meeting the pilots makes a world of difference. Whenever I heard a noise, I could picture their faces knowing what it was, and doing what they needed to do about it. To make a long story short, the flights went well and we had a great trip and visit with my son.

In order to be successful in any aspect of your life you need to be fully committed and be willing to work hard to achieve your goals. The key is to work hard in the right direction. Captain Tom and SOAR gave me that direction. It was nice to know that I am not so different than everyone else.

Fear of flying courses, like the one this architect took, were introduced at Pan Am and US Airways around 1975. They were helpful only if a person's flight difficulties were mild. I worked as a volunteer on the course at Pan Am. It disturbed me that many on the "graduation flight"—though they were using the techniques we had taught them—suffered massive anxiety or panic. Information about safety was not enough. Relaxation exercises did not work.

For every person these well-intended courses have helped, another person has been left feeling that they are very different and terribly flawed. The course that failed Harold impacted his life for twenty-three years. Such a failure—through no fault of his own—can affect a person for the rest of his life.

When I established SOAR, no one had broken the code on how to treat flight phobia. I thought that by being both an airline captain and a licensed therapist, perhaps with enough study, I might be able to do it. Through work with thousands of clients, and by studying how the mind works, I found a way to control high anxiety, claustrophobia, and panic by inhibiting the release of stress hormones. At this point, SOAR is more than a fear-of-flying course. It is the most advanced method of treating flight phobia.

Some cases are like others. Some are unique. Some clients had not flown for more than thirty years. A few had a complete breakdown and were helped off the plane. Out of ten thousand clients, I can count on one hand those who were in a crash of some kind. Usually it was a private plane, because airline crashes are very rare. I have worked with clients who believed they were on flights that were life-threatening. When we examine the evidence, the risk—if any—was minor, or was dealt with effectively by the flight crew members. I have worked with clients who were in the World Trade Center when it was attacked on 9/11. All these clients are flying successfully.

These examples do not begin to exhaust the reasons why, but most clients believe their situation is unique and thus untreatable. As unique or as impossible as you may believe your case to be, I probably have worked successfully with precisely what you believe cannot be fixed. At this point, I have to go back many years to find a client who I was not able to help. Therefore, I believe what you find in this book will help you, too. Every day, there are e-mails like this one:

We are back from our trip to Australia, about as far as one can fly from Illinois! Besides having the time of our lives, the good news is that my husband has declared me CURED from my phobia.

Not once did I medicate (except a Lunesta to sleep . . . nothing for anxiety). Nor did I sob or grip the armrests. In the past, I would remain "frozen" and keep my mind focused on "keeping the plane up." So, of course I couldn't carry on a conversation, read, watch the movie, or even eat. This trip, I did all those things! In addition to the preparatory exercises, I did two things that were very helpful. I put a glass half filled with water on my tray and observed it during turbulence—the water moved not at all! And on channel 9, I could listen to the talk in the cockpit, and heard only routine, procedural stuff. Both were very reassuring. So, I got my money's worth from your program. Count me a very satisfied client.

As you read through this book, I will lead you through the steps you need to take to overcome fear of flying. Having received reports like the one above from literally thousands of clients, I'm sure that SOAR can help anyone and everyone be far more comfortable in flight.

CHAPTER 2

Ending Your Fear of Flying

I have to say SOAR has done a lot for me and has gotten me on planes, reduced my anticipatory anxiety, and improved my life—thank you! I now look to plan vacations all over the place regardless of flight time, etc. Looking back, I realize that one of the things that keeps me flying is the pride I get from making that choice to go to the airport and get on that plane. At first it was for others—my family or those I was traveling with—but I notice lately it is now primarily for me. I know that this upcoming trip will just be another success for which I can be proud. I have found the SOAR program helpful in other areas of my life. My therapist thinks the program is brilliant.

Overall, there are two things you need. One is intellectual and one is emotional. Intellectually, you need to be satisfied that flying—though not absolutely safe—is safe enough to do. Airline pilots do their job day in and day out. They are neither foolish nor fearless. You never see pilots leaving the job due to concerns about safety. To become as confident as pilots are about safety, you need to become a mini-expert in how flying works. You will learn about the various systems needed for flight, and how they are checked and rechecked. You will know that if a system fails during the flight, the plane switches automatically to a second system. If the second system doesn't work properly, the pilots switch to one of the backup systems. And, if that backup system doesn't solve the problem, they can switch to another backup system, or if necessary, to an emergency backup system. Pilots know the score. They feel more secure in the air than on the ground. Why? Because, in the air, they have more control than on the ground. The greater the control, the greater the safety. The greater your knowledge of the "ins and outs," the greater your feeling of safety.

When driving, you feel secure because your most basic system of emotional control—the Mobilization System—seems available as a backup. If you crash your car, you can imagine stepping out of it onto the ground. Though everyone knows some crashes are more serious, being able to imagine stepping out of the car is helpful in controlling anxiety. On the other hand, whether it is an elevator or a plane, the thought of one's exit being blocked causes distress. Though there is no *physical* exit during flight, there is an *engineering* exit. For every device needed for flight, there is a backup device. These backup devices are just as physical as the earth is. Though you can't step out onto these devices like you can step out onto the earth, pilots know they can "step" from the device they have been using to a duplicate device that has been just sitting there waiting to be used. The idea of stepping from an incapacitated device to a second, or a third, or a fourth one needs to become as real to your Mobilization System as stepping from an incapacitated car onto the earth. As you come to appreciate the control the pilots have, you will be satisfied intellectually about your safety.

But, what about emotional safety? Fear, anxiety, claustrophobia, and panic are caused by excessive stress hormones released by two small clusters of brain cells. Each is the size and shape of an almond. Thus they are called, after the Greek word for almond, the amygdalae. The amygdalae have an important job to do. I think of them as having a job similar to that of the smoke alarm in your house. When your smoke alarm detects particles in the air, it attracts your attention by making a loud noise. When the amygdalae sense anything non-routine, they attract your attention by releasing stress hormones.

If you were a flight crew member, your amygdalae would regard the noises and motions of flight as routine. But as a passenger, your amygdalae regard them as non-routine; they respond with a release of stress hormones. During takeoff and turbulence, a series of noises and motions can cause one release of stress hormones after another. Stress hormones can build up. When they do, they cause high anxiety or panic. To control these feelings, we will train the amygdalae to limit the release of stress hormones when flying. Later, I will teach you, step-by-step, how to train the amygdalae. The procedure you will use to train the amygdalae is called the Strengthening Exercise. In two or three sessions, each lasting twenty to thirty minutes, the Strengthening Exercise will establish links to automatically regulate the release of stress hormones so you are protected from high anxiety and panic when you fly. The Strengthening Exercise is mentioned in the following e-mail, one that illustrates what you can look forward to. The e-mail also mentions an exercise I will teach you in the next chapter, the 5-4-3-2-1 Exercise:

I did it. I flew by myself without anxiety. It is unbelievable to me and I am still in shock. I have been terrified of flying for many years. I have flown before, but not without terror and I have avoided flying whenever possible. I have tried everything—hypnosis, alcohol, and tranquilizers. Nothing worked to alleviate the terror.

I was skeptical of the SOAR program. How could this possibly work? But, I took a leap of faith. I dutifully did the Strengthening Exercises over and over. That's where SOAR separates itself from the rest of the programs out there. The Strengthening Exercises are the key.

On the day of the flight, I had some anxiety, very little compared to my usual. The plane was late and then they announced we would have to wait for a while because there were mechanical issues with the plane. I began to go into my old way of thinking, that this was an omen that I shouldn't get on the plane, that the mechanical issues were going to make the plane crash. Then I thought, the mechanical issues could be something as simple as a burned-out lightbulb or a toilet that had overflowed. I did the 5-4-3-2-1 Exercise and stopped the "fake" movie in my head. I separated reality from fiction and, miracle of miracles, my stomach stopped hurting and I was able to immediately calm myself.

During the flight, I was calm. When the pilot said we were cleared for landing, I was calm. When I felt the plane not land, but head up again, I was calm. When the captain came on and said the winds had changed and he had to come around at another angle, I was calm. I can't even believe I am writing these words. I was calm.

When I bought the SOAR program, I only wanted to be able to get on the plane and fly without terror. But, it has given me so much more than I could have ever expected. I actually look forward to my next flight and when I look up at the sky and see a plane flying, I get excited that the whole world is now open to me.

Twin Fears

Two fears are likely to arise. One is that you will fail. To try one's best and still fail is devastating. The other fear is that you will succeed. That may seem strange, but if fear keeps you from flying, you may think fear is protecting you, keeping you from doing something you shouldn't do.

Life assigns us certain jobs. It might appear that our task is to avoid all risk. If that seems reasonable, take another look. It is not life, but an overprotective parent that assigned such an impossible task. Life cannot be lived without risk. Everything we do—and everything we don't do—involves risk. If we exercise, we risk injury.

If we don't exercise, we risk heart disease. The task life assigns us is not to avoid all risk but to balance risk and reward. Travel can be rewarding. Flying is one of the safest things you can do. As you become a mini-expert in how flying works, you will know why.

If You Have Never Flown, or Haven't Flown in Years

I just wanted to say "Thank you!" This past weekend I flew for the first time in thirty-nine years. I was somewhat nervous on my first flight from New York to St. Louis, mostly with anticipatory anxiety. But, you're right. Once I was on the plane I was really fine. I couldn't believe that I didn't think about the trip back even once while I was away.

Since stress hormones are released by what is non-routine, it should be no surprise that stress hormones are released when facing the unknown. In medieval times, it was common practice for cartographers to draw sea serpents on maps in areas that had not been explored. Stepping into the unknown can make your first post-SOAR flight difficult. Subsequent flights are a breeze. The e-mail quoted above continues:

Getting on the plane to come back to New York was no problem at all. I actually thought I was beyond help and would never be able to get on a plane, but now I can't wait to make plans for another trip. Unbelievable! Thank you again.

The Schedule for Ending Your Fear of Flying

The process of ending your fear of flying needs to be under your control. My recommendation is that you complete the project in a week to ten days, enough time to finish this book and to do the exercise that establishes automatic control. If you complete the process quickly, you reduce the risk that you will set it aside thinking, "Maybe I should wait until I have to fly." Not a good idea. Finish as far ahead of flying as possible, so as to minimize anticipatory anxiety.

Preparation is everything. What you do ahead of the flight protects you automatically during the flight. There is nothing you need to do on the flight itself. Preparation will train your amygdalae—the part of the brain responsible for releasing stress hormones—to disregard the noises and movements of the plane. Once the amygdalae have been trained, you will be able to fly as others do.

There are only two things you need to do: Finish the book to take care of the intellectual part of the process, and complete the Strengthening Exercise to take care of the emotional part of the process. Though some readers might like to have every step of this process spelled out, detailed instructions can feed a person's perfectionism. In this endeavor, it's not necessary to do things perfectly to reach success. As to the Strengthening Exercise, two or three times is enough. If you want to do it more, that's fine. If several weeks pass between your Strengthening Exercise practice and a flight, do the exercise once or twice shortly before your flight as a refresher.

You will feel anxiety as you prepare. Anxiety does not mean you are not doing the exercise correctly. You will feel some anxiety when you have completed your preparation. Anxiety does not mean you are not adequately prepared. In both cases, anxiety is the result of the amygdalae doing their job. They produce stress hormones whenever you do something non-routine, or even imagine doing something non-routine. Preparation is a process. It is important for you to be in control; do not allow anxiety during the process to control you. Do not let anxiety prevent you from completing the preparation.

Everyone seems to think that SOAR might work for others, but it won't work for them. Expect to think that. Expect anxiety as you think forward to taking a flight. Doubts may persist until you have completed a few flights, enough to be convinced that the automatic control will work every time.

We can control stress hormones during flight once we have trained the amygdalae. But we can't control anxiety on the ground while you are training your amygdalae. As you do your training, if you feel anxiety, immediately use the 5-4-3-2-1 Exercise in the next chapter. Why? Once stress hormones are released, they force you to focus on whatever triggered their release. That focus causes . . . guess what? More stress hormones. It's a vicious cycle. Use the 5-4-3-2-1 to break the cycle. As the stress hormones burn off, you will regain the ability to focus your mind as you wish. Use this window of opportunity wisely. Don't return to the thoughts that caused anxiety in the first place. As you finish the 5-4-3-2-1, plan ahead. Find something better to occupy your mind.

CHAPTER 3

Manual Regulation—The 5-4-3-2-1 Exercise

Our objective is to control feelings automatically when you fly. But in aviation, for every automatic system, we have a manual backup. For feelings, your manual backup is the 5-4-3-2-1 Exercise.

Stress hormones can unbalance your thinking and control your focus. The 5-4-3-2-1 Exercise is nothing more than an exercise to fully occupy your mind so that, as hormones caused by disturbing thoughts are being burned off, they are not replaced. After a minute or two of the exercise, you will again be able to focus your thoughts as you choose. Don't let yourself return to thoughts that trigger anxiety. As you are finishing the exercise, find something useful or pleasurable to do.

Doing the Exercise

To complete the exercise, simply follow these steps:

- Sit or recline comfortably.
- Focus on some physical object in front of you.
- Keep your focus on the object throughout the exercise.

If your eyes drift off, just bring them back. Do the exercise out loud the first time. Then try it silently. See which works better for you.

- Say "I see" and name something in your peripheral vision.
- Say "I see" and name something else in your peripheral vision.

Continue until you have made five statements. For example: "I see the lamp, I see the table, I see a spot on the lamp shade, I see a book on the table, I see a picture on the table." Continue focusing on the object in front of you, and switch to hearing.

- Say, "I hear" and name something you hear.
- Say, "I hear" and name something else you hear.

Continue until you have made five statements. Note: It's okay to repeat something if there are not five different things you hear. For example: "I hear the clock ticking, I hear the refrigerator, I hear a dog barking, I hear a car, I hear the clock ticking." Continue focusing on the object in front of you, and switch to statements about physical contact.

- Say, "I feel" and name something you feel.
- Say, "I feel" and name something else you feel.

Continue until you have made five statements. Note: The focus is on external objects in physical contact, not internal feelings such as heartbeat or tension in the body. For example, say, "I feel the chair under me, I feel my arm against my leg, I feel the breeze from the ceiling fan," and so on.

That completes one cycle. The exercise requires intense concentration. As you concentrate on non-threatening things, stress hormones are used up without being replaced.

What about the next cycle? If you continued the exercise in exactly the same way, you soon could do it without intense concentration. Unwanted thoughts might be able to get a foothold. To keep concentration intense, make one change. Instead of five statements, make four statements. Then, in the next cycle, make three statements. Next, make two statements. Then, in the last cycle, make one statement.

Remember the order of each cycle: seeing, hearing, and feeling. Keeping track of the order and the count is part of the concentration required. If you lose count, or can't remember what comes next, that's a good sign because it means you're getting relaxed. When you are as relaxed as you want to be, stop. If you want to become more relaxed—or to fall asleep—start again with five repetitions. This strategy needs to become so automatic that it comes to mind and is used at the first sign of anticipatory anxiety. To help it become automatic, overuse it to begin with by doing it every few minutes, whether you need it or not.

When to Use the 5-4-3-2-1 Exercise

First, use the 5-4-3-2-1 Exercise as a backup, as mentioned above. Second, use it to combat anticipatory anxiety. Start by using it every fifteen minutes for an hour. Then, use it every thirty minutes for an hour. Next, use it once an hour for the remainder of the day. This will prove to you that you have absolute control over anticipatory anxiety, provided you do the necessary work. It will also help you remember to use it when anxiety arises.

This exercise should also be used in the days and weeks prior to your flight. It is vitally important to avoid repeated imagination of a crash, or of a panic attack. Be vigilant. As soon as you notice imagination of disaster, immediately use the 5-4-3-2-1 Exercise. Use it to regain your ability to focus your mind as you choose.

CHAPTER 4
Automatic Regulation—Its Discovery

In 1982, SOAR introduced flight-anxiety control strategies based on Cognitive Behavioral Therapy (CBT). CBT employs high-level thinking—called Executive Function—to replace impressions that produce anxiety with well-examined thoughts. Some clients were helped by these techniques, but there were two major limitations. First, some anxiety-producing thoughts (being up high, not in control, and no means of escape) are factual. Second, high levels of stress hormones caused by a rapid series of noises or motions can overwhelm the high-level thinking CBT depends upon. For example, during takeoff, there is one unfamiliar noise after another. In turbulence, there is one unexpected movement after another. Each noise and each motion triggers a release of stress hormones. Executive Function, hard-pressed to keep up, may be unable to prevent its own collapse. As a result, the CBT-based techniques failed some clients just when they needed them most.

For CBT-based techniques to remain viable during takeoff and when in turbulence, cognitive processes must be protected from stress hormone overload. What can prevent stress hormone release?

Systematic Desensitization

Systematic Desensitization trains the amygdalae to become accustomed to a situation they react to as non-routine. Treatment begins with exposure too mild to trigger a reaction. As treatment continues, the exposure is progressively increased, but so slightly that the amygdalae do not notice the difference. Finally, if treatment is successful, full exposure does not trigger an amygdalae response.

Though Systematic Desensitization can train the amygdalae to regard some situations as routine, it is not a practical treatment for flight phobia. A phobic flier could be exposed to slowly increased periods of time on a parked airliner, then to slowly increased periods of time of taxiing on the ground. The problem is that at some point, the next incremental increase in exposure would require a takeoff, a few seconds in the air, and a landing. This increase in exposure would be too great for the amygdalae to ignore and would ruin the treatment. Practicality aside, months of incrementally increased exposure to an airliner would be prohibitively expensive.

Simulated Flight

Exposure to simulated flight, using computer-generated images, is easily adjusted. Since the images are unmistakably artificial, and since exposure takes place in an office, there is no desensitization to the aspects of flight that anxious fliers find challenging: the risk of disaster, the loss of control, and the inability to escape. Despite elaborate claims of success, anxious fliers exposed to simulated flight were— according to research—no better able to fly than those exposed to a parked airliner. A number of SOAR clients had previously tried simulated flight and found it both expensive and unhelpful:

I just have to write and say thank you again for helping me to enjoy flying. It's been two years since I took your course and I haven't stopped flying. Just returned from a cross-country flight from Atlanta to San Francisco. I now can say I do enjoy it. I've even had some people say that I must have not really had a fear. Ha! I had gone twenty-five years without flying. Really became fearful when I was in college. It grew progressively worse and I just stopped. I went through Virtual Reality Exposure Therapy here in Georgia. Very expensive and did nothing for my fear. I then decided that I was going to do SOAR and just try it. I have to say I didn't think it would work. How could something that didn't cost a lot, not face-to-face with someone, work? But it did. I now look at flying as my time. It's a time when I can't get a phone call or do anything else. I've enjoyed using this time to catch up on my reading and to get excited about the places I am going!

Thought Stopping

Phobia therapist Jerilyn Ross promoted a technique called "thought stopping." Clients were instructed to wear a rubber band on their wrist, and upon first awareness of an anxiety-producing thought, to snap the rubber band. By being associated with pain, it was believed troublesome thoughts would be inhibited. This method helped some clients control thoughts that led to anticipatory anxiety, but the rubber band technique did not reduce anxiety *during* flight.

Relaxation Exercises

Similarly, relaxation exercises may reduce anxiety on the days leading up to a flight, but not anxiety during the flight. Though a relaxed state can reduce anxiety-producing thoughts, relaxation cannot keep the amygdalae from performing their duty. The amygdalae have a job to do. They protect us by alerting us to anything that is non-routine. Whether the person is relaxed or not, the amygdalae will release stress hormones whenever they sense anything non-routine.

The Breakthrough—Systematic Inhibition

Finally, a breakthrough occurred. An attempt was made to reduce stress hormone release by redirecting anxiety-producing thoughts. The plan was to establish a habit pattern that would draw the mind from anxiety-producing thoughts toward recall of a powerful positive memory. The first experiment was with a marathon runner. She was asked to first imagine a flight scene and then quickly focus on her marathon experience. This was repeated with one flight image after another. After she reported reduced in-flight anxiety, thought redirection was tried with other clients.

The results were widely varied. Surprisingly, effectiveness depended on the type—not on the intensity—of the experience toward which thoughts were redirected. An equestrian who linked images of flight to competitive riding received no relief at all. Clients who chose sunning at a beach, peaceful moments of solitude, religious experiences, or meditation reported only slight improvement.

But a father who linked flying to the face of his son running toward him when returning home from work reported complete relief from anxiety when flying. The same was true for another man who imagined the face of his bride coming down the aisle. Another client used her loved one's face at the moment they became engaged; it was profoundly effective. Time after time, when the face of a loved one was comprehensively linked to flight, clients reported in-flight anxiety as greatly reduced or eliminated, and no panic at all.

When a client decided to link flying to the memory of nursing her newborn child, I was concerned that the association might cause her to think, while aloft, that she might never see her child again. One by one, she linked various moments of flight, imagined as photographs in a magazine, to a memory of nursing her child. To my surprise, she reported complete freedom from anxiety on her flight. Because of her success, I started encouraging women who had nursed a child to link moments of flight to that memory. Time after time, women who linked flight to nursing gained complete relief. What could explain the protection provided by these links?

The Role of Oxytocin

It has been known for some time that the level of the hormone oxytocin is exceptionally high when a mother nurses an infant. Research by Kerstin Uvnäs-Moberg and Carol Sue Carter has helped us understand the anti-anxiety benefits of this hormone. Oxytocin, they found, plays a central role in the action of the parasympathetic nervous system, which Uvnäs-Moberg calls the "calm and connection system." According to their research, the release of oxytocin inhibits the amygdalae, "conveying the sense that there is less to be afraid of." It has been shown that when women are nursing, their blood pressure decreases and the level of the stress hormone cortisol in the blood drops.

Oxytocin is also produced during romantic moments, sexual foreplay, marriage proposals, and wedding vows. In such moments, the release of oxytocin inhibits the amygdalae, and prevents it from releasing stress hormones. In the absence of stress hormones, the Mobilization System produces no urge to escape.

Empathic Attunement—Connecting with a Loved One

In addition to reproduction-related situations that produce the anti-anxiety hormone oxytocin, calming can also be provided in a non-hormonal way. According to researcher Stephen Porges, the Social Engagement System responds to moments of empathic attunement with a neurological action that lowers the heart rate. This lowering of the heart rate produces a calming effect throughout the parasympathetic nervous system.

The success of the clients who have linked flight to a profound face-to-face moment has made it clear that something more than thought redirection is at work. Now, experience with thousands of SOAR clients has proven that linking challenging moments of flight to the memory of a beloved face can moderate or eliminate flight anxiety, claustrophobia, and panic. Once appropriate links have been established, the face of a loved one can neutralize anxiety-producing thoughts and strip in-flight noises and motions of their power to release stress hormones.

Ancient Greek mythology told us a face could launch a thousand ships. We have now learned an empathically attuned face can quell a thousand fears. This breakthrough, now called Systematic Inhibition, taps into our genetically encoded ability to be calmed by empathic attunement.

A single release of stress hormones does not cause distress. It activates Executive Function, causing whatever is non-routine to be examined. It is one stress hormone release on top of another, and then another, that causes high anxiety, claustrophobia, or panic. A series of stress hormone releases can cause Executive Function, which plays an important role in the regulation of anxiety, to be overwhelmed. Thus Systematic Inhibition can relieve distress by inhibiting stress hormone release, and by protecting your inner ability (what I call your inner CEO) to use Executive Function to regulate anxiety.

CHAPTER 5

How Your Inner CEO Regulates Stress Hormones

Corporations have a CEO. So do you. An inner one. Think of your inner CEO as responsible for making assessments, decisions, and commitments. It carries out this work in its executive suite: the prefrontal cortex. Like most CEOs, yours is freed up from having to attend to routine tasks. In the subcortex of your brain, a sort of mental autopilot carries out routine tasks for you with little or no conscious attention.

Your Autopilot

How does your autopilot learn to perform routine tasks? When first carrying out a new task, you do so by focusing on it. The same is true the second time. But as you continue repeating the task, repetition causes some steps to be memorized. The memorized steps are carried out automatically. The unmemorized steps, as before, are done consciously. As repetition continues and more steps are memorized, more of the task is performed automatically. Finally, the entire task is done with little or no conscious thought.

Think of teaching a child to tie a shoelace. You have to go over it again and again. Finally, the child can do it for herself, albeit slowly and methodically. Soon, however, it becomes automatic. Before long, the child can carry on a conversation while tying her shoelaces.

Over time, many activities are committed to memory. In some cases, sets of memorized steps can be sequenced to produce a lengthy routine. For example, when first learning the waltz, you stumble your way through three basic steps (the man: left foot forward, right foot forward and to the side, left foot together with the right; the woman: right foot back, left foot backward and to the side, right foot together with the left). Three steps follow this with the woman going forward and the man going backward.

Your cortex is, of course, doing this consciously. Three steps in one direction and three steps in the other direction are a total of six steps. On the conscious level, in what is called working memory, the number of things the cortex can keep in play at one time is around seven (plus or minus two). If seven is the limit of what a person can juggle consciously in the cortex, how do we do more complex things? How do we recite a poem of more than seven words? How do we master the waltz?

Fortunately, unconscious procedural memory in your subcortex can hold millions of steps. By repetition, you transfer a few words at a time, or a few steps at a time, from conscious working memory (in the cortex) to unconscious procedural memory (in the subcortex). Repetition signals your subcortex to memorize what you are doing.

Have those first six steps been memorized? At your next lesson, you check, and sure enough, the steps are in place. Now you are ready to try them while turning left. After turning left a few times, you try turning right. By the end of the second lesson, you have six additional steps transferred to unconscious procedural memory. Think about the word *unconscious:* Before long, this amazing memory system will enable you to perform an extended routine with little or no conscious thought. To add some sophistication, you need a couple of fancy steps, the whisk (three steps) and the chassé (five steps). Once again, through conscious repetition, you transfer these steps to unconscious procedural memory.

At this point, your instructor shows you how to use all the steps you have learned in a sequence. The sequence has twenty-some steps, ending with the chassé. The chassé leads you back to the beginning of the sequence, thus allowing the sequence to be repeated seamlessly. Though it might have seemed impossible at the outset, you can now let the music float you around the dance floor, as you and your partner perform the sequence again and again without a thought. Through repetition, the dance routine has become, literally, routine. While your subcortex is moving you around the floor, your CEO is free to focus on more important things, such as the face of the person in your arms. That's the magic of ballroom dance.

Your Inner CEO and Autopilot as Partners

When you go from a private studio to a crowded ballroom, if your subcortex simply carries out the routine, you are going to collide with other dancers. You have to use your cortex *and* your subcortex. Your CEO (in the cortex) needs to fit the memorized steps stored (in the subcortex) into a sequence that navigates you and your partner around the other dancers. Once the plan is complete, your CEO commits to it, and the subcortex carries it out.

Let's consider a different example: driving on a multilane highway. The autopilot in your subcortex is doing the driving. Your CEO is thinking about dinner; "Umm, how about a nice filet of sole, with a little white wine, butter, and lemon juice?" Your inner CEO gets so deep into the thought of Sole Française that you can almost taste it. Uh, oh. Target fixation! If you can remember a time on a multilane highway when you missed your planned exit, you can understand how your CEO, fixated on Sole Française, might not notice a car drifting into your lane. Though the autopilot in your subcortex sees this happen, it has no decision-making capacity. It is like a deer frozen in the headlights. It cannot make a change.

Some out-of-the-box thinking is called for. Who is going to make the call? Your CEO is busy thinking about Sole Française. Fortunately, the amygdalae are monitoring what is going on. If everything is routine, the amygdalae, while remaining alert for anything out of the ordinary, chill out. But if they notice anything non-routine, they notify your inner CEO.

To bring a non-routine situation to the CEO's attention, the amygdalae do not politely knock on the door. Rather, they zap your CEO with a shot of stress hormones. Thoughts of Sole Française vanish. All you are aware of is a car coming at you! You think, "Where the hell did that come from?" Well, simple. It came from the lane next to you, but since you were otherwise occupied when it first started drifting toward you, you didn't notice it. How it got so close feels like a mystery. Never mind. There's work to be done.

Your Inner CEO's ABCs

When signaled by your amygdalae, your inner CEO functions like a real CEO. It uses its Executive Function to quickly do three things:

A. It *assesses* whether this non-routine situation is an opportunity, irrelevance, or a threat. (The amygdalae only know whether something is routine or non-routine.)

B. It *builds a plan* of action—or inaction—based on what is most likely to produce desired results.

C. It *commits* to action or to inaction. (In some cases, the commitment is to watchful waiting, or to dismissal of the situation as irrelevant.)

Assessment? That's easy. The car coming into your lane is a threat. Build a plan of action? You could blow the horn. You could turn the wheel to move away. You could hit the brakes to drop behind where the other car is headed. You could do all three. Once you decide, the next step is commitment. Commitment puts your plan into action. Then, something remarkable happens.

Commitment Terminates Stress Hormone Release

There is a dedicated neurological pathway from your inner CEO's office, the orbitofrontal cortex, to the amygdalae. This is one of the pathways built early in life between areas of conscious thought and areas where unconscious processes regulate emotion. This neurological pathway has but one purpose: At the moment of commitment, it is used to send a signal to the amygdalae that causes them to *automatically* reset. Stress hormone release stops. The amygdalae return to monitoring, ready to alert you to the next non-routine situation.

There is a reason why stress hormone release stops, even if the situation requires further action. If stress hormones were to continue post-commitment, they would be a distraction that would get in the way of carrying out the plan. When a phone rings, at the moment you take action and answer it, the ringing stops. Think how distracting it would be to carry on a conversation with the phone still ringing.

That's how your inner CEO responds to stress hormone release. You may need a shot of stress hormones to get your inner CEO's attention, but once it is on the case, it needs no further hormones to maintain its focus. As necessary, your inner CEO reassesses the situation, reevaluates the plan of action, and recommits until the job is done, and things are again routine.

In case your inner CEO comes up with a plan that requires physical exertion, your body is prepared. When the stress hormones alerted your inner CEO, they also increased your heart rate and breathing rate. Take note: Neither the release of stress hormones, nor the feelings or the elevated heart and breathing rates they cause, signify danger. They only mean a non-routine situation has been detected. The amygdalae don't have enough brainpower to assess whether something is safe or unsafe, nor can they make a decision about what to do. After all, each amygdala is merely the size and shape of an almond. Assessment requires far greater resources, those in the cortex, under the command of your inner CEO.

Self-Activation

I don't understand. I can get on my motorcycle and go one hundred mph and I'm fine. But I can't get on an airplane.

Some anxious fliers can ski, ride a motorcycle, or go rock climbing without undue anxiety. They wonder why flying is so different. It appears that being in control keeps them from feeling anxious. To some degree this is true, but being in control does not necessarily regulate anxiety. When in control, if you can't decide what to do, anxiety persists.

A risky activity requires continuous ABC activity. Some kind of assessment, decision, and commitment takes place every few seconds. With almost continuous commitment signals being sent to the amygdalae, stress hormones—and thus feelings of fear—are kept at bay.

A well-disciplined person can stay focused on a task even if it does not involve risk, and even if it is not exciting. Airline pilots have an expression. When they see a pilot leave the cockpit, they jokingly ask, "Who's minding the store?" The pilot making that comment knows, of course, that someone is still at the controls. But this inside joke has a point. Airline flying is boring. We intend to keep it that way.

In the cockpit, duties are shared. One pilot monitors the radio and handles the communications with Air Traffic Control. Another pilot stays focused on the instruments to make sure the plane's speed, altitude, and navigation are as they should be. Though this is boring business, it has to be done to make sure there are no nasty surprises. Since being an airline pilot is, if anything, less exciting than being a storekeeper, we jokingly refer to it as "minding the store."

Stress hormones rarely are triggered when a disciplined individual "minds the store." Events that would trigger stress hormones are preempted by constant management. When your inner CEO "minds the store," it is as if it is telling the amygdalae, "Hey. I'm on the case. You don't need to zap me with stress hormones. I'm already paying attention."

On the road, an expert driver doesn't wait for stress hormones to activate Executive Function. The driver is constantly doing his ABCs. He is continuously assessing, continuously building plans of action, and continuously committing to them. A commitment of some kind is taking place every few seconds. This means the amygdalae are almost perpetually being signaled to hold back the stress hormones. When driving, if you "mind the store," you are not subjected to the release of stress hormones. If the car in the next lane starts to drift toward you, you notice it right from the beginning. Though it is non-routine for the car to be moving toward you, its position is so nearly the same as its previous position that, though it is perceptible to you, the amygdalae do not react to it. When you "mind the store," you can sense smaller differences than your amygdalae can.

By self-activating and "minding the store," you can avoid stress hormone release altogether. You take notice of non-routine situations and act on them before they reach the threshold at which the amygdalae can sense them. Executive Function beats the amygdalae to the draw.

● ● ●

The Social Engagement System can moderately or completely inhibit stress hormone release. Executive Function can terminate stress hormone release if it can do all three ABC steps. Self-activation by your inner CEO can preempt stress hormone release by "minding the store."

We all know that if we can keep something out of mind, it doesn't bother us. This leads anxious fliers to focus on other things, and try to keep the flight out of mind. During taking off and when in turbulence, the "keep it out of mind" strategy doesn't work. Non-routine noises and motions trigger the amygdalae; they release stress hormones that forcibly bring the facts of flight to mind. Would it not be a better strategy to do the opposite and "mind the store"? By staying keenly aware—taking conscious note of every noise and motion of flight—Executive Function beats the amygdalae to the draw, and keeps stress hormones from being released.

The Mobilization System can regulate anxiety only if the person is assured of immediate escape. Executive Function can regulate anxiety only if the person is in control. The Social Engagement System, however, can regulate anxiety even when not in control or when unable to escape.

CHAPTER 6

Understanding Executive Function

In addition to situations that are non-routine, the amygdalae react to certain genetically encoded stimuli. For example, if you are walking in the woods, an S-shaped object on the ground will trigger a stress hormone release. In a few thousandths of a second, without will on your part, your hormones shut down the mental autopilot that has been walking you forward and stop you in your tracks. For a moment, you don't know why: It takes one-tenth of a second for the brain to turn data from the eyes into a usable image. Another tenth of a second is needed to identify the image. If the image turns out to be a vine, you may feel foolish for having overreacted. But if, after backing away, you see a snake, you'll feel relief, and maybe even a little proud of your performance. But, really, feeling prideful or foolish is neither here nor there. Your amygdalae were just doing their job, which is to be quick—not right.

The opposite is true for Executive Function. Its job, like that of a corporate executive, is to be right—not quick. Even so, a good CEO doesn't let problems build up. Some say the sign of a good executive is an empty desk. Through deliberate assessment, building a plan of action, and commitment, good Executive Function clears the desk to be ready to deal with what comes next.

It is important to process each issue brought to your attention as it is brought to your attention. In this way, stress from unresolved issues does not build up. With your desk cleared, when your amygdalae bring something to your attention, you are free to fully focus on the matter; then you can resolve it, and return—like any good executive—to an empty desk.

Your Inner CEO's Executive Suite

Think of your orbitofrontal cortex—that part of the brain directly over your eyes—as your inner CEO's executive suite. There your inner CEO has a desk. And on the desk, there's an intercom. It is directly wired to the intercom at your assistant's desk. Let's call your personal assistant Amy (short for amygdalae). Amy's job is to alert your CEO to anything that is non-routine. If the situation calls for action, your CEO builds a plan of action, and commits to it.

Amy isn't the problem solver, but she's a great gatekeeper and is very efficient. She sorts through the myriad e-mails, phone calls, and letters that constantly come to your office, not bothering you with these mundane, routine items, knowing that you have better things to do. But when something unusual pops up, something non-routine that only you, the inner CEO, can deal with, she pushes the intercom button: The intercom in your mental office goes off. But unlike an ordinary intercom or a smoke alarm that produces noise, when this intercom goes off, it zaps your CEO with stress hormones. When the stress hormones hit, your inner CEO jumps into action, assesses the situation, builds a plan of action, and commits resources to carrying it out. Commitment automatically signals Amy that the plan is being carried out. This lets her off the hook. So Amy takes her finger off the intercom button and goes back to her gatekeeper role. Your inner CEO takes a break or focuses on whatever is of interest.

So we have Amy, the gatekeeper, ever-vigilant, on the lookout for non-routine situations; the intercom, the alert system, signaling the CEO to situations that require his immediate attention; and the

CEO, the executive, the big kahuna, the only one capable of solving the situation by practicing his ABCs, quickly assessing what's going on, making a plan, and committing to an action. That's your inner office at work, 24/7.

Consider Amy coming across an ad saying, "Today Only! Your own portable television set, a $129.99 value for just $69.99!" Like any other non-routine situation, the ad gets Amy's attention: She pushes the intercom, compelling your CEO to take note. In spite of the impulse to hurry to the store and take advantage of the non-routine offer, your CEO may say, "No, I already have one." With good Executive Function, your CEO makes its commitment and signals Amy to turn off the intercom. Nevertheless, residual hormones—like the noise from Amy's intercom—are still echoing around the building. They remain an influence for a few seconds. In the case of an exciting opportunity, residual hormones can influence your thinking for a few seconds, tempting you to reconsider. In a risk-assessment situation, residual hormones keep you temporarily on edge. This is a time when impulsivity could get the better of you. But good Executive Function, in spite of the lingering effect, stands fast and does not ruminate; to do so would bring the non-routine matter back into focus, triggering a new round of stress hormones. When the residual hormones are given time to subside, there is a return to homeostasis, which is a state of internal equilibrium.

How does all this relate to the fear of flying? If you were able to fly in the cockpit, anxiety would be easily controlled. Upon sensing something non-routine, a glance at the pilots would provide you with an assessment that there is no problem. Your Executive Function would then be able to correctly decide to take no action. Commitment to that decision would quiet the amygdalae.

But in the passenger section, information is limited. When a noise or motion triggers a stress hormone release, an anxious flier may not have enough information to be sure there is no problem. Without a good assessment, no plan—either of action or inaction—can be built. With no plan, no commitment can be made. And with no commitment, no signal can be sent to the amygdalae to discontinue stress hormone release.

Probability versus Possibility

A good CEO recognizes that every course of action—or inaction—involves some level of uncertainty. Your Executive Function, if it is to serve you well, must accept that there are no guarantees. When a good CEO builds a plan, the plan is based not on certainty but on what can be reasonably expected. The next step is to commit—not in the naïve "nothing bad can ever happen" sense, but in the mature acceptance that this commitment, like any other, could work out badly. If the plan carries a high risk of failure, Executive Function may wisely decide to not take the risk. But if the risk of failure is exceptionally low, it is dismissed as not worth consideration.

Impaired Executive Function doesn't like probability. It wants certainty. Make no mistake, if an outcome were certain, what need would there be for Executive Function? In other words, if the score of the Super Bowl had been established before the kickoff, there would be no need for quarterbacks.

As it looks for certainty, impaired Executive Function misses the big picture. It fixates instead on the small—in fact, minuscule—picture. It brushes aside what is by far the most likely outcome—that the plane will arrive just fine—and focuses instead on the tiny possibility of disaster. Though a fatality occurs once in twenty-some million flights, when Executive Function is impaired, its logic seems to be, if something is possible, it can happen. If it can happen, it can happen to me. At that point, the disaster becomes personal; the thought of being in a plane that is crashing triggers the release of stress hormones. Stress hormones, because they force Executive Function to focus on what the amygdalae are responding to, compel impaired Executive Function to view images of personal disaster, which make it appear that any plan of action will result in disaster. Seeing disaster as the only possibility, the second ABC step—building a plan of action—comes to a halt. With no plan to commit to, no signal can be sent to quiet the amygdalae. Stress hormones continue, fixation on disaster continues; no relief comes until the person decides to abandon the plan. Professors George Loewenstein and Jennifer Lerner summarize the process, saying "As the intensity of immediate emotions intensifies, they progressively take control of decision making and override rational decision making."

Here is an example of impaired Executive Function. This dialogue is from the SOAR Chat. To maintain her privacy, her name has been changed to Jeanette. She is not a client. She was unable to deal with two decisions: her flight, and whether or not to enroll in SOAR. The following are dialogues from two different chat sessions.

FIRST CHAT SESSION

Jeanette. Every time I feel I'm making progress, I get worse again. It is a horrible feeling to let fear take over your life. My flight is supposed to be in June, but I am procrastinating and haven't bought the tickets yet. I'm so afraid to get my tickets. If I give up at the last minute, I won't get my money back, and I'll miss work on unpaid vacation. I'm always like that when it comes to making big decisions. I am starting to think that my main fear is turbulence even though there are millions of things in my head right now. I know that once I buy the tickets, then I will be anxious about packing, walking at the airport, boarding, etc.

Captain Tom Bunn. Jeanette, we were just talking about how the amygdalae, the part of the brain that triggers stress hormones, has a job to do. Not unlike the smoke alarm in your home, whenever anything non-routine is picked up, they alert you. The smoke alarm with noise. The amygdala with stress hormones. Then you do your ABCs. A. You assess what the alarm means. B. You build a plan. C. You commit to the plan. Commitment resets the amygdalae. The stress hormones stop. The feelings, which are caused by stress hormones, go away.

Jeanette. I wish I had a capacity and power to control the feelings. I know that half of what I feel is part of my imagination. I have this fear of being inside the plane and trying to get out and it is too late. I always make everything too complicated. I tend to do that with other issues, too. I started imagining how nice it would be to drive to another place closer instead of flying overseas, and I felt my anxiety level drop when I took the idea of flying out of my head. But I get so depressed for feeling I am a failure and a disappointment to the loved ones anxious to see me.

SECOND CHAT SESSION

Jeanette. Today my stress level is huge. I booked my tickets yesterday and that already made my heart race.

Captain Tom Bunn. Jeanette, what comes to mind as the problem?

Jeanette. Oh, Captain Tom, I could stay here forever listing you all my fears. Turbulence is a big thing. Worried about bad weather. The fact of being on a plane for nine hours. I don't see me standing nine hours without feeling sick. But I have neglected flying for three years and I haven't seen my parents that long due to this awful fear. I blame it on myself. I cry every day and I put pressure on myself. But what if the weather is bad and we are already up in the air?

Captain Tom Bunn. Jeanette, the weather forecast has to be okay. And if there is any chance at all that it might go bad, you have to have an alternate airport specified.

Jeanette. Sometimes I feel it is out of the pilot's hands when it comes to Mother Nature, like in a storm, and it gets me so anxious to imagine the possibility of having a massive turbulence, etc. The feeling is so intense and getting stronger over the years that the fear took control over my life.

Captain Tom Bunn. Jeanette, of course you can imagine the possibility of massive turbulence. So can I. But, I can do it without stress hormone release. I can teach you to do that, too. One way we control these feelings is we tap into the Social Engagement System. It is a system that shuts down stress hormone production in certain interpersonal situations. We teach the amygdalae to link each thing that happens on a flight—or that you imagine could happen on a flight—with something the amygdalae regard as benign. We want to teach the amygdalae to regard being on the plane as being alone with someone you are profoundly secure with. Recalling such a moment shuts down the release of stress hormones. By shutting down the release of hormones, we control the feelings. The other way we control feelings is to teach your high-level thinking, called Executive Function, to recognize the difference between what can go wrong, and what could go wrong, and what will go wrong. What you are contemplating is extremely unlikely, and your Executive Function needs to be able to base decisions on what is by far the most likely outcome instead of expectation of a most unlikely outcome.

Jeanette. I think that training could be almost impossible in a person so fearful like myself. I can't even stand up without my legs shaking. I get stuck in my seat. I don't get up to use the restroom. I don't eat and I stay staring at everybody waiting for something to happen. I get so scared that I feel—I know it is silly—that if I get up I won't feel the ground below my feet.

• • •

Jeanette's remarks show, that for emotional control, she is dependent upon the Mobilization System. She knows only one way to control fear and anxiety, and that is to always be able to escape. The very idea that her feelings could be controlled in some other way is unthinkable. She needs her feet on the ground. To her, security means being able to go toward what is interesting or desirable—she would like to see her family again—and being able to move away from anything that frightens her (in this case, being on the plane). The two things, confinement on the plane to reach her family and escape from the plane to stop anxiety, are in direct conflict.

Psychological Fixation

Though impaired Executive Function can become fixed on physical disaster, for many anxious fliers, the fixation is on psychological disaster: claustrophobia, high anxiety, or panic. Such folks have panic at times in day-to-day life. When they do, they seek relief by getting away from where they are. The relief that comes with this action causes a gross misunderstanding. Because the amygdalae stop releasing stress hormones when commitment to an action is taken, panic stops immediately upon commitment to escape. Ironically, the panic would stop just as quickly if the person made a commitment to stay put. As has been pointed out, it is *commitment* that ends the release of stress hormones, whether it is to escape or to hold one's ground.

Notice that panic stops not when arriving at a safe haven but upon leaving to go there. Logically, if it feels unsafe here, there should be no reason to feel safe until well away from here. The fact that panic is relieved at the moment escape is initiated shows us that commitment to action, not completion of the action, ends stress hormone release. The belief that panic can be stopped only by escape causes fear of being any place where escape is not instantly available. It could be an elevator. It could be a bridge. It could be a tunnel. It could be a multilane highway with no immediate exit. It could, for some, even be speed, and the awareness that it would take a moving vehicle several seconds to stop and let them off. It could be the insecurity of another person in control of the vehicle; will he respond instantly if the person insists she wants to get off? And, even if escape is not blocked by a physical barrier, it can be blocked by a psychological barrier: embarrassment. Some clients have said they cannot go to church because, if the need to escape arose, they could not leave because of embarrassment. Even if sitting in the back row, someone—and perhaps several people—would notice.

The very thought of restrictions triggers anxiety. In time, the thought of being any place where escape is not instantly available may cause feelings of panic. Thus, knowing they cannot get off the plane, the very thought of being on the plane can bring them to the edge of panic. I can no longer count the number of people who have told me they cannot bear to look up in the sky because they might see an airplane, and have the thought of being unable to instantly escape from it.

Believing panic could last until able to get off the plane, an anxious flier may fear that a long flight could mean being in a state of panic for hours. Like fixation on an image of physical disaster, fixation on images of psychological disaster can keep Executive Function from doing its job.

What else can prevent your inner CEO from doing its ABCs? Some inner CEOs can build a good plan of action but not be able to commit to it. High probability that the plan will succeed may not be enough. Some CEOs cannot commit unless the desired outcome seems certain. Amy keeps her finger pressed on the intercom button waiting to hear the CEO has made a commitment. The CEO can't decide. This goes on and on. Finally, when the noise from the intercom becomes intolerable, the CEO falls apart. Incapacitated in his office, no one can signal Amy to stop, so her finger stays on the intercom. In other words, when a person's Executive Function cannot produce a commitment, stress hormones keep building up, and the buildup causes Executive Function to collapse. Control reverts to the Mobilization System. This primitive system, having but one solution, demands escape. If escape if blocked, no regulation of stress hormones is possible; the result is panic.

Though some anxious fliers must have immediate escape, others can maintain themselves as long as the flight is making progress. They calm themselves by keeping the goal—getting off the plane at the destination—in mind. Emotions are controlled as long as there is "light at the end of the tunnel" and the progress toward the end of the tunnel is constant. They run into trouble when, for example, the plane goes into a holding pattern, or there is an indefinite delay before takeoff. If there is any pause in progress, the plan is thrown into doubt, and the image in their mind of being able to get off the plane disappears. Success seems no longer guaranteed. Commitment to the plan comes undone. When commitment is lost, stress hormones return.

A similar example is being on an elevator, and just when you expect the door to open, nothing happens. The image of being stuck replaces the expectation of being able to get out. So many anxious fliers say, "I don't know what to expect." Some check the weather constantly in an effort to find out what to expect. It is as if the ability to be calm depends upon the ability to expect—and to hold in one's mind—the desired outcome.

Panic: Multiple Stress Hormone Release

The amygdalae, located in the brain just behind the eyes, receive incoming visual data directly. Think of this as the front door. Images coming in the front door, because they come from your eye, are limited by reality. But the amygdalae have a back door, too, and through the back door images from the mind's eye enter. These images are not limited by reality. Much of what is presented to the amygdalae by the mind's eye is imagination. Yet, the amygdalae—in determining whether to react and release stress hormones or ignore the situation and release none—make no distinction between the images from reality and the images from your imagination.

First, let's consider reality. Unless you're a first responder or a spy or a soldier in the midst of battle, life does not present one life-threatening situation after another. For most of us, threats coming into the amygdalae through the front door are rare. What comes in the front door is limited to what is actually going on. But what about the mind's eye? Threats coming into the amygdalae through the back door are limited by nothing other than the limits of your creative imagination. Amygdalae exposure to reality rarely causes panic. But amygdalae exposure to what comes in through the back door from your imagination can. Panic is a back door problem, which is to say it is a mind's eye problem, which is to say it is a particular kind of imagination problem, one in which a person accepts what is imagined as if it were real.

Whether triggered by your physical eye or your mind's eye, a single non-routine image is only a single source of stress hormones. A single source does not cause panic. Instead, it only alerts Executive Function; your CEO assesses the non-routine situation and determines its strategy.

Though an armed assailant is a serious threat, it is only one source of stress hormones. When facing a threat that is real, arousal goes no higher than two, on a scale of zero to ten. But when the assailant leaves, the person's focus is no longer constrained by the emergency. The person can imagine "what if" things had been different. For example, what if the assailant had pulled the trigger? Even though it's conjecture, the image nonetheless causes the amygdalae to release stress hormones. If your CEO cannot adequately explain why the thief did not shoot, imagination can run wild and produce a whole series of images about being shot, rushed to a hospital, living or dying, and so on. Each image produces a shot of stress hormones. Multiple shots of stress hormones can cause arousal to skyrocket and overwhelm Executive Function. If Executive Function collapses, the person has no ability to stop stress hormone production. The amygdalae may drive arousal even higher. The result may be panic or dissociation. Consider this series:

Thought A: "What if I had done something different?"

Thought B: "He might have shot me."

Thought C: "I could be dead right now."

Thought D: "I might be bleeding to death on the sidewalk."

Thought E: "What will my family feel when they hear what happened?"

Thought A takes arousal from zero to two. Thought B takes arousal from two to four. Thought C takes arousal from four to six. Thought D takes it from six to eight. At eight, stress hormones cause psychic equivalence to take place, shifting thought E from imagination to actuality. Psychic equivalence, according to psychologist Peter Fonagy, is a state in which imagination is experienced as if it were reality.

Executive Function Overload
Even though takeoff is not a life-threatening situation, the plane makes one noise after another. In turbulence, there is one movement

after another. These noises and movements—routine to a crew member's amygdalae—may be non-routine to a passenger's amygdalae. When the amygdalae notice an unfamiliar noise, stress hormones are released that focus 100 percent of the inner CEO's attention on the noise. If the CEO recognizes what the noise is, and understands it is nothing to be concerned about, she knows no action is called for. Her plan, then, is to disregard the noise, and to return to what she was doing before. But, as she is about to commit to her plan to disregard the noise—a commitment that would end stress hormone release—she hears another noise. The amygdalae again release stress hormones. Stress hormones give the inner CEO no choice; they force the inner CEO to focus 100 percent of her attention to this new noise. Her plan to disregard the first noise vanishes from her mind. Since her ABCs had not been completed, and commitment had not been reached, the stress hormones from the first noise continue. Then, before she can reach commitment about the second problem, a third problem is presented.

If this continues—as it can during takeoff or in turbulence—the inner CEO can't stick with any problem long enough to complete the ABCs. She can't reach commitment, the point at which stress hormone release would stop. Instead, the stress hormones build to a higher and higher level. The sequence in ordinary turbulence might be:

Thought A: "Oh, no. Turbulence!"

Thought B: "I wonder if it will get worse?"

Thought C: "I don't know if I can take it!"

Thought D: "I think something is wrong."

Thought E: "The plane is falling!"

In an actual life-threatening situation, reality limits awareness to one thought. In an imaginary life-threatening situation, an unlimited number of thoughts are possible. Each triggers a stress hormone release. Multiple sources of stress hormones cause high anxiety or panic.

Takeoff is brief. Even though there are several noises and movements, the ordeal is over fairly quickly. Turbulence, though, is a different matter. It can go on for an extended period of time. The description above involves imagination. During any non-routine situation in which there is one motion or noise after another, however, Executive Function can become overloaded. The inner CEO may be unable to reach commitment and signal the amygdalae to cease stress hormone production.

But, even if stress hormone production can be stopped, the hormones already released have a residual effect. After commitment has been reached, it may take one to two minutes for the hormones to wear off. Even if the inner CEO recognizes every motion and every noise, and is able to complete the ABC process and reach the point of commitment every time there is a noise or motion, the residual effect can be formidable. It is possible that the residual effect can be enough, at least over an extended period of time in turbulence, for Executive Function to collapse and accomplish no further ABC steps at all.

Imagine what it would be like at home if you had a dozen smoke alarms. If one went off, you would use your Executive Function. You would assess the situation to see if the toaster was burning toast or if there was a serious fire. But what if, after one smoke alarm went off, another one went off a second later, and another after that until all twelve were blaring? Even if you were sure you were not in physical danger, the noise would be too much. You would just leave. That's what happens psychologically when Executive Function reacts—even successfully—to one situation after another. The combination of fatigue and residual hormone buildup can cause your inner CEO to collapse. The result would be high anxiety or panic. Fortunately, automatic control via Systematic Inhibition can override or prevent stress hormone release and provide the protection necessary for your inner CEO to continue working.

CHAPTER 7
Onset

Flying can become a problem after a bad flight. But in most cases, the problem begins in a different way, when a person discovers—to his amazement—that he just can't get on the plane. What's going on?

Anxiety is regulated by a combination of internal psychological resources, external support from others, and compensatory strategies. Flying becomes a problem when internal resources falter, external support is lost, or compensatory strategies lose their effectiveness. This can happen for a number of reasons, as we shall see.

No Apparent Reason

I flew for years with no problem. I never really liked it, but I could do it. Now I just can't see myself getting on a plane.

It strikes anxious fliers as strange that it starts this way, but this is how the problem usually begins: After flying for years with little or no anxiety, suddenly it becomes a problem. Stresses can build up over time, often without the buildup being noticed. Compensatory strategies—possibly unconscious ones—keep us from noticing the buildup. If the accumulated load becomes too great, compensatory strategies—the various personal security blankets we depend on—may crumple under the load of accumulated concerns. When young, a person may know of only one plane crash. But as years go by, she hears about others. Each time the person flies, these crashes come to mind. When facing an upcoming flight, information about one additional crash can be too much. Just as one purchase—large or small—can put your credit card over the limit, one single concern can put you over the top when it comes to regulating anxiety. Suddenly and unexpectedly, you just can't take the flight.

Onset Due to Loss

My father died suddenly of a heart attack. I flew to his funeral. There was nothing special about the flight. I wasn't afraid, as best I can remember, but I haven't been able to fly since. Though he spent his life doing everything correct medically and maintained a healthy lifestyle, he passed away at fifty-seven. Somewhere in my head I connected the possibility that the worst thing in life can happen despite your best efforts to protect yourself from it. From then on, my somewhat dormant fear of flying ballooned into a full-blown problem. Suddenly, I couldn't board a plane much less look at them take off or land, not even on TV or in movies. It was that bad! I had to lie to get myself out of plans because I was too embarrassed to admit my fear. I felt terrible; I didn't know what was wrong with me. I didn't know how I lost a grip on a seemingly simple thing and I felt very alone. On top of it all, I was losing money on blown trips. I may never get back to see places like Costa Rica or Sweden.

In an optimal childhood, challenges become linked to parental support. In theory, if the supportive parenting were fully internalized, a child would grow up having little or no ongoing need for his or her parents. In practice, however, support is only partly internalized, and we never completely outgrow our need for external support.

For the sake of illustration, let's imagine a person has internalized 50 percent of the emotional support he or she needs, and is dependent on the physical presence of the parents for the remaining 50 percent. Upon their death, the 50 percent provided by the physical presence of the parents is lost. Though the 50 percent that's built in remains, it isn't accessible. Until the cycle of grieving is complete, whenever the parents come to mind—which is often, at this juncture—there are painful feelings of loss rather than comforting feelings of support. He continued his story as follows:

> *I won't lie: I didn't follow the SOAR steps down to the letter. Though there were some bad moments, I was able to slowly trust the lessons in my head over the irrational fear I couldn't control. Each time the fear came around I was able to combat it. On some rare moments, I even felt my love of flying and looking out the window come back. I just got back from my latest flight. Something strange happened before my flight departed: My normal level of fear was gone. That gnawing feeling of anticipatory anxiety was gone. It felt strange, almost like I missed it. I doubt every flight will be that smooth, but that's not the point. I have my life back and the fear is now manageable. That's all I ever wanted.*

Childhood Onset

We're planning a trip, and my child doesn't want to go. He says he's afraid to fly. I don't understand it, because although I don't really like to fly, I've kept it from him. When we've flown before as a family, I've always sat away from him so he doesn't see me afraid.

When a child expresses fear of flying, it should be recognized as a wake-up call because the problem is not just flying. The child has not adequately developed his or her ability to regulate anxiety. Professional assistance is essential. Otherwise, as a teenager, emotional regulation will become a problem neither the child nor the parents can control. Whatever the teenager needs to do to get relief will be done, which may mean drugs and other self-destructive behavior. Parents are fortunate when the emotional regulation surfaces as a fear-of-flying problem, rather than a drugs, alcohol, or behavior problem.

Teen Onset

When I was thirteen, I just started having panic attacks. I don't want to get one on the plane.

For many teenagers, everything seems out of control. There's stress from competition with other teens. There's stress due to conflicts with parents. Indeed, the teenager's body can be out of control. If panic becomes a problem, so does flying. On the plane, there is neither control to prevent panic, nor escape to relieve it.

Adult Onset

I had never really thought about being out in the world on my own. I guess I thought college was going to go on forever.

Onset when beginning college is due to inadequate internal replicas when physically separating from people needed for emotional support, and the uncertainties the young adult discovers in a larger world. In a commencement address at Harvard in 2010, Justice David Souter said, "Is there any one of us who has not lived through moments, or years, of longing for a world without ambiguity . . . ? I don't forget my own longings for certainty, which heartily resisted the pronouncement of Justice Holmes, that certainty generally is illusion and repose is not our destiny."

Parents offer children a simplified world in which behaviors are either right or wrong, and activities are either safe or dangerous. As children grow up, simplicity needs to give way to complexity. Parents who themselves have failed to come to grips with complexity cannot prepare their children for a transition into the real world.

Though absolutes exist only conceptually, the temptation to cling to them is strong. Belief is a life preserver that keeps non-swimmers from drowning in the Sea of Complexity. It is easy to find help when in need of an illusion to believe. We have not only newly fashioned cults but also long-accepted traditions that purvey their particular illusion of certainty as a commodity.

If unprepared, young adults develop anxiety when confronting complexity. As a child, following rules ensured success. As an adult, compliance means being overtaken by those with no rules at all. Where there used to be certainty, ambiguity abounds. The question needs to shift from "Is flying safe?" to "How safe is flying relative to other forms of transportation or to not traveling?" The young adult may not be ready for that shift. As long as a person frames safety in absolute terms, his Executive Function remains impaired by the logic that whatever is not absolutely safe is unsafe.

No matter how high the probability of safe arrival, probability is unacceptable. Impaired Executive Function requires absolute safety. Though absolute safety does not exist, impaired Executive Function operates on the illusion that control equals safety, and if control is not absolute, escape equals safety.

Onset Due to Recognition of Vulnerability

It never even crossed my mind to jog facing traffic. I always ran in the same direction as the traffic. One day, when I came to a dead animal in my way, I put just one foot out on the pavement to avoid it, and got hit by a truck. Until then, my favorite sport had been skydiving. But after that, I couldn't even fly as a passenger.

The prudent jogger faces oncoming traffic in case a driver strays from the road. This person—an athletic young woman—had no thoughts of caution. She was—in her own mind—invulnerable. Until the accident, belief in her invulnerability kept fear and anxiety neatly in check. Though she developed physical strength, the illusion of invulnerability kept her from developing emotional strength.

Most youths share the illusion that they are invulnerable. Kids, particularly boys, compensate for an inability to regulate anxiety by identifying with superheroes who, being invulnerable, are fearless and equal to any challenge. The fantasy of invulnerability, like the belief that bad things happen only to others, may extend into adulthood. In time, collisions with reality shatter the fantasy. This may explain why the average age of onset for fear of flying is not until age twenty-seven.

Marriage Onset

I'm supposed to get married in Jamaica on June 1st, which requires us to fly out on the 30th. That's only eight days away. I've played tough and tried not to think about it, but as it nears, I'm getting more and more scared. I have a contingency plan, which is to reschedule and have it on a beach somewhere in Florida, where I can drive. I am afraid of regretting doing that. And it's going to kill me to tell her she can't have her dream wedding she's so excited about because of me not being able to handle a simple three-hour flight. I'm already thinking about boarding the flight. The dry mouth, the racing heart, stomach jumping up into my throat, the dings and dongs in the cabin, etc. I was thinking of staying up all night the night before so that I'd be so tired that I'd just fall asleep on the plane, but I'm not even sure that would work.

In both marriage and flight, some degree of control is relinquished. Living together, usually in a limited space, makes it harder to regulate anxiety by a change in physical distance. But how did it work out? Here is what this client said two years later:

I did the SOAR program and since then I've taken about twelve flights, each of which was better than the last. In fact, I feel the most stressful part of the trip now is getting to the airport and dealing with the rigamarole of checking in, security, and hoping the plane is on time. Once I've boarded I feel much more relaxed. I will say that the difficult part of the flight for me now is definitely takeoff. Sometimes I wonder "Are we climbing? Should the engines be spooling down already? Why are we turning this soon after takeoff? Is something wrong? Are we going back to the airport?" But inevitably after several minutes of worrying over nothing the "ding" occurs, the crew tells us it's okay to get out our electronics, and I get out my iPod and watch something to help me laugh.

The program worked wonders for me. I had originally cancelled my wedding in Jamaica after failing to get on a plane at DFW during boarding. I'm not joking. I came home, did the program, rescheduled for a month later, got nervous at the airport. Called Capt. Tom prior to boarding, settled down, got on the plane, and enjoyed AA flight 1232 to Montego Bay without issues. Since then I've flown back to Cancun, San Diego, Ft. Lauderdale, Houston, Denver, and other places and have enjoyed the convenience and lack of headaches that flying provides. I feel like it's the pilot's job to get us where we're going and that's what he gets paid for, because I'm done scheduling days off work just for travel time, fighting through traffic, and risking the inherent dangers that come with road travel, especially in unfamiliar places .

I've resigned myself to the fact that some aspects of flying are just going to make me a little nervous, and that's okay. Being in a metal tube, traveling 500 mph at 37,000 feet isn't exactly natural, plus I'm not a pilot so I think it's okay to be a little nervous every so often about it. But a little bit of nerves that subside quickly after takeoff is much different from a crippling fear that leaves you running from the airport on what's supposed to be the eve of your wedding because you're scared of a plane ride.

Onset When Learning to Care

The loss of someone dear to us hurts. One way to limit anxiety about losing someone is pretending not to care. Not caring makes it easier to take chances. By taking chances, we may get life to be the way we want it to be. Then we don't want anything to change.

We start caring again, perhaps more than we knew we could. Knowing we could lose someone we treasure can trigger the onset of fear of flying.

Pregnancy Onset

Ever since my son was born (nineteen months ago) I have had some trouble flying. I've never really enjoyed it, but now I'm starting to believe I am going to panic on my next flight (Italy from Chicago in June). I can get on the plane just fine, and I can act like nothing is wrong, but my palms are sweaty, and I'm sitting there listening very carefully to any sound that signals impending danger. I consider myself an ultracautious person. Anything "unsafe" bothers me. I make sure to drive a car with a five-star crash rating in order to protect my child.

Becoming a parent means greater responsibilities, loss of control, and increased caring. All of these stressors can explain onset. But parenthood can initiate fear of flying in a unique way. Brain scan research has shown that in the final weeks of pregnancy, hormones that cause an obsession with safety are released in the brain. Anything that remotely could be a risk to the baby grabs the expectant mother's attention. Fortunately, this happens to some degree in the father as well. A few weeks after delivery, those hormones disappear. But the patterns produced by the hormones may endure. The increased concern about safety is generally protective for the new baby. However, reason needs to trump raw fear. Taking a flight—short or long—is equal in terms of fatality to a mere 10.8 miles of interstate driving. This is not to suggest driving is dangerous; it isn't. It is to point out, though, that while it may seem counterintuitive, the family is far better protected when travel is done by airliner than by car. New parents need to know they are making a responsible choice when they choose to fly.

Why Now?

Each of us has a certain ability to regulate emotion. Strategies can compensate to some degree. But compensatory strategies that work on the ground may not work in the air. Fear of flying develops when the sum of built-in ability, plus compensatory strategies, become insufficient to bear the stress load.

CHAPTER 8
Going into Your Own Movie

When you were a child, you probably saw a movie in which animals were lost. If you started to cry, an adult might touch you and say, "Honey, it's just a movie!" By touching you, the grown-up presented you with something real to help you notice the difference between a real experience and an imaginary one. When flying, if you produce a movie of your own in your head and get lost in it, you need to find your way back to what is real. First, recognize that what you have taken for real is not real, but imaginary. Second, like touch offered to a child by an adult, you need to let reality replace imagination.

The solution is to experience the flight just as it is, adding nothing, and subtracting nothing. Distress comes when a person adds the imagination of impending disaster, or attempts to keep the flight out of mind and fails. But your own movie is adding something. Here is how going into your own movie works: In a movie theater, as film runs through the projector, a sequence of individual photographs flashes on the screen. The mind assembles them into a moving picture.

Imagine you are examining a strip of movie film taken during a few seconds of a flight. Each photographic image on the filmstrip is called a "frame." We are going to study seven different frames.

Frame One: A passenger is reading a magazine.

Frame Two: There is a noise.

Frame Three: There is nothing happening.

Frame Four: There is nothing happening.

Frame Five: There is nothing happening.

Frame Six: There is nothing happening.

Frame Seven: A flight attendant asks, "Would you like some orange juice?"

The Reality Movie

Since this is what really happened, let's call this "The Reality Movie." A person who's not anxious stays in or close to reality and experiences what happens as it happens.

Frame One: The passenger is reading a magazine.

Frame Two: The person hears a noise.

Frame Three: The person thinks, "What's that?"

Frame Four: The person thinks, "Oh, I don't know."

Frame Five: The person turns his or her attention back to the magazine.

Frame Six: The person is reading the magazine.

Frame Seven: Asked about orange juice, the person responds, "Oh, thanks."

Your Own Movie

A person who is anxious has trouble sticking with "The Reality Movie." Experience is split between reality and expectation of something awful.

Frame One: The passenger is reading a magazine.

Frame Two: The person hears the noise.

Frame Three: The person thinks, "What's that?"

Frame Four: In response to the thought "What's that?" what comes to mind, psychologists tell us, depends upon what the person's mind is "primed" for. The confident flier is not primed to come up with anything, and unable to answer the question "What's that?" returns to reading. But the anxious flier *is* expecting something to go wrong. Of the things that could go wrong, let's say he or she most fears engine problems. So when the anxious flier thinks, "What's that?" engine failure comes to mind. The amygdalae respond to this non-routine thought and release stress hormones.

Reflective function—the mind's quality-control system—has already been weakened by anxiety. When imagination of engine failure triggers the release of stress hormones, self-examination of thought processing ends, and imagination masquerades as reality. Now, certain of engine failure, there is no attempt to explore alternative explanations. Thus, the internally produced movie begins. Stress hormones keep the mind focused on the movie.

Does the person have enough reflective function to say, "Wait, this is just my imagination," and exit from the theater of the mind?

If so, the person's reflective function is operating like a caregiver who says, "Honey, it's just a movie."

If you catch yourself in your own movie, don't let stress hormones keep you there. Turn to the 5-4-3-2-1 Exercise to intentionally focus on things that are both real and non-threatening long enough to burn off the stress hormones. Once stress hormones are reduced, you can again choose where to focus your attention—perhaps, like the confident flier, back to a magazine. But if reflective function is insufficient, imagination is experienced as though it were reality. This triggers even more stress hormones, locking the movie even more solidly in place.

Frame Five: Heart rate increases; breathing rate goes up; the person feels tense, his mind locked onto this false reality with no key to unlock it. What was imagined, then feared, then expected, arrives. It becomes the only available reality.

Frame Six. The person is deep inside the terror of his or her own movie. Contact with external reality has been lost. The person stares, unfocused, straight ahead.

Frame Seven. The flight attendant asks, "Would you like some orange juice?" If no one has intervened, the person neither hears the words nor is aware of the flight attendant's presence. The person is away from reality, locked inside the terror movie.

How Another Person Can Intervene during Flight

When an anxious flier goes into her own movie, another person can intervene by intrusion. The fearful flier needs to be taken from the internal movie back to something that is real. To intervene, someone must get directly in the person's face. He can hold up two or three fingers, and demand, "How many fingers do I have up? How many fingers? How many? Count them! How many fingers do I have up?" The person embroiled in her own movie may say, "Uh . . . Uh . . . Uh . . . t – t – t – t – two."

The demand to come out of the internal movie may need to be repeated. If so, someone can hold up a different number of fingers and demand an answer again. Or point at an object and say, "What color is that? What color is that?" When the person comes out of the terror movie, she will be shaken, but the spell will have been broken. At least for the moment. If you fly with other people, explain this to them and have them try it with you.

Don't Go into Your Movie before the Flight

I am afraid the plane is going to crash or be used in a terrorist attack. I know the chances of that happening are small, especially when you compare it to the chances of being in a car accident, or just in the wrong place at the wrong time. But I still feel that it is almost certain the plane will crash while I am on it.

Going into your own movie can happen before your flight. It happens if you unwittingly allow imagination to masquerade as reality. When my wife, Marie, was in art school, she was given an assignment to create an imaginary room. She was then told—using only her imagination—to decorate the room with furniture, lamps, textiles, and so on. So her instructor could see what she had come up with, she was asked to produce sketches of the room as she had imagined it.

As she worked on the drawings, it took less and less effort to bring the room to mind. By the time the drawings were finished, the room and all of its decorations came to mind effortlessly. The room no longer seemed like one she had created in her imagination. It seemed like a room she had previously been in. Why? Through repetition, her imagination of the room had been memorized.

When an anxious flier repeatedly imagines an upcoming flight ending in disaster, the imagination becomes memorized. Once imagination is memorized, it takes on a life of its own. What may have started out as mere possibility becomes probability. As stress hormones begin to rise, probability becomes certainty, and the person "just knows" his flight will crash.

He may be unable to board, or he may board and then get off. If he remains on the flight, he expects disaster at every moment. The mind is spring-loaded, like a mousetrap. The slightest ripple of turbulence can trip the latch and—snap—the person is trapped like a hapless mouse, held captive not in the jaws of a trap but by a nightmare: the plane falling out of the sky, which has been made real in his mind. The example below illustrates what happens when you go into your own movie before a flight:

> *I have to fly from Chicago to Orlando on September 12th and then back on September 14th. I am now to the point where the anxiety is starting to overwhelm me. I am unable to even see past those two dates. I am convinced I am going to die on either of those dates, so why bother looking forward to the concert tickets I have for later in the month?*

When your inner CEO does his ABCs, the first step is to assess—not what he imagines is going on—what is really going on. The second step, build a plan, does involve imagination—not free imagination but disciplined imagination of cause and effect. Your inner CEO may think, "If I carry out this set of actions, I should get results like that." You imagine what you are going to do, and you imagine that causing certain things to happen. This disciplined imagination of cause and effect sets the stage for the third step: commitment to carry out a plan. And commitment rests the amygdalae and stops the release of stress hormones.

But free imagination, undisciplined by cause and effect, gains nothing. Undisciplined imagination does not reveal the outcome of the flight. Imagination of "what if" does not prepare a person for the flight. It does the opposite. If allowed free range in one's mind, "what if" replaces "what is." When imagination becomes reality, flight can become difficult or impossible. The anxious flier is wise to take notice when free imagination begins, and limit it to cause and effect, or stop it by turning to the 5-4-3-2-1 Exercise.

CHAPTER 9
Staying Out of Your Own Movie in Turbulence

Turbulence, the thing many anxious fliers fear most, does not threaten the plane. Why, then, such fear? Reflective function is fragile. Anxiety can cause it to collapse, more easily in some than in others. When reflective function collapses, psychic equivalence takes place and imagination is experienced as if it were reality. Imagination that the plane *might* fall morphs into an experience that the plane *is actually* falling. Panic results.

For the person whose ability to regulate anxiety was not sufficiently developed during childhood, control of anxiety requires control of the situation. If adequate control is unavailable, the person needs an instant means of escape—and that is not an option in flight. When the person thinks about being unable to escape, she feels trapped. Since feeling trapped can cause panic, the person knows that when flying, she must keep awareness of the situation out of mind.

This is a fragile strategy at best; it depends upon the person's ability to not think about being in the situation she is in. Success rests upon the person's ability to constantly focus on other things or to psychologically dissociate while on the plane.

When turbulence forces the person to recognize the situation she is in, her selective focus—or her psychological dissociation—fails.

This form of control, like a house of cards, crashes down. Anxious fliers, knowing this is not a dependable strategy, obsess about the weather. Their emotional well-being depends on a turbulence-free flight. A more substantial plan is needed. Some have found the following strategies helpful for staying out of your own movie during turbulence.

Visualize the "Solidness" of Air—the "Gelatin" Exercise

The plane is so heavy. I just can't see how air can hold something up that is so big and heavy.

On October 14, 1947, Chuck Yeager was the first person to fly faster than the speed of sound. It was said he "broke the sound barrier" because, until then, it was theorized that air might become as solid as a brick wall when approaching the speed of sound. It isn't solid—but it is thick! Since airliners cruise close to the speed of sound, the air supporting the plane can be compared to gelatin.

As speed through air increases, passage becomes more difficult. When you're walking through air at five mph, it's effortless; biking through air at twenty-five mph requires all the effort a non-racer can muster. In a car, at fifty mph, if you put your hand out the window and push forward, it takes the same effort as putting your hand under water in a swimming pool and pushing forward. This means, to a vehicle penetrating it, fifty mph air is as thick as water in a pool. At eighty mph, air becomes like oil or molasses. At takeoff speed, between 140 and 200 mph, as far as the plane is concerned, air has been transformed into something as solid as gelatin.

Imagine a plate of gelatin in front of you. A cube of pineapple is suspended in the gelatin. Pick up the plate and shake it. No matter how hard you shake, you can't dislodge the pineapple from the gelatin. Now, replace the pineapple with a toy airplane. Again, shake the gelatin. As with the pineapple, there's nothing you can do to make the airplane plunge. The gelatin holding the toy airplane sits on a plate. The gelatin-like air holding the real airplane sits on the earth. Turbulence cannot break the hold of the gelatin. In gelatin-thick air, it is not possible to fall.

Once a plane reaches "gelatin-speed," it has to go where it is pointed. Imagine poking bare shish-kebab skewers into the gelatin behind the toy airplane. Put the tips against the rear of the engines. When you apply force, you can make the toy plane cut forward through the gelatin. This is what happens in flight. Engines make the plane cut forward through the gelatin-like air. Flying is as simple as accelerating to gelatin-speed on the runway, and pointing the nose where the plane needs to go. That's it. An accident can happen under only two circumstances:

1. The plane is pointed in the wrong direction, such as at a mountain (of course, as you've learned, there are warnings to prevent that);

2. The plane goes too slowly and the air is no longer gelatin-like. That never happens with professional pilots. Nevertheless, there are warnings if the plane begins to fly too slowly.

If your concern persists that the plane could fall, buy some gelatin mix—Knox, Jell-O, or in Australia the most popular brand is Aeroplane Jelly—a small model airplane, and some skewers. Place the toy in the gelatin, allowing it to set there. Once it's set, simulate the engines pushing the plane forward by placing the skewers against the rear of the toy plane's engines and pushing.

When onboard and taking a flight, don't wait for turbulence to begin "thinking gelatin." Picture the air getting thicker and thicker as you accelerate. Know the plane is in gelatin-like air before the nose is even lifted off the runway. Think of your toy airplane, safely suspended in gelatin, just as you are. You can jiggle in it, but you can't fall through it.

Calibrate Your Instrument

Turbulence is the worst because it feels like the plane is falling out of the sky.

What the plane is actually doing and what it *feels* like the plane is doing is very different. In the early days of aviation, instruments had not been developed for flying in clouds or landing in fog. In such conditions, pilots were said to be "flying by the seat of their pants." The human body experiences up-and-down motions as physical sensations of heaviness and lightness. So to some degree, when in clouds and unable to see, a pilot could get some idea of what the plane was doing from the physical feelings transmitted by the seat in which he or she sat.

As a passenger, you can easily misinterpret what is going on unless you first calibrate the "instrument" used when flying by the seat of your pants. Here's how: While the plane is parked at the terminal, lift your arms up off the armrest and lift your legs up off the floor. This puts all your weight on the seat. Memorize the amount of weight you feel in the seat. Once you have memorized that, your "instrument" has been calibrated. You can then compare that feeling with what you feel during flight.

During flight, if you get the impression the plane is falling, you tense up. That tension causes some of the weight that would ordinarily be in the seat to be transferred to the floor, via the stiffness in your legs, and some of the weight that would ordinarily be in the seat is transferred onto the armrest, due to the stiffness in your arms. The resultant lightness in your seat makes it feel like the plane is falling, even though it isn't. Thus, if the plane descends even for a moment, your reaction of tensing up causes the descent feeling to continue.

If you get the impression the plane is falling, lift your arms off the armrest and lift your feet off the floor. This places all your weight onto the seat. Compare what you feel with the calibration you did while parked at the terminal. This makes flying by the seat of your pants more accurate and not influenced by weight transferred from the seat to your limbs by tension.

Use a Sticky Note

I get worried that turbulence will get so bad that the plane can't handle it and something will break.

Airliners are built to withstand 5.0 Gs or more. The term G-force is used to state how much stress an object is being subjected to. The term can also describe the amount of stress an airplane or a person can withstand. The amount of stress we are subjected to when simply standing on the earth is 1.0 G. An airliner is built to sustain 2.5 Gs (two-and-one-half times the stress of level flight) with no damage whatsoever, and 5.0 G s (five times that amount of stress) with some damage to the structure of the plane but without breaking apart. In ordinary turbulence, the forces on the plane are in the 1.2 to 1.4 Gs range. But what about extreme turbulence? What is the worst turbulence can be? In determining the tie-downs needed to restrain extremely heavy cargo (combat vehicles, tanks, ammunition, and so on) on planes, the maximum possible turbulence has to be taken into consideration. The figure used by the military is 2.0 Gs. This means the worst possible turbulence cannot match the strength capacity built into every airliner.

As G-force on the body increases, blood is pulled downward. It drains away from the brain and pools in the legs and abdomen. Fighter pilots wear a G-suit to keep from losing vision during high-G maneuvers. One part of the G-suit wraps around the abdomen; other parts encircle the legs. When "pulling Gs," a bladder built into the G-suit inflates, compressing the legs and the abdomen to keep blood from flowing downward. Since you don't have a G-suit, if an airliner reached even half of the G-force it's built to withstand, you would first gray out and then black out.

Write this phrase on a sticky note: "If I can read this, it is not yet time to worry about the plane." Place the note on the back of the seat in front of you. During the flight, as long as you can read that note—or even see what color it is—it is not yet time for you to worry.

Prove How Little the Plane Moves

The plane dropped this huge amount. It must have been a hundred feet!

A bump during turbulence feels a lot like a speed bump feels when you're in your car. A five-inch speed bump produces a solid jolt at 5 mph. A one-inch bump would produce a similar jolt at 50 mph. A half-inch bump would do the same at 100 mph, or a quarter-inch at 200 mph. At cruise speed of 550 mph, the bump would need to be between an eighth and a sixteenth of an inch. Though it feels like the plane moves hundreds of feet in turbulence, the actual movement is a fraction of an inch.

Would slowing down help? It isn't possible to improve the ride when in turbulence by slowing down. The required speed—Turbulence Penetration Speed—is equidistant between too fast for the wing to produce lift and too slow for the wing to produce lift. That speed, only 2 to 4 percent slower than normal cruise speed, makes no noticeable difference

Even great improvement in the ride would not resolve anxiety about turbulence. Anxious fliers can be extraordinarily sensitive and alarmed by movements that a pilot would not even notice. When I've flown with anxious fliers, some have said, "What's that turbulence?" To which I replied, "What turbulence?" Even when they said, "There, that!" to point out the moment when they felt something disturbing, I still didn't notice any movement at all.

It isn't possible to fly a plane in a manner that will not trigger stress release in a highly sensitive flier. Regardless of how much you may think flying should be different, the difference has to come from you in the form of increased ability to regulate emotion when encountering movement that is unfamiliar.

Where does such sensitivity to—and fear of—the unfamiliar come from? The amygdalae are key to how we respond to what is non-routine. They are "experience dependent" in their development. Research shows in orphanages, where we know children do not get the psychological connection they need, and in homes where mothers are depressed, emotional development does not progress as it should, and the amygdalae—like a muscle that develops when it is used more—become enlarged. Enlarged amygdalae are associated with greater sensitivity to what is unfamiliar.

Growing up secure makes the unfamiliar intriguing. Growing up insecure makes the unfamiliar seem dangerous. To grow up secure, children require personalized attention. The famous child psychiatrist Donald Winnicott wrote about "the holding environment," the world of the child made safe for exploration by what he called "the good enough mother": one who is responsive to the child's expressed needs but careful not to impinge on the child's need to explore the unfamiliar.

Since pilots can't give you relief from turbulence by slowing down, you need to be convinced how little the plane moves in turbulence. Here's how you can prove it to yourself. Hold a cup half filled with water high over a bathtub. As quickly as you can, plunge the cup downward toward the tub (you do not need to hit bottom). Note how some of the water sloshes over the side of the cup. During flight, hold a cup half full of liquid against the edge of the tray table. If the plane goes up or down, so does the tray table, so it serves as a measure. If the plane were to plunge even one foot, you would see the water rise up above the cup. Note how, during even the most intense turbulence, the liquid, while it may wave, stays in the cup. Surprisingly, you will find that drinking from the cup, in turbulence, is less difficult than doing so while riding in a car. Here's an e-mail from a client who tried this out:

I have gained so much through this course, and my flights have been more manageable. I found the 5-4-3-2-1 Exercise most helpful, and I bring an interior decorating magazine on the plane because the pictures have lots of different items to describe when doing the exercise. Unfortunately, my biggest fear is turbulence. I remember you telling me that the plane was typically only moving a fraction of an inch. I remember stopping you and repeatedly asking: "What do you mean it's only moving a fraction of an inch?" I thought you MUST have meant relative to how high we were in the sky. But no, you really meant that the plane wasn't moving that much. For me, it feels like a cork in the ocean, wildly bobbing up and down. On my last flight, we hit turbulence, not bad enough for the flight attendants to be seated, but bad enough that the seat belt sign came on. I asked the flight attendant if we were okay, and then I sort of fell apart. I became a total borderline, unglued, tearful passenger. She was wonderful. But I was mortified. Unlike a true borderline, I didn't want attention; I wanted to blend in and be "normal."

On the next flight, I got a clear plastic cup, half-full of water. I told myself that I would NOT allow myself to freak out if the water didn't come out of the cup. I simply REFUSED to allow myself to freak out over a plane that was moving only less than an inch. I was taking charge! Anyway, it got turbulent, flight attendants–seated kind of turbulence. And the water never came out of my cup. I stared at my cup and I counted . . . one-one-thousand, two-one-thousand, three-one-thousand. I figured most turbulence doesn't last more than five minutes, so I stared at my cup and counted to sixty-one-thousand five times and if I needed to start over, I did.

I honestly feel like a switch was flipped, like some faulty neurological pathway that associated turbulence with immediate panic was reset. I flew from Houston to Cancun and back from Cancun to Chicago to Cedar Rapids and ALL of the flights were turbulent and I didn't panic. I was OK. No pounding chest. No tears. No "I'm going to die right now" feeling.

I wanted to pass this on in hopes that it might help others. It may look a bit OCD to stare non-stop at a cup while counting but so be it! It's less embarrassing than sobbing and yelling!

Build a Library of Turbulence "Chunks"

If the flight is smooth, I'm fine. I always check the weather. If it looks like a storm is brewing, I worry about turbulence. I know if the flight is turbulent, I'm going to have an awful time.

We are constantly bombarded with stimuli. Since we can't pay attention to everything, information that enters our eyes, ears, and other senses needs to be automatically filtered so we can focus on what's important. The Reticular Activating System (RAS) operates a lot like a spam filter—one that really works. A sample is taken of incoming sensory data. Each sample is called "a chunk." Chunks are stored in memory. When a chunk fails to match any of the stored chunks, the RAS signals the brain to take notice. But if a chunk matches a chunk taken in the past, and nothing of importance took place at that time, the RAS filters that chunk as irrelevant. It's filtered out so as not to enter your awareness. Thus, most of what is going on at any particular moment is filtered out. The RAS more or less says, "Been there, done that," and ignores it.

If turbulence were consistent, like a steady vibration, we would get used to it in a very short time. Every new encounter with turbulence would produce a chunk that was a match with the initial turbulence chunk. The RAS would simply ignore it. But turbulence doesn't follow a consistent pattern. Each moment of turbulence can feel very different from another. It takes many chunks to cover all the permutations of turbulence. Because I've had so many experiences with turbulence as a pilot, I have stored enough turbulence samples to match almost any new sample. My RAS ignores the turbulence that alarms my clients.

In order to remember to turn on the seat belt sign, pilots, because they have a comprehensive set of "turbulence chunks," have to program themselves to tune in to turbulence. More than once, an irritated flight attendant has called on the intercom to ask why the captain hasn't turned on the seat belt sign. The turbulence simply had not been noticed.

Whose view should prevail? That of the passenger who flies only occasionally and has few if any memory chunks to filter out turbulence, and so is alarmed by it? Or the view of a captain who flies day in and day out, tends not to notice turbulence, and is not alarmed by it? It isn't easy for passengers to store a turbulence chunk, never mind a whole library of them, for two reasons. First, as mentioned, turbulence is irregular and it takes considerable experience to memorize it in all its permutations. Second, the often-used strategy of trying to keep the flight out of mind interferes with chunk production. So does anti-anxiety medication. Research shows it interferes with the process of getting used to the motions—including motions during turbulence—that are a normal part of flying.

In turbulence, movements of different intensity and different direction are normal. Study each variation on the theme. Memorize the characteristics of each movement. This will help your RAS build its library of turbulence chunks.

Organize a strategy ahead of time. Limit the number of things you expose yourself to at any one moment so your RAS can keep up. For example, take plenty of time getting to the airport so there is never a rushed moment that overloads the RAS. At the airport, stop as soon as you step inside the terminal. Focus on what you can see: other passengers, luggage, computer check-in stations, airline personnel, and arrival and departure boards. Get used to all the visual information. One by one identify each thing you can see. Then, after naming each of the things you see, let yourself experience the things you see as though they were the meaningless shapes and colors of an abstract painting. Notice how this shift to meaninglessness brings your stress level nearer to zero. Then close your eyes and focus solely on what you hear. Identify each sound: PA announcements, the chatter of people, and instructions from security guards. Then listen to the sounds as though they were meaningless, like the sound of the ocean. Notice again what a difference this makes to your stress level. Next, notice the atmosphere of the room: the temperature, the level of humidity, any scent present, movement of air—or lack thereof. Once the atmosphere of the room is familiar, breathe it in as known and safe. Doing this allows the RAS to form any new "chunks" it needs. This sequence gets your stress level back near zero so you bring as little stress as possible along with you as you head toward the airplane. Repeat this exercise at each juncture of the preflight—from check-in, to security, to boarding area.

Adopt a Scientific Attitude

I just hate turbulence. I just want it to go away.

A scientist's aim is to gather and analyze information from a neutral stance. Pretend you are a scientist assigned to study the sounds and movements of routine flight. Instead of trying to keep the flight off your mind, eagerly observe every sound and motion while maintaining a sense of scientific detachment. This will help keep the "chunks" you establish free of emotion.

Conceptualize Physical Sensations

My body gets so tense when I fly. I just can't help it.

Movement of the plane is physically experienced in the passenger's body. This physical experience is intensified when there's no concept of what is causing it. Conversely, a realistic concept of what is going on limits the intensity of the physical experience. The best way I can think of to make this important principle clear is to tell you a personal experience. When I was sixteen, some friends were talking about French kissing. I said, "What's that?" One of the girls said, "You don't know what a French kiss is?" I said, "No." She grasped my head in her hands, pressed her mouth to mine, and the next thing I knew, it felt like the top of my head had blown off. I had never felt anything that intense in my life! Kisses that came later never approached that kiss in intensity. Why? As soon as the kiss was over, I conceptualized what she had done. I understood its cause and effect. And, of course, there was a name for the experience. As a result, no subsequent French kisses approached the intensity of that first one.

If we resist or dissociate during an experience, it can take place again with the same intensity. But when we take an experience in, Executive Function can map it out visually and use words to label it. If the experience can be figured out, its cause-and-effect explanation is understood. All this organizes the experience conceptually in the mind. Once it's conceptually organized, the intensity of the experience is deconstructed. No subsequent iteration will be as intense. Physical intensity must compete with mental activity as Executive Function tracks the experience. As long as Executive Function remains active and able to compare the current experience with pre-existing conceptualizations, awareness cannot be flooded with physical sensation.

This principle points again to the important role played by Executive Function. Just as a person wanting *more* intense physical sensation may employ alcohol or drugs to deactivate Executive Function, a passenger who wants to *limit* the intensity of physical sensation must keep Executive Function active by avoiding alcohol and drugs and by using the methodology described in this book to prepare for flight.

When a passenger experiencing turbulence has no accurate mental picture of what is going on, awareness is filled with physical sensations. Pilots, because they have a thorough mental organization of what is going on, have a hard time understanding why passengers are troubled in the least by turbulence. In the cockpit, they can see the plane is not deviating from its intended path or from its intended altitude.

Even though you're not in the cockpit, you can provide yourself with a visual conceptualization of what is going on. Using a pen and a sheet of paper, track the movement of the plane. Start the pen on the left side of the paper; let it move slowly over toward the right side, drawing a line to depict the forward movement of the plane. As the plane moves up or moves down, let your pen move ever so slightly up or down to track the up and down movements of the plane. When you reach the right side of the paper, start again on the left side, and make another graph of the plane's movement below the first one.

In addition to this visual conceptualization, give yourself a verbal cause-and-effect conceptualization. Tell yourself that the line you're drawing on the paper represents the movement of the plane across the planet. As the plane moves forward, it encounters air that is moving up or down at a speed of only one foot per second. The slow-moving air causes the fast-moving plane to bump. The bump lasts only a fraction of a second. The upward or downward movement caused by the bump is only a fraction of the forward speed of the plane. This is depicted by the graph you produce during turbulence. Doing this during turbulence will help you form a turbulence "chunk." In time, when you have accumulated enough "chunks" to represent all the different kinds of turbulence, awareness of turbulence will be filtered out of your mind by the Reticular Activating System.

Conceptualize Navigation

All I know is the plane is up somewhere. Picture where the plane is? Why would I do that?

Anxiety can be regulated in part by maintaining an orientation of where the plane is relative to its point of departure, its destination, and en route checkpoints. Some airliners offer visual displays that show the plane's progress. Even if your airliner has this, you can strengthen your regulation of anxiety by independently maintaining a sense of where the plane is. You will need a map. One can usually be found in the airline's in-flight magazine. If you plan ahead you can purchase or download a more detailed map to bring with you. When the plane takes off, look at your watch. Write the takeoff time on the map at the departure point. Add the total flying time to your takeoff time, and write that time on the map at the destination. Draw a line from your departure point to your destination. Divide the line up into one-hour segments. For example, if the flying time is four hours, mark the line between your departure point and your destination into four parts. At the first mark, add an hour to your takeoff time and write down that time. Add another hour and write that time at the second mark, etc. Once the map shows the time you will be at each of the marks, you can use your own watch at any time during the flight to figure out where you are on the map.

Conceptualize Anxiety Level

I'm more tense on some flights than on others. I don't know why. I just I hope I don't panic.

Keep track of your level of anxiety on a scale of zero to ten, with zero being completely relaxed and ten being the most anxiety you have ever experienced. If tempted at times to say that on a scale of zero to ten you're at a fourteen, then revise the scale so that fourteen becomes the new ten. If you like, you can write down your anxiety level on the map at takeoff and at the various checkpoints along the way. Otherwise, write it down, along with the time, on a piece of paper. As in any experience, as long as your Executive Function is able to assess your current anxiety level and compare it with the pre-existing zero-to-ten conceptualization, you cannot be overwhelmed. If, at any time, your level of arousal is higher than acceptable, turn to the 5-4-3-2-1 Exercise in order to bring it down to an acceptable level.

Go High Tech

There are apps that measure G-force, many of them free, that can be put on a smartphone. You can simply set your phone to Airplane Mode. In turbulence, you can read the actual G-load being put on the plane. You will be amazed how low the readings are. For information on apps that measure G-force go to fearofflying.com/app.

By the way, some anxious fliers worry that cell phones could interfere with the operation of the plane. That is not true. Cell phones operate on radio frequencies different from those used by planes. If left on, cell phones do no harm.

● ● ●

Turbulence, though it may not feel safe, is safe. If turbulence continues to seem unsafe in spite of the facts, what can you do? The key is to experience flight—turbulence included—just as it is, without adding imagination and without subtracting awareness by trying to keep it out of mind. These techniques, plus the Strengthening Exercise, are designed to turn flying around so that instead of it growing worse and worse with each flight, it becomes better and better as you continue to fly.

CHAPTER 10

Rumination

Flight phobia can develop by rumination, repeatedly imagining that one's flight could have ended in disaster. For example, the person may think:

Thought A: I felt the plane fall.

Thought B: What if it kept falling?

Thought C: What if it crashed?

Thought D: What if I'd been killed?

Thought E: I narrowly escaped death.

Thought F: I almost got killed!

When repeated, the sequence of thoughts becomes memorized. Once memorized, it can run on its own, trigger the release of stress hormones, disable reflective function, and cause psychic equivalence to take place, where the imaginary becomes real in your mind. The sequence then becomes the person's reality. Though never in any danger, the flight is carved in stone in the person's mind as a near-death experience. This fabrication can produce phobia.

Don't let rumination create phobia. Break rumination with the 5-4-3-2-1 Exercise. It enables you to shed the accumulated stress hormones and regain the ability to direct what your mind is focused on. Then apply Executive Function. Do your ABCs. Fully assess the situation. Consider the available courses of action. Build a plan of action (or non-action) based on the most likely outcome. Make a decision and commit to it. If unable to complete your ABCs and reach a commitment, shift your focus to some non-flying subject of interest so as to avoid returning to rumination.

If it's hard for you to recognize this pattern of rumination because, perhaps, it's so close to home, picture this: Suppose a CEO is expecting a call from his accountant telling him he owes millions in back taxes and is on the verge of bankruptcy. He expects the call to come in at any minute. He tells Amy, his ever-vigilant assistant, to be on the lookout for this call and to let him know the minute it comes in. Following instructions, Amy sits with one hand on the phone and one hand on the intercom. Unbeknownst to Amy, the CEO has decided that if the call comes through, he is going to leap out the window of his fiftieth-story office. The phone rings. It's the lottery calling to tell the CEO he has won a hundred million dollars. Amy picks up the phone and, at the same moment, presses the intercom. The CEO, expecting the worst, jumps out the window.

While that may be the kind of thing one would expect to see in a Mel Brooks comedy sketch (where it would be funny), that is how some of us live: spring-loaded, expecting disaster at every moment. So whenever Amy calls, we know we are doomed. Because we anticipate the message, we can't take in the accurate information. So when experiencing turbulence during flight, we "know" the plane is falling out of the sky.

Can a plane fall out of the sky? Can a wing break off? It is tempting to think that if something can happen in the mind, it can happen in the real world. Not so. Planes cannot fall out of the sky and wings cannot break off. The answer is, "No."

CHAPTER 11

Executive Function Overload

Anxiety can be controlled by commitment. When a non-routine situation arises, the amygdalae release stress hormones that force Executive Function to focus 100 percent of its attention on the situation. Executive Function, in the orbitofrontal cortex, then does its ABCs. It assesses whether the non-routine situation is an opportunity, an irrelevance, or a threat. After building a plan of action—or inaction—Executive Function commits the plan to the subcortex for execution. This commitment signals the amygdalae, also part of the subcortex, to end the release of stress hormones. Once the previously released stress hormones dissipate, anxiety disappears.

Multitask Overload

It might seem ideal for your inner CEO to have no stress at all, but psychological research shows that with no stress hormones at all, Executive Function is dormant. A moderate amount of stress hormones is needed to activate Executive Function and to keep it operating. But if stress hormones rise above the optimal level, Executive Function slows down. If stress hormones become excessive, your inner CEO shuts down completely. When that happens, there is no mental capacity remaining that can limit arousal, and panic is often the result.

Executive Function does not multitask. When two non-routine situations arise simultaneously or in rapid succession, both demand Executive Function's exclusive attention. Reflective function establishes priority, allowing Executive Function to focus its attention on one of the situations, build a plan, and make a commitment. Upon commitment to action or inaction, the amygdalae are signaled to discontinue stress hormone release about that situation; however, they may continue releasing stress hormones about the other non-routine situation that reflective function temporarily put on the back burner. Now Executive Function can focus on the other situation. After making a commitment about the second non-routine situation as well, Executive Function once again signals the amygdalae, and this time stress hormone release is halted altogether.

As you can see, multiple non-routine situations—whether real or imaginary—can present a problem. Reflective function is sensitive to stress hormones. If reflective function, weakened by stress hormones from multiple sources, is unable to prioritize, Executive Function cannot establish the necessary focus.

Good reflective function is like a CEO's assistant who says, "You have a lot to do today, but don't worry. I have it all spread out. At 9:00 a.m. you meet with Joe. At 10:00 a.m. you have a conference call. At 11:00 a.m. you meet with the accountant, and at noon you have lunch with Frank. At 2:00 p.m. you meet with Mary, at 3:00 p.m. with Edward, and at 4:00 p.m. with Judith." The CEO can devote full attention to each meeting and deal with each effectively. But if all seven things happened at once, the CEO would be overwhelmed. Each of the situations would remain unresolved. Each would continue to cause stress hormone release.

A common situation that can cause multiple source overload is a vista that presents a multitude of things to see. That is why some people have trouble with high places. For example, if a person climbs up the stairs inside the Notre Dame Cathedral in Paris and steps out onto the balcony, she suddenly—and perhaps unexpectedly—can see for miles. Thousands of structures are instantly presented to her mind. Strong reflective function can deal with this by establishing a priority. It allows the person to focus first on this, then that, and then the next thing. Like the CEO's assistant, reflective function limits the scope of a person's focus. It spreads things out, organizing them into an acceptable sequence over time. But a person with limited reflective function is like an executive with no assistant. Everything in view hits the person all at once; it's overwhelming! Obviously this can cause a fear of heights.

Action movies are chock-full of non-routine situations. Indiana Jones encounters poison darts, an out-of-control truck, assassins, explosions, gunfire, and giant rolling boulders. He has great Executive Function; he handles everything the bad guys throw at him. If we willfully suspend disbelief, we let the movie trigger our amygdalae. We let the movie excite us. If we get too excited, we try to remind ourselves it isn't real.

Though many life-threatening things can happen in the movies, we rarely encounter them in day-to-day living. Though you may imagine otherwise, life-threatening situations are rare when flying. The main complaint airline pilots have about their job is that it is boring.

You might find it boring, too, if it were possible for you to do all your flights in the cockpit. In the cockpit, reality constrains your imagination. If a noise triggers the release of stress hormones, your Executive Function is called on to do its ABCs. Assessment? One glance at the pilots would tell you that the noise you heard is routine to them. Build a plan? Simply stay put. Commit to that plan? Sure, why not?

It's different in the passenger cabin. If a noise triggers stress hormones, your Executive Function is again called on to do its ABCs. Assessment? If you recognize the noise as the flaps being retracted, you know the noise is not a threat. Build a plan? Action isn't needed. You decide to return to what you were doing. Committing to that, your amygdalae reset; stress hormones subside.

But what if you are unable to recognize the noise? Good Executive Function considers what is most probably the case. Since noises are usually routine, the unknown noise is probably routine. Assessing the situation as probably routine, good Executive Function returns to its original plan and recommits to doing what you were doing before hearing the noise.

But impaired Executive Function isn't satisfied with probability. Instead of assessing the situation based on what is most likely, its assessment consists of imagining everything the noise could mean. As a passenger, only one plan is available: to remain on the plane. Before being able to comfortably commit to that plan, it must rule out each and every disaster the noise could mean— not just as improbable—but as impossible. This situation illustrates the double-bind nature of Executive function impairment. It demands—of itself—an impossible task. As it seeks to build a plan, it must imagine every possible disaster; as it considers commitment, it must be certain every imaginable disaster is impossible. Unable to commit, stress hormones build up. Executive Function becomes unable to override the Mobilization System. It has only one way to control stress hormones: escape. But with escape impossible, stress hormones continue to rise, and high anxiety or panic results.

Frozen Executive Function

When the amygdalae detect a non-routine situation, stress hormones force the mind to focus on it. The focus remains—producing additional hormones—until Executive Function builds a plan of action and commits to it. If stress hormones build to the point that anxiety fills the mind to capacity, no capacity exists to build a plan. With no plan, there is no commitment; with no commitment, there is no signal to end stress hormone release. When Amy's finger is stuck on the intercom button, stress hormones keep pumping out.

Executive Function can freeze for other reasons. Research at Florida State University has shown that some of us have a hard time going from a decision to a commitment. Researcher Joyce Ehrlinger says some of us are "maximizers" and some are "satisficers." (*Note:* Ehrlinger coined this term to suggest a high degree of probability *suffices* to *satisfy* the person when making a commitment.) Maximizers obsess over decisions big or small and then fret about their choices later. Satisficers, however, tend to make a decision and live by it. "Maximizers," says Ehrlinger, "want to be certain they have made the right choice. High-level maximizers certainly cause themselves a lot of grief. Identifying the 'right' choice can become a never-ending task."

For most maximizers, this need for a perfect solution can be set aside if pressured by circumstances. For example, a car barreling toward you can trump the need for a plan that can't miss. But, in truly extreme cases of impairment, Executive Function can remain frozen—unable to do its ABCs—regardless of the circumstances. This is the deer-in-the-headlights phenomenon. To illustrate, a friend lived in a third-floor apartment that had no fire escape. Fire on a lower floor could block the stairway, leaving no escape other than her apartment window. Since jumping from the third floor would cause serious injury, I suggested that she install a chain ladder fire escape. One end of the chain ladder would be attached to the floor near a window. In case of a fire, the chain ladder would be tossed out the window so she could climb down the ladder to the ground below, thus escaping disaster.

She said a chain ladder wouldn't work. She said even if there were a fire in her apartment, she would not be able to use the ladder because she would be so frightened, she was certain she wouldn't be able to hold on. Images of falling from the ladder flooded her with terror. Unable to even imagine using the ladder, her Executive Function was paralyzed.

Since escaping from fire would require action, and being burned to death required no action, like a deer frozen in the headlights, she would be unable to take any action to escape the danger.

Good Executive Function is important. It assesses what goes on around us, builds plans that work for us, and commits to actions necessary to carry out our plans. To do its job, Executive Function needs protection. In an upcoming chapter, you will learn how to automatically protect Executive Function from stress hormone overload when flying.

CHAPTER 12

Regulating Anxiety with the Strengthening Exercise

Before you even get on the plane, there are a number of non-routine situations that keep Amy very busy pushing your intercom. You hit traffic on your way to the airport. Checking in did not go smoothly. Security, always stressful, pulled you aside for an extra scan. Waiting in the boarding area seems perfectly designed to push your anticipatory anxiety buttons. Finally, your section is called to board, and you encounter one non-routine thing after another. The passenger boarding bridge is a forbidding undecorated tube with no windows. It may be tilted, challenging your balance. The aisle of the plane is crowded. Passengers trying to stow their belongings in already over-crowded compartments may block you. Someone may be sitting in your seat. You find yourself seated next to a person whose size makes you feel even more squished in than usual.

Every one of these non-routine encounters triggers a release of stress hormones. Each encounter grabs your attention. After all, that is what stress hormones released by the amygdalae are supposed to do. Make no mistake; we get hit by a stress hormone release hundreds of times a day. In most cases, you don't notice the stress hormone release or your inner CEO ending it. We are fairly masterful at it. But, if too many things happen too fast, your Executive Function can't keep up. If the stress hormones build up, your Executive Function weakens. Then, just one more thing is too much. You nearly explode at a person who has brought on more items than allowed and has to put them away while you stand there crowded in the aisle.

This can be tough. You know this is your last chance to escape. If you bolt, you will feel instant relief. But, you also know that, after the instant relief, you will feel worse for a very long time.

During takeoff, passengers get bombarded. There is one sound and physical sensation after another. The amygdalae regard each of these as a separate non-routine situation deserving of its own shot of stress hormones. As takeoff begins, the engines rev up to a high-pitched scream. Exhaust from the engines roars. Acceleration pushes passengers back in their seats. Overhead compartments flex and make noises. During the first few seconds of takeoff, Executive Function receives several demands for 100 percent of its attention.

Consider just the first non-routine alert during takeoff. When the engines rev up, Executive Function needs to evaluate the sound, decide it is not a threat, and, by committing to do nothing, signal the amygdalae to discontinue stress hormone release. If that is dispensed with, Executive Function will be ready to focus fully on the second non-routine alert: a thunderous roar. It will conclude the roar is not a threat, commit to doing nothing, and again signal the amygdalae to quiet down.

But if the second alert hits before Executive Function has dismissed the first, two situations demand its full attention simultaneously. It's as though the CEO, already dealing with a touchy client, has to deal with another who shows up unexpectedly, demanding her attention. Imagine, then, what happens when a third, even more demanding client appears—one who muscles his way into your office.

The third stressful in-flight situation—being pushed back in the seat—is more complex than the first two because it is so physical. Few of us are completely free of trauma due to physical intrusion. In order to dismiss this physical intrusion, Executive Function has to separate it from earlier ones—not an easy task. With stress hormones from three non-routine situations to deal with, Executive

Function may be at risk of collapse when a fourth alert takes place: noises from the overhead compartments. So now the CEO is grappling with three demanding clients, one of whom is quite physical, and then the phones start ringing, the fax machine goes off, and Amy is pushing the intercom every which way.

In this case, knowledge is not power. Knowledge, since it is stored in an area of the brain separate from the amygdalae, isn't enough to prevent them from releasing stress hormones. Things happen too fast during takeoff. Yes, if the non-routine situations that occur during takeoff could be spread out so that, instead of taking place seconds apart, they happened minutes apart, your inner CEO might be able to keep up. But they don't. They occur in rapid-fire succession. Processing them as fast as they take place is a lot to expect from your CEO. Stress hormones from unprocessed non-routine situations build up. When stress hormones accumulate, Executive Function slows down. That makes it even harder for your CEO to keep up. The answer is obvious; we need to reduce the load on your CEO by decreasing or, even better, preventing stress hormone release during takeoff, and then later, during turbulence. We need to make it more like it is for a pilot. A pilot's Executive Function keeps up—still not because of knowledge—but because the noises and motions are routine to his or her amygdalae.

Since it is unlikely that you will fly often enough for your amygdalae to regard takeoff as routine, we reduce the load on your inner CEO another way. We link the things that happen during takeoff, during turbulence, and in other flight situations to an experience that inhibits amygdalae response.

How SOAR Prevents the Release of Stress Hormones

Systematic Desensitization reduces amygdalae response to a non-routine situation by slowly making it routine. This transformation is accomplished by exposure to the non-routine situation at a very low level, followed by gradual increases in intensity or duration until, at the end of treatment, an ordinary level of exposure has become routine to the amygdalae. But for flight phobia, Systematic Desensitization is not a practical treatment. Even with an airliner and crew at one's disposal (a highly unlikely prospect), exposure to flight stimuli cannot be adjusted finely enough to achieve desensitization.

Fortunately, the methodology developed by the SOAR program serves as a practical substitute for Systematic Desensitization. Unlike desensitization, SOAR does not try to get you used to the flight. What we are doing is dramatically different. Instead of training the amygdalae to regard flying as routine, we are linking flight situations to an experience that either counterbalances the effect of the stress hormones or, preferably, inhibits the stress hormone release. Then, when a flight situation that previously triggered stress hormones is encountered, because it is linked to something that bars the amygdalae from producing stress hormones, the amygdalae get shut down by proxy.

Ultimately, desensitization does occur, for when a person has had a series of flights in which stress hormone release has been regulated by the SOAR methodology, flight does become regarded as routine by the amygdalae.

Social Engagement Overrides Stress Hormones

The amygdalae release stress hormones when something that is non-routine takes place or someone unfamiliar arrives on the scene. Thus, the appearance of an unfamiliar person triggers stress hormones, which activate the Mobilization System. This causes an urge to escape. Stress hormones also activate Executive Function. It overrides the urge to escape in favor of time to make a conscious assessment of the new person. The stress hormones also cause an increase in heart rate and breathing rate. The body is prepared to run or to fight in case Executive Function decides this person is a threat.

In addition to the conscious assessment made by Executive Function, a system that operates completely unconsciously assesses the person. This unconscious system, the Social Engagement System, senses the person's facial expression, body language, and voice characteristics. If it likes what it senses, it counteracts the hormonally caused increase in heart rate. According to researcher Stephen Porges, the Social Engagement System applies a braking action to the vagus nerve, a nerve that regulates the heart. This slowing of the heart causes a general calming effect in the brain and in the body. The urge to escape disappears, and interest in interacting socially with the person begins to develop.

Automatically, the brain overrides the effect of stress hormones when signals we unconsciously receive from others indicate that they are trustworthy. People who once were strangers, through the calming action of the Social Engagement System, can become friends or business partners, and can set the stage for even more.

Oxytocin: The Anti-Anxiety Hormone

The Social Engagement System also facilitates reproduction. If the signals passed between two people indicate exclusivity and devotion, a social relationship can become a romantic relationship. When mutual gaze suggests each person regards the other as if they are the only person in the world, the anti-anxiety hormone oxytocin is produced. Oxytocin, when present in sufficient amounts, inhibits the amygdalae, making stress hormone release impossible. Fear, worry, and anxiety disappear. In their absence, desire—if present—is acted upon. Oxytocin is also produced after sexual intercourse. By lying calmly together, bonding takes place, and conception is more likely.

Thus, there are two ways the Social Engagement System calms. First, when it senses a person is trustworthy enough to be a friend, or a partner in some enterprise, it slows the heart rate by applying a braking action to the vagus nerve that regulates the heart. Second, when it senses a person is trustworthy as a reproductive partner, the Social Engagement System produces oxytocin that temporarily makes all fear—including fear of sexual activity—disappear.

Nature also uses oxytocin to facilitate nurturing. High levels of oxytocin are produced when a mother nurses her baby. Oxytocin inhibits the amygdalae so she can calmly provide the physical and psychological nourishment her baby needs.

The Strengthening Exercise, instead of turning non-routine situations into routine situations, controls stress by *linking* non-routine flight situations to a moment in which heart rate was slowed by an empathically attuned face—a deep, sympathetic connection with another person—or in which amygdalae response was inhibited by oxytocin in a romantic or sexual situation.

To set up the Strengthening Exercise, we need to identify a moment in your life when the Social Engagement System was unmistakably activated. We might expect there to be many such moments. But this is not always the case. The existence of flight anxiety in an individual suggests that empathic attunement was more the exception than the rule. Nevertheless, even one suitable moment allows the links needed to regulate flight anxiety to be established.

Look now for a moment of empathic attunement. Scan through your life experience. We need a moment not when you were happy or relaxed because there was no stress, but a moment when a person's presence caused you to feel both connected and calm. The amygdalae are very interested in faces. A person's face can express things that words cannot. Look for a moment of eye-to-eye contact when someone was gazing at you as though you were the only person in the world; their eyes told you that you were wanted and cared about. The moment may have been brief. It may have been during a quiet conversation. Other possibilities are a romantic dinner, taking a walk together, a marriage proposal or wedding vows, the first moments alone together after the wedding ceremony, sexual foreplay or afterglow, or the contact between parents when holding a newborn child. One moment is particularly worth consideration: Nursing an infant produces more oxytocin than any other human experience. If you have nursed a baby, that is probably the most powerful moment you can use.

Finding a Moment of Connection

Dear Capt. Tom. I'm having trouble with the Strengthening Exercise because I don't have any of those moments you talk about. I've been divorced for two years so I can't use marriage vows or engagement. I've never had children so I can't use THAT. I don't have a boyfriend I feel that good about. I'm a happy person. I have lots of good times with friends, and it is relaxing to me to lie on the beach, or watch TV, or read a book. But I can't come up with a moment like the ones you describe to use in the exercise.

I had to explain to this client that emotional strength is based on relationships, and if we had to depend only on relationships we have right now, many of us wouldn't have much strength to draw on. To increase emotional strength when flying, we need a moment—regardless of how short it was or how it ended—in which the fear system shut down. It shuts down when a lover's eyes tell you—not necessarily consciously, because chemistry is unconscious—that you are the only person in the world. Yes, I know. It may not have been the same the next morning, or the next year. But in such moments, the shutting down of the fear system allows us—for better or for worse—to become physically close. That is how the Social Engagement System works. It overrides the Mobilization System and completely inhibits stress hormone release. When fear is out of the picture, the remaining emotion is desire.

Even though her marriage did not work out, my client salvaged something valuable. By going back to when she was dating her ex-husband, and remembering a moment when the way he looked at her caused her to melt, she was able to find what she needed to end fear of flying.

Attunement between two people can be brief. Don't discard or invalidate a moment because the relationship did not last. Even if things ended badly, the moment of attunement you were able to achieve was real. It is yours. Even a chance encounter will do. Even if the person is no longer part of your life, you have a right to use a moment of attunement, and to draw strength from it. That is what emotional strength is built from—moments of attunement. We need to draw upon empathically attuned moments, whenever they arose, whomever they were with. Don't insist on permanence. Don't discount a moment because of impermanence. It's fine to go back and use a moment with people who are no longer alive; they can still contribute to your emotional strength. If unable to find a memory that inhibits stress hormone release, look for a moment of friendship. The Social Engagement System overrides the effect of stress hormones when it senses another person is empathically attuned to you.

Perhaps, after a thorough search, you've found no suitable moments with another person. There's a reason we say dogs are man's—or woman's—best friend. People may let us down, but pets don't. They are often our most reliable source of calming. Clients have reported good in-flight results when a pet was used in the Strengthening Exercise. Research reported in the journal *Hormones and Behavior* has shown that owners of dogs had increased levels of oxytocin when gazing into their dog's eyes. Because of the oxytocin factor, even if you find a moment of empathic attunement with a person, if you have a pet, do some Strengthening Exercise sessions linking your pet's eyes to in-flight scenes as well. I will show you exactly how to do this in the Strengthening Exercise later in the chapter.

If You Need Help

If you really can't recall a moment of connection with someone, you may want to consider seeing a psychotherapist to help you locate a moment that is hidden. To illustrate how a moment can be hidden, one employer referred a young executive to therapy because her inability to control her alcohol use was impacting her career. When she came to see me, I asked her what her childhood was like, and she said, "Oh, my mom was great; we had a great time together." I asked her to give an example of a great moment with her mom. She replied, "I can't remember an exact moment, but things were great between her and me." When I persisted, she became angry, continuing to insist that she had had a great childhood, a great mother, had a lot of fun, and that the fact that she could not offer an example meant nothing.

Actually, it means a great deal. When an adult claims a good childhood and a good relationship with a parent but cannot recall specific details, it indicates profound childhood depression; the memories of their entire childhood are shrouded in depression.

For the Strengthening Exercise, we need a moment that, because of the empathic connection, slows the heart rate, or a romantic moment, because it produces oxytocin, which simply shuts down your alarm system. When someone is attuned and empathic, he or she would not hurt you because it would hurt them as well. In a romantic moment, the fear system turns off. *Do not make the mistake of choosing a "happy moment" or thoughts of a situation that relaxes you.* Neither happiness nor relaxation can activate the vagal brake to slow the heart rate or release oxytocin to shut down the amygdalae. When happy or relaxed, the amygdalae are still on guard. It is only when another person's face and eyes communicate what words cannot express that the amygdalae completely shut down. Do not use an imaginary moment. Your amygdalae respond, and shut down, only to the real deal. You need a moment not from imagination but from history.

For example, we respond differently to a genuine smile versus a social smile. When another person smiles at you, if his smile is spontaneous, certain muscles on his face contract that cannot be made to operate intentionally. They operate only when a smile is spontaneous. If there is eye contact, his smile triggers an automatic response;

you reflexively smile in response to his smile. Your smile mirrors his smile. When you reflexively mirror his spontaneous smile, the corresponding involuntary muscles contract on your face. Contraction of these muscles is associated with times when you smiled spontaneously out of delight. Thus, when your muscles contract, you get a good feeling. The other person's genuine smile evokes good feelings in you. Not so with a social smile, even if, intellectually, the smile looks great. The muscles that contract in a spontaneous smile cannot be made to operate intentionally. When you reflexively mirror a put-on social smile, you feel nothing.

When you find a moment, remember exact details of what was happening and what you saw on his or her face. Then imagine that person touching a photograph or a cartoon of a flight scene to his or her cheek. As you imagine the person's face and eyes together with the flight scene, it establishes a link to help protect you from anxiety during actual flight.

If, for the purposes of the Strengthening Exercise, you are unable to locate and vividly recall a moment of empathic attunement, I believe you would be wise to spend a few sessions with a therapist, not only to help you find a suitable moment to use in the exercise but also to determine whether you are—or were—unknowingly suffering from depression. If, indeed, there have been no moments of empathic attunement, develop a new relationship with the therapist, one built on trust and empathic attunement, which can then be used in the Strengthening Exercise.

Linking Flight to a Regulatory Moment

Once you find a regulatory moment of either type—one that inhibits stress hormone release or one that overrides the effect of stress hormones—the next step is to link the moment to each situation that could trigger the release of stress hormones during flight. Once these links have been established, the amygdalae respond to flight as they do to the regulatory moment. If linked to an oxytocin-producing moment, the flight situation triggers the release of oxytocin. Oxytocin keeps the amygdalae from releasing stress hormones. If linked to a moment of attunement, the flight situation activates the vegal brake. This slows the heart rate, and provides calming in spite of stress hormones. Links to a moment of profound empathic attunement may both activate the vagal brake and cause the release of oxytocin.

During flight, the amygdalae release stress hormones in response to anything they consider non-routine. Let's call these things NORs (short for NOn-Routine). Certain moments with another person help us regulate anxiety. Let's call such a moment RM (short for Regulatory Moment). To regulate your anxiety during flight, we are going to link each NOR to a RM. The links are established by using the Strengthening Exercise. By linking a NOR with a RM, it is transformed into a NORM (short for normal). Though your amygdalae react to NORs, they do not react to NORMs.

First, vividly recall your RM, a moment of sexual attunement or empathic attunement. Notice how the person's eyes show they are attuned to you, care about you and sense what you are feeling. Imagine he or she is holding a NOR photo next to their cheek. Be aware of the person's face and the photograph at the same time.

If the RM involves a baby, imagine the photo of the NOR is being held by the baby's face so you see both at the same time. By simultaneously being aware of the photo (NOR) and face (RM), the NOR and the RM become a NORM (NORMal) to which the amygdala will not react.

A less technical–sounding explanation may help you understand how the Strengthening Exercise works. By way of analogy, let's say you own a coffee and doughnut shop. Every day, you have regular customers who come in. You see them day in and day out. You talk with them and they talk with each other. Since the regulars like to socialize with each other, it's not essential that you talk with them each day to keep them coming back. As the business grows, you find you need to be in the back office more, so you hire a woman named Amy to help out at the counter. You tell Amy that in the next few days, she'll see the same people coming in each morning; they are the regulars. They'll come in every day whether you're there to greet them or not. So you instruct Amy that when regulars come in, just to take care of their order—and not to bother you in the back office. But, you add, if a person you don't recognize as a regular comes in, that's different; you want to know about it because you want to greet that person and hopefully get him to be a regular customer.

So, being an obedient employee, Amy doesn't notify you when a routine customer comes in, but calls it to your attention every time a new (non-routine) customer enters.

Then, one day while Amy is on duty, you walk in with a person she's never seen before. Clearly, Amy isn't going to run over to you and tell you that you're with someone new. It's obvious to Amy that this "new" person is a routine person to you. So she says nothing and just continues with her work. The same would hold true if your business partner entered the shop with an unknown person. Recognizing your partner, Amy would realize that while she doesn't recognize the new person, he is probably known to you or, if not, at least is safe, since he's known to your partner.

To further the analogy, let's say Amy has a boyfriend. She has repeatedly had this wonderful experience with him in which, when he looks into her eyes, she feels he sees her very soul. When he does that, she melts. So when Amy is on duty at the doughnut shop and her boyfriend unexpectedly comes in with someone she's never seen before, she just feels good. Of course, she's supposed to call the boss and tell him about the new person, but when her boyfriend looks at her in that special way, she forgets all about her duties—the last thing on her mind is the boss. And, of course, it is okay, because the new person wasn't going to become a customer anyway. Her boyfriend just dropped by to say hello and his friend happened to be with him.

Occurrences such as these can be considered "routine by proxy." Since we can't use systematic *desensitization* (it isn't possible to gently and gradually make routine to the amygdalae all the things that happen during flight), we use Systematic *Inhibition* to make each thing routine by proxy.

Conducting the Strengthening Exercise

The Strengthening Exercise has three required phases and a fourth optional one—all of which must be completed prior to your flight:

1. Phase One links things that happen on a normal flight to a moment of empathic attunement. Though these things are normal and routine, they are not routine to your amygdalae. Your amygdalae regard these things as NORs. We want to transform them into NOR-RMs.

2. Phase Two links a moment of empathic attunement to the specific things you fear might go wrong. Anyone's amygdalae—even a pilot's—would regard these as non-routine. Again, we are transforming NORs into NOR-RMs so that your amygdalae will not react.

3. Phase Three links empathic attunement to each element of a panic attack. Each element is a NOR that needs to be neutralized by being linked to an RM.

4. Phase Four is optional.

As you begin, though you may be tempted to use a photograph as an aid in remembering a person's face, don't: An image recorded by a camera will probably lack the eye-to-eye intimacy that captivates the amygdalae. In a moment of true intimacy, no one says,

"Hold that pose; let me get a shot of that." Involuntary changes take place in the face and eyes during genuine empathic attunement. The amygdalae sense these changes. What is needed to make the link work is an image recorded by your mind when someone's eyes said something that words cannot say.

Bring an empathically attuned moment with one person to mind. (If the moment you have in mind involves more than one person, select one person to focus on.) Vividly recall the person's face, lips, eyes, and warmth of expression. What do you see in the person's eyes? What do you feel? What do you hear? Is there a scent present? Relive the moment as though it were happening now. The details of a moment of attunement may elicit surprisingly powerful feelings. You may want to protect the feelings in your heart by placing your hands there.

While the presence of feelings is a strong indication that the moment will be an effective one to use in the Strengthening Exercise, some equally effective moments do not elicit any noticeable feelings. And, as you conduct the exercise, feelings—if present initially—will naturally wane. That's fine. Remember: We are linking one image with another image; feelings are not necessarily part of the exercise.

Phase One Strengthening Exercise—Routine Flight Situations

Though these flight situations are things that happen routinely on every flight, your amygdalae may regard some of them as nonroutine, or NORs. Link each item on this list to your Regulatory Moment of empathic or sexual attunement (RM). You'll notice that we say "a stranger" in some cases below; we do this intentionally so as not to trigger any anxiety or stress hormone release while doing the exercise. It's also best to think of these items in reverse order, so that your mind can't fast-forward to a moment of disaster. Start at the end of the flight and work backward

- A plane taxiing to the terminal after the flight
- A plane slowing down on the runway after landing
- A plane about to land, aborts the landing, and goes back up
- A plane about to land, wheels just a foot or two off the runway
- Landing gear being extended
- A plane gliding down for landing
- A plane cruising in smooth air
- A plane cruising in rough air (notice that the two cruise "pictures" are identical to the eye)
- A stranger (or a cartoon character in these situations) hearing a noise he or she doesn't recognize
- A stranger hearing the engines change speed
- A stranger thinking the speed of the plane is changing too much
- A stranger feeling heavy in the seat as the plane starts climbing
- A stranger feeling light-headed as the plane levels off after climbing
- A stranger imagining the airplane will tip over when making a turn
- Wing flaps being retracted after takeoff (sound: like a blender)
- Engine power being reduced after takeoff (sound: less engine noise)
- A stranger feeling light-headed (like a swiftly upward-moving elevator arriving at an upper floor)
- A plane's landing gear going up after takeoff (sound: like water running through a pipe as hydraulic fluid is flowing to raise the gear; follow by watching a stranger who hears a clunk as the gear is locked in the up position, and less airflow noise as the gear doors close)
- A plane's nose wheel lifting off the runway
- A plane's landing gear leaving the ground (sound: a clunk as the gear strut extends to its limit as the weight of the plane is transferred to the wings)

- A plane rolling down the runway (sound: overhead compartments may rattle, but that is just "furniture"—not the structure of the plane; the nose wheel going bump, bump, bump, over the lights installed in the centerline of the runway)
- A plane beginning takeoff (sound: engines rev up, higher pitched sound)
- A stranger being pushed back in the seat by acceleration of the plane
- A plane waiting to take off
- A plane taxiing out for takeoff
- Announcement by the captain
- Announcement by a flight attendant
- Plane pushing back from the terminal
- Engines starting
- Cabin door being closed
- Flight attendants taking their seats
- Someone waiting on the plane for departure
- A view of the seat back in front of a passenger
- A view of the window beside a passenger
- A view of the compartment over a passenger's head
- A view of the armrest under a passenger's arm
- A view of the seat belt fastened over a passenger's lap
- Someone getting into his or her assigned seat
- Someone looking at the assigned seat
- Someone finding the right seat
- Someone walking in the aisle of the plane
- Someone thinking there are too many people on the plane
- Someone boarding the plane
- Someone in the Jetway
- People waiting in the boarding lounge
- People checking in
- People arriving at the airport
- Someone riding to the airport

- Someone leaving home
- Someone packing
- Someone waking up the morning of the flight
- Someone the day before the flight
- Someone making arrangements to fly
- Someone thinking of flying

Occasionally, when about to land, the pilot must discontinue the landing. This is usually because the plane landing ahead of you has not yet left the runway. Just as you were expecting to be on the ground, the plane goes back up. This needs to be put into our Phase One practice.

If claustrophobia is a problem, pay special attention to what you will see when in your seat, such as the window, the aisle, the overhead compartment, the seat back in front of you, and another passenger beside you. Link each of these to your moment of empathic attunement. The following may help you understand how powerful links to your immediate environment can be.

From time to time, a student pilot who flies comfortably with an instructor but is extremely anxious when flying solo has asked me for help. Naturally, it feels safer with the instructor aboard; a new pilot is right to trust their instructor more than they trust themselves. But solo flight is a necessary part of training. How can the anxiety be relieved? The answer is to go out to the airport on a day when they are not going to fly, to get into the plane, and to take out the checklist. If the student pilot is male, and married, I ask him to picture his wife's face when she is attuned to him. I might suggest he go back in time to when they were dating and to recall the moment when he realized, from what he saw in her eyes, that they were about to make love for the first time. Holding that image in mind, I ask him to read the first item on the checklist, the position of the throttle. I ask him to place his hand on the throttle and to picture her face and eyes. Then, going to the next item, perhaps the ignition switch, touch it and again picture her face and eyes. This is continued with every item on the checklist, so as—as it were—to embed her face and her spirit into every control and instrument in the cockpit. Then, when the student pilot is in the cockpit to do his solo flight, instead of the controls and instruments taking emotional strength from him, her presence in them provides him with emotional strength.

Similarly, I would like each of the things you see when in your seat to give you—rather than take away—emotional strength. I want you to be so comfortable in the seat that there is no sense of a need to be anywhere else. Look at the seat back in front on you. There is a tray table stowed there. Use that flat surface as if it were a movie screen. Take the image of the empathically attuned face you have in your mind, and imaginarily project that face onto the tray table. Then look to the side, and project the face onto the wall beside the window. Then, look overhead, and project the face onto the overhead compartment. Do this now, as if you were on a plane. And, when you are actually seated on a plane, do this again. Project the face onto the tray table, the wall, and the overhead compartment there on the plane. During the flight, from time to time, seeing these surfaces will unconsciously trigger oxytocin.

Phase Two Strengthening Exercise—Non-Routine Flight
Since Phase Two scenes can cause anxiety, use cartoons. When awful things happen to cartoon characters, we laugh. We know they'll bounce back. For example, Road Runner rolls a boulder off the top of a mesa. It plunges down and smashes Wile E. Coyote into the desert. Undaunted, Wile E. emerges and resumes the chase. There are of course things you, as an anxious flier, might be troubled by. But with a cartoon chaacter as your stand-in, the troubling things can be brought to mind without causing you anxiety. Presented to the amygdalae in this way, any item can be linked to a moment of

empathic attunement while maintaining the stress-free atmosphere needed while doing the Strengthening Exercise.

Consider Snoopy sitting in a first-class seat, thinking, "I like to sit on top of my doghouse and pretend I'm a World War I fighter pilot shooting at the Red Baron. But that is pretend; I can control what I pretend. But this is real! I'm not in control and I don't like it." He is nervously biting his toenails, saying, "They are going to close the door of this plane; my doghouse doesn't even have a door!" Snoopy thinks, "My doghouse is only two feet high. I can jump down from there. But this plane is going to go twenty thousand feet up. I can't jump down from there." Picture a balloon over his head in which there is a drawing of:

- Snoopy out of control
- Snoopy imagining the door of the plane being closed
- Snoopy imagining his plane plunging

Here's a suggested list of cartoon characters:

- Lucy
- Linus
- Snoopy
- Charlie Brown
- Donald Duck
- Mickey Mouse
- Fred Flintstone
- Wilma Flintstone
- Homer Simpson
- Marge Simpson
- Bart Simpson
- Lisa Simpson
- Superman
- Spider-Man

- Batman
- Scooby Doo
- Shrek

Since different people have different concerns, you will need to compose your own list of potential things that make you anxious when flying. The list below is a good starting point: Add or subtract items to make the list fit you.

- What if this doesn't work?
- What if I panic?
- What if I fail?
- Plane falling
- Pilots fighting for control in the cockpit
- Things flying around the cabin
- People screaming
- Never seeing loved ones again
- Loved ones feeling grief
- Engine problem
- Plane can't get off the ground
- Plane gets off the ground and slides back
- Plane shaking
- Can't get out
- Making a fool of myself
- A mechanical noise
- Plane flipping upside down
- Hitting another plane in the air
- Waiting for something to go wrong
- Explosion
- Flight attendant looking upset
- Feeling isolated and alone

Fine-Tuning Your Phase Two List

Review your list. Break down each item into its component parts. For example, the item "What if the plane crashes?" can be broken down into more detail: What things could cause you to think the plane is crashing? A certain noise? An expression on a flight attendant's face? Someone screaming? A feeling of falling? Again, what would cause you to think the plane is falling? A feeling of light-headedness? Turbulence?

After breaking down the item into its component parts, treat each component as a separate item in the exercise. Amygdalae operation is highly visual. Note any imagery associated with an item.

When learning to fly, student pilots, with an instructor onboard, experiment with flying too slow. When too slow, air flowing over the wing causes a low frequency rumble that can be heard and felt. Practice trains the student pilot to recognize this sound and feeling, and to increase the speed.

On my first flight as a passenger on a Boeing 777, as the plane was coming in for a landing, I sensed this same low-frequency sound and rumble. Immediately, because of my training, I became concerned. But, the rumble continued, and the plane continued flying fine. Though most landings are done with the flaps set at thirty degrees, some situations call for forty degrees. When the forty-degree setting is used, air flowing over the flaps causes a slight rumble on most planes I was flying. I was not aware that when the 777 is landing with flaps at forty degrees, the rumble is far more pronounced. When I realized what was going on, I was confident the plane was in no danger. But I continued to feel anxious until the plane was on the ground. Though I knew the plane was fine, that knowledge did not alleviate the anxiety. What could explain this? In his research on emotional control, Stephen Porges, has found that low-frequency sound triggers the release of stress hormones. He believes this is because low frequency sounds are associated with predators such as lions, tigers, and panthers, and with earthquakes.

A defensive reaction to low-frequency sound and vibration appears to be built into our genes. No matter how I try to convince anxious fliers that they are safe in turbulence, some remain anxious. This may be due to a low-frequency rumble that is heard and felt intermittently when in turbulence. Each time the plane hits a bump, just for a moment, the airflow over the wing is altered so that it causes a rumble. To help you recognize it, recall the sound and feeling when you have opened one window of your car when driving.

Can we change this defensive reaction? Can we get rid of the feeling of danger and need to escape? Yes, we need to link both hearing this sound and feeling this rumble to an empathically attuned face. Try to recall a very low frequency sound or rumble. Now, picture a cartoon of Homer Simpson or Charlie Brown sitting on a plane. Imagine he is hearing that low-frequency sound. Pretend the person you use in your Strengthening Exercise is holding that cartoon touching his or her cheek. This links the low-frequency sound to an experience that is calming. Repeat this with feeling the low-frequency rumble. In turbulence, there are other noises inside the plane, such as the overhead compartments rattling. Link those as well.

Phase Two Options

The following cartoon ideas are examples of how thoughts of crashing can be brought to mind without distress, so they can be more easily linked to a memory of empathic attunement.

Plunging. Snoopy is on his doghouse pretending he is flying his Sopwith Camel. He feels it shaking in turbulence and worries his doghouse will plunge out of control. Imagine this as a cartoon held beside an attuned face. Or, make it turn out right when Charlie Brown, bringing a bowl of dog food, interrupts Snoopy's plunge. Snoopy feels relieved, knowing the disaster was just his imagination taking over. Even cartoon dogs get psychic equivalence!

Panic. Imagine Linus on a plane with his security blanket. Lucy grabs it. Linus imagines he will panic. Imagine the cartoon is alongside an empathically attuned face. But amazingly, he doesn't panic, and the moment of empathic attunement comes to mind. When Lucy realizes she can no longer upset Linus by snatching his security blanket, she gives it back. Though Linus is glad to have his security blanket back, he has a huge smile on his face knowing the emotional strength he needs is now built inside him.

Claustrophobia. Tweetie Pie is in her cage. Normally she feels cozy and protected in there. But as her cage is being put on an airplane, she feels panic. Though Tweetie Pie can fly, she can't fly here because she is trapped. Put the cartoon by an empathically attuned face. A kindly flight attendant takes Tweetie Pie and her cage up to the cockpit, where she meets the captain. Tweetie Pie recognizes the captain can fly just as well as she can. Feeling confident about the captain, she no longer feels the need to get out.

Difficulty Letting Go of Control. Green Lantern flies with his magic ring. It keeps him aloft through his sheer force of will. If something interfered with his concentration, he'd drop like a stone. He sits in the plane gripping the armrests, maintaining his concentration to keep the plane in the air. He sees other passengers are not doing the same thing and thinks, "Don't they understand what will happen if they don't concentrate on holding the plane in the air?!" Put the cartoon by an empathically attuned face. The person sitting next to Green Lantern explains the Gelatin Exercise to him and tells him the plane can't do anything but go where it's pointed when going that fast through the air. "Oh," he says, relaxing his grip, "I didn't know that."

Something Going Wrong Technically. Iron Man flies using a suit of armor that requires maintenance by a team of highly trained technicians. He knows if someone sabotages his jet boots, he won't be able to stay in the air. That leads him to imagine someone not fixing something on the plane, so that it won't stay in the air. Have the cartoon next to an empathically attuned face. The person sitting next to him explains that—unlike his jet boots—the airplane has multiple backup systems for everything that is needed for flight and recommends he get some backup systems built into his jet boots.

Bad Weather. Storm, from the *X-Men,* is able to slip between the winds. If the weather is bad though, she'll have a rocky time of it. If there's a tornado, she's as helpless as anyone else. Imagine this cartoon by an empathically attuned face. She asks if she can meet the captain and talk this over. The captain explains she will be fine because airliners fly far above the tornadoes below.

Something Unknown Causing Disaster. Harry Potter is an expert flier, but if an enemy hits him with the right spell at the wrong time, he'll be jolted off his broom and crash onto the quidditch patch. He worries that the plane could be jolted if "anything" happens. Picture the cartoon by an empathically attuned face. But of course, everything always works out in the end for Harry Potter. So, use your imagination and figure out how.

Kinesthetic Thinking

Some people think in physical—kinesthetic—terms. They're not troubled by images of the plane crashing; it is what they *physically* feel that causes them to react. If your thinking does not seem to use images or other visual representation, the Strengthening Exercise may need to be modified. You will need to get a handle on the physical experience so it can be neutralized. If your thinking is predominately kinesthetic, here's how to modify Phase Two of the Strengthening Exercise:

1. Go back in your memory and re-live a flight when the plane moved in a way that bothered you.

2. When you find a moment when movement of the plane bothered you, freeze on it. Do whatever you can to "grab"

the physical feeling. Is the plane dropping out from under you? Is your stomach tight? Is your chest tight? Are you gripping the armrest? To give yourself relief, I want you to take yourself out of the situation and put a cartoon character in your place. Why does this help? When cartoon characters are in a bad situation, we know that they will get out okay. Using a cartoon character makes the situation less serious. This way, the situation we want to link to the person's face is registered with the amygdalae without causing you distress.

3. Pretend the cartoon character is in the situation that you were in. Pretend the cartoon character is feeling what you were feeling.

4. Next, think of a person you have a good connection with. Remember their eyes when there are good feelings between the two of you. Imagine he or she is holding a comic strip touching their face, and in the comic strip, the cartoon character is feeling what you were feeling. Notice the comic strip and the person's eyes at the same time.

5. One of the most difficult things to link is the feeling of the plane dropping out from under you. We can, of course, picture Snoopy sitting in first class. Suddenly, the plane drops, and Snoopy finds himself in midair, several inches off his seat. Snoopy, who pretends he is a World War One fighter pilot when atop his doghouse, thinks, "My doghouse doesn't do this when I'm flying it. Something is wrong!" Try to imagine what Snoopy feels when the plane drops out from under him. Link that physical feeling to your moment of empathic attunement. One more suggestion. With a person you are emotionally close with, stand side by side on

a curb or on a step. Put an arm around the person's waist. Have the person put an arm around your waist. Then, on a count of three, jump off the curb or off the stair. Just for a moment, the two of you will experience weightlessness together. Thus, the experience of feeling weightless, as when the plane drops out from under you momentarily in turbulence, is now linked to another person.

Phase Three Strengthening Exercise—Protection against Panic

In Phase Three of the Strengthening Exercise, we separate and neutralize each component of panic. This prevents a domino effect in which one component triggers another. Use the cartoon situations below to link these components to a moment that inhibits the amygdalae.

Rapid Heartbeat. Superman, disguised as Clark Kent, is sitting on an airplane in his business suit. He is confident that if anything goes wrong, he can become Superman, grab the plane, and place it safely on the ground. But then he notices his increase in heart rate. That can mean only one thing: Some evil person on this plane has kryptonite, the one substance that strips away his powers. To show panic, the cartoonist has drawn exclamation marks on Clark Kent's chest, and curved lines beside his chest, to indicate a pounding heart.

Rapid or Difficult Breathing. Imagine Popeye seated on a plane beside Olive Oyl. Popeye doesn't want Olive to know he's anxious. He decides to fortify himself with some spinach. Reaching into his pocket, he finds it empty. No spinach! Popeye panics. Stress hormones push him to breathe faster than is possible. Unable to keep up with this rate, he thinks he is suffocating. To illustrate this, the cartoonist draws Popeye with his fist wrapped around his neck, saying, "Olive Oyl, I can't breathe!"

Hot and Sweaty, Cold and Clammy. Imagine SpongeBob on a plane and in a state of panic with sweat dripping across his face.

Derealization, Dissociation, Disorientation. Feeling Unreal or Surreal. Looking at Your Self from Outside Yourself. Imagine Scooby Doo in a kennel by the nose wheel of an airliner. Baggage handlers pick up his kennel, put it in the baggage compartment and slam the door shut. It's dark in there. Scooby can't see a thing. The engines start up. The plane starts to move, and then, with lots of unfamiliar noise, the plane takes off. This is something Scooby has never experienced. The cartoonist draws stars and exclamation marks spiraling around Scooby's head to indicate that things feel unreal, or surreal.

Tension in the Body. Imagine Bruce Banner seated on a plane with body tension turning him into the Hulk.

Anxiety about Time. What if the flight is too long? What if feelings build up? What if panic lasts the whole flight? Obviously a longer flight seems more threatening. Longer flights are actually easier, but anticipatory anxiety is greater about long flights than short ones. Imagine Cinderella is flying with the prince. They are in first class, sipping champagne. Suddenly the plane is stuck in midair. If it doesn't land before midnight, Cinderella's identity will be revealed, her gown will turn to rags, and the plane will turn into a pumpkin.

To understand how Phase Three prevents panic, consider this: If you buy a string of imitation pearls, if the string were to break, several beads would come off at once and go flying in all directions. Not so with quality pearls. When expensive cultured pearls are strung, a knot is placed between each pearl. The main reason for the knots is to protect the pearls from rubbing against each other. But knots also serve another purpose. If the string were to break, only one pearl would come loose. At most, only one pearl would be lost. Phase Three of the Strengthening Exercise places a psychological knot between each of the five things that could occur in a panic attack. Instead of five things happening, at most, only one takes place.

Strengthening Exercise—Phase Four (Optional)

My big sister was sick in the hospital. My mother and father went to see her. They took me along but, once we got there, they said I couldn't go to her room and that I had to wait in a hallway. As they started to leave, I said, 'When will you be back?' My father said, 'Count to one hundred. When you get to one hundred, we'll be back.' They left. I sat down on the floor and started counting. I got confused and started again. I got stuck, so I started again. I got stuck again. I started again and again. But each time, I couldn't remember what came next. I couldn't count to one hundred. It was then I realized they weren't ever coming back.

In this example of early relational trauma, the client was able to remember the event and the feelings of abandonment when it seemed her parents would never return.

Abandonment feelings can arise when flying because we are indeed alone. We are not sure anyone will respond to our needs. We are disconnected, far from the ground, which we may not even be able to see. The situation can trigger a flashback to childhood moments of hopelessness and helplessness. When high up, we, like the girl alone at the hospital, have no way to find comfort. Feelings of isolation from childhood replay and make cruise, the safest phase of flight physically, the most threatening phase of flight emotionally.

How do we protect ourselves from these feelings? We need to link a moment of empathic connection to these feelings of abandonment. There are at least two profound versions. In one, there is someone you need, but can't find. In the other, no one exists to connect to; connection is impossible. To find the imagery needed to link your type of abandonment to a moment of empathic attunement, you are literally on your own. Start by considering images of hopelessness, helplessness, emptiness, fear, guilt, passivity, anger, rage, and depression. These terms, as Dr. James Masterson has pointed out, are "too abstract to convey the intensity and immediacy of these feelings." Some examples below may offer a better sense of what those terms mean.

Abandonment Example One

A cartoon character, about six years old, has just awakened from a bad dream and doesn't know where he or she is or where its mother is. Imagine this cartoon touching the empathically attuned face.

Abandonment Example Two

Imagine a cartoon character who is a young mother. She fears something will happen that will cause her to never see her child again; she imagines what her child would feel. Imagine this cartoon by the face of an empathically attuned person.

Abandonment Example Three

In a comic book, you see an astronaut exiting a spacecraft to repair a solar panel. Floating weightless in space, she advances toward the panel. She is not entirely focused. It has been hard to sleep in weightlessness. That was a surprise. She had thought floating would produce delightful sleep. But a yearning for physical contact has made sleep difficult. She reaches toward the solar panel's attachment to the fuselage of the spaceship. During launch, the attachment was retracted into the fuselage. Once in orbit, the device unfolded its solar panels like a glistening oriental fan. Without warning, the device slams back to its retracted position, trapping her fingers in a vice-like grip. Instinctively, she jerks free. Good. She is free. But the spacecraft is just out of reach, and she is moving away a fraction of an inch each second. Her tether will catch her, she thinks. It will put an end to this drifting away from the space cart. She looks toward the tether and sees it, too, is floating, unattached.

First, she is angry. How did she fail to attach the tether? Anger quickly turns to panic. She has no options. The momentum of the drift from the spacecraft is infinite. Nothing she can do will end this separation. If she calls out, her voice will not pass through space, for there is no air to carry her words. The air in her life support system will become stale and finally toxic. She will perish within some undefined period of time. She is cosmically alone. Place the comic strip by an empathically attuned face.

Strengthening Exercise Details

Before beginning this exercise, free yourself of stress hormones by using the 5-4-3-2-1 Exercise. Once having done so, use the following guidelines to work your way through the three phases of the Strengthening Exercise.

- *Regulatory Moments (RMs).* Find more than one, if you can. Emotional strength comes from moments of connection. Using more than one moment increases the power of the Strengthening Exercise.
- *Warm Feelings.* Moments of empathic connection do not always produce warm feelings. But if the moment initially brings warm feelings, the feelings will fade as you do the exercise. That is to be expected and will not cause a problem. The object is to link flight situations to the person's face, not to a feeling.
- *Take a Break.* If you lose focus, take a break and pick up later where you left off.
- *Physical Presence.* If there's a person currently in your life with whom you share attunement, in addition to practicing the exercise in your imagination, do the exercise face-to-face with that person.
- *Timing.* Ideally, practice the exercise once a day for a week. If you need to fly soon, practice the exercise twice a day. More than twice a day is not recommended.
- *Emotional Management.* Aim for an anxiety-free exercise. Weaken the airplane scenes (the NORs) with the following visual techniques.

- *Exclude Yourself.* Do not include yourself in an imaginary situation (NOR) as you link it to your regulatory moment (RM). Instead, you can either use an imaginary photo taken from the outside of the plane or use an imaginary photo of someone else in the situation on the plane. In either case, assume you're not on the plane.
- *Size.* Keep each imaginary photo small, not life-size. Imagine a white margin around photos, or imagine them on a magazine page.
- *Avoid Color.* Keep the imaginary flight-scene photos black-and-white. If a scene causes anxiety, did you let the image become life-size, or become color rather than stay black-and-white?
- *Use Cartoons.* If it is hard to keep an image small and black-and-white, or if a situation still causes anxiety, use a cartoon for that scene. Imagine a cartoon character sitting on a plane, someone like Goofy or Shrek. Picture what cartoonists call a "balloon," an oval or cloud-shaped area over the character's head containing words or marks; the contents indicate that it is the cartoon character—not you—that is worried about the flight situation.
- *Make a Recording.* To help you focus on the Strengthening Exercise, consider making a voice recording that guides you through the steps.
- *Make a Set of Index Cards.* On each card, draw a rough sketch, or write a couple of words, to suggest each non-routine flight situation (NOR). Use the cards to guide you through the steps.
- *Stick to the Exercise.* As you go through the exercise, even if you stumble through the steps, the links are nevertheless established. Two to three sessions may be adequate to establish the links if things go smoothly. If you are unsure, continue until you have done six to eight sessions.

What should you expect to feel on your flight? Provided each moment that could trigger stress hormone release has been linked to a suitable moment of empathic attunement, you should feel complete protection from high anxiety and from panic.

A selection of images suitable for use in the Strengthening Exercise is available at www.fearofflying.com/photos/.

Troubleshooting

If you continue to feel anxiety when flying, revisit the selection of a moment intended to inhibit stress hormone release. Read again the criteria. An activity that you find relaxing may not inhibit the amygdalae. Remember that the amygdalae are very visual in their operation. A moment with more than one person will work only if you limit the image you use to one person's face. And, that person's face must be attuned to you, and it must show caring for you.

Also, list the moments of flight when you felt anxious. Identify the cause. Break down the cause into its elements. Link each element separately in the Strengthening Exercise.

Occasionally, you may encounter an unforeseen non-routine situation, one you did not include in your practice of the Strengthening Exercise. If so, a single stress hormone release may occur. As soon as you notice any indication of a stress hormone release, use your backup, the 5-4-3-2-1 Exercise, to get rid of the anxiety. Quickly, write down what triggered the release. A note will help you add it to your Strengthening Exercise practice before your next flight. As soon as you have written it down, use the 5-4-3-2-1 Exercise.

There's no need to worry. One thought doesn't cause high anxiety or panic. Here's an example, and you may even find it amusing. A client was in the boarding area waiting for her first post-SOAR flight and very pleased with herself for feeling quite calm. Then, there was an announcement, "Passengers for flight 123, please proceed to gate 16. There has been a gate change." At that point, she felt the stress hormones rush through her. Her first thought was that this was a panic attack. But, no. Just one shot of stress hormones. Since that left her Executive Function intact, she was able to think, "How dangerous is it for me to walk one hundred yards," and regain her composure. This was simply a case of something happening— a non-routine event that triggered the amygdalae to release stress hormones—that we had not thought to put into the Strengthening Exercise.

It may help to do this. Take along a piece of paper. Write 5-4-3-2-1 on the top. If you feel anxiety, write down the cause. Then quickly turn to the 5-4-3-2-1 Exercise to bring yourself back to a calm state. Having it written on top of the page may make the difference between the stress hormones snowballing into high anxiety and being able to reinstate your Executive Function. Then, before your next flight, reference your notes. Carefully break down any item that caused stress hormone release into its elements. Add each element, as a separate item, to your next practice session. Sooner or later, everything that could cause anxiety will be included.

After practice of the Strengthening Exercise, though you may feel more confident about flying, it is completely normal to still feel anxious. Why? Because the exercise keeps the amygdalae from reacting to what happens during the flight, not what you imagine before the flight.

Anticipatory anxiety and flight anxiety are different. No matter how much anticipatory anxiety you feel, it does not mean there will be anxiety on the flight.

• • •

Though it is easy to doubt that something as simple as linking the challenges of flight (NORs) to a regulatory moment of empathic or sexual attunement (RM) can work, it does. It might just as easily seem doubtful that Systematic Desensitization would work; it does, too. Both are ways to retrain the amygdalae. This way of retraining the amygdalae is based on the most fundamental of all human characteristics: the need for relationship. The Strengthening Exercise taps into genetic programming that, in certain relational moments, causes the amygdalae to shut down. Were it not for this programming, humans would have become extinct. When a person's eyes unmistakably tell us we are the only person in their world, oxytocin, the powerful anti-anxiety hormone, pushes fear aside and allows us to mate.

Performers say that what gets them to Carnegie Hall is practice, practice, practice. That's what will get you good results on the plane. It is all in the practice you complete before the "performance." Once the links are established, there is nothing you need to do on the plane. Practice the exercise only when and where you can devote your full focus on it, not when driving a car or when under stress at home or at the office. Stress hormones can get in the way. Use the 5-4-3-2-1 Exercise to burn them off before starting the exercise.

How many practice sessions are needed to establish the links? How many sessions would you need to link a dozen words of a foreign language to your native language? It takes no more practice than that to establish links using the Strengthening Exercise.

When you practice the Strengthening Exercise, as you simultaneously present the amygdalae with a NOR and an RM, they merge into a NORM. As you continue your practice, they unify into a NORM. In other words, what the amygdalae previously regarded as non-routine, it now regards as normal.

CHAPTER 13

Stopping Anxiety and Panic in Everyday Situations

The Strengthening Exercise can be used to protect against high anxiety and panic in situations such as elevators, bridges, tunnels, car trips, MRI scans, or visits to the doctor or dentist. Sometimes, if you feel anxiety in more than one situation, it's a little easier to try the Strengthening Exercise first in something like an elevator before attempting to use it for flying. And then if you find that it's successful in regulating your anxiety in an elevator, it may be easier for you to trust that it will work on the plane.

Focus on the situation in which high anxiety or panic occurs. Use the same approach as for flying. Break the situation down into a sequence of steps. Make a list of the steps involved entering the situation, in the situation, and leaving the situation. Reverse the order so that the exercise starts at the end of the situation and works backward toward the beginning. As needed, insulate yourself emotionally by imagining a comic book character is worried about the situation.

Bring to mind and relive a regulatory moment of attunement with someone. Imagine he or she picks up a photo (or comic) of a situation listed below, holds it near his or her face, and puts it down. Continue until the list has been completed. The following is for high anxiety or panic in elevators.

Phase One for Elevators

- outside the building
- leaving the building
- heading for the building exit
- just out of the elevator
- stepping out of the elevator: one foot out, one foot still in
- in the elevator with no one in your way
- in the elevator with someone blocking your exit
- in the elevator with the door opening
- elevator stopped with the door closed
- elevator stopping; heavy feeling
- elevator passing the third floor
- elevator passing the fifth floor
- elevator passing the eighth floor
- elevator starting downward; light-headed feeling
- elevator door closed, not moving
- elevator door closing
- waiting in the elevator
- others getting in the elevator
- selecting the ground floor
- stepping in the elevator
- seeing the elevator ready for you to get in
- the elevator door opening
- waiting for the elevator to arrive
- pressing the button for the elevator to come
- walking toward the elevator
- thinking about returning to the elevator
- walking around the tenth floor
- stepping out of the elevator onto the tenth floor
- in the elevator with no one in your way
- in the elevator with someone blocking your exit
- in the elevator with the door opening

- elevator stopped with the door closed
- elevator slows its ascent; light-headed feeling
- elevator passing the eighth floor
- elevator passing the fifth floor
- elevator passing the third floor
- elevator starting upward; heavy feeling
- elevator not moving, with the door closed
- elevator door closing
- in the elevator, waiting for door to close
- in the elevator, more people getting in
- selecting the tenth floor
- stepping into the elevator
- seeing the elevator ready for you to get in
- the elevator door opening
- waiting for the elevator
- pressing the button for the elevator to come
- walking to the elevator
- outside the building

Phase Two for Elevators

List everything that could go wrong and cause panic. Examples are:

- embarrassment
- can't immediately leave
- people will notice
- what if I can't breathe?
- what if I have a heart attack?
- what if I can't get help?
- what if I lose control?
- what if I go crazy?
- there are too many people in here

Phase Three for Elevators

Just as it is done for flight anxiety, apply Phase Three of the Strengthening Exercise to the five components of panic (rapid heartbeat, difficulty breathing, sweaty, dizziness, and body tension) one at a time with the cartoon character experiencing that component. This neutralizes and separates each of the five main elements of a panic attack.

• • •

Now you can see that the Strengthening Exercise is valuable in many different anxiety-inducing situations. You can take the leap of faith and fly!

CHAPTER 14
Erasure Exercise

The object of this optional exercise is to partly erase a traumatic memory. If recall of a flight causes distress, the Erasure Exercise can reduce the emotional impact when you recall it. Before getting started, bring the traumatic flight to mind and make an assessment, zero to ten, of your anxiety while you are remembering the worst part. Like a novel or a movie, your memory of the flight runs forward in time from the beginning to the end. This exercise artificially creates a memory of the flight that runs backward in time, from the end, then backward through the entire flight to the beginning.

First, we create a backward version of the flight. Make a step-by-step outline of what happened. For example, you checked in at the airport, went through security, and sat down in the boarding area. After waiting, you boarded the plane. The plane taxied out, took off, climbed to cruise altitude. Everything was fine. Suddenly there was some turbulence. An announcement was made to fasten your seat belt. The turbulence became so intense you began to worry. You imagined the plane might plunge. You had thoughts about not seeing loved ones again. Then the turbulence stabilized. The plane landed. You got off. You got in a car or taxi and went to the place you would spend the night. You woke up the next morning.

Using your notes, begin assembling a backward version of the flight—visually—in your mind. Start with waking up the next morning. Since everything will run backward, imagine the clock is running backward, it is getting darker, and you fall asleep. You sleep backward through the night. You get out of bed and walk backward to the bathroom, where you brush your teeth. When you finish, there is toothpaste on the brush. You touch the toothpaste tube to the brush and the paste goes back into the tube. You put on your clothes and go to the dinner table, where a finished plate is presented. As you eat backward, and the food comes out of your mouth, back onto the plate, and you finish the meal by giving up a perfectly untouched plate of food.

You walk backward out to a car or taxi. It goes down the road backward. When you look out the windshield, everything is going away from you, except the cars are coming backward toward you.

You ride backward to the airport. You get out of the vehicle backward. You go backward into the terminal. You put your bag on the baggage carousel. As it spins, your bag disappears. You go backward up the escalator, backward to the gate, backward through the passenger boarding bridge, backward through the aisle of the plane, and backward to your seat.

The door closes, and the plane taxis backward to the runway. Making lots of noise, it rushes faster and faster backward down the runway, and bumps into the air. It climbs backward to cruise altitude. In most cases, a traumatic flight involves turbulence. As you visualize your flight backward, it is important that you visualize turbulence backward. This is probably the most important piece of the Erasure Exercise. On an actual flight, when the plane moves down, you feel light-headed, and get the impression that the plane is falling. When the plane moves upward, you feel heavier in your seat and are not alarmed. But when visualizing your flight backward, you must reverse this. In other words, what you feel in turbulence when the plane moves up and down is reversed. When you visualize the plane moving upward, imagine feeling light-headedness and alarm that the plane will fall. When you visualize the plane moving downward, imagine feeling heavy in your seat, and no alarm at all. Spend extra time on this part of the Erasure Exercise so as to solidly connect falling with upward motion, and heaviness with downward motion, as you visualize the plane flying backward.

Next, picture the plane descending backward, landing, and taxiing backward to the terminal. You get off backward, go backward through security, and back to check in, and, backward, back to where you started the day.

Now that you have it assembled, you are ready to record the backward version on top of the forward version. Pretend you have a video of the traumatic flight on a cell phone. View a few seconds of it on the small cell phone screen. Then, without delay, run the backward version. See it in your imagination—not on the small cell phone screen—but life-size. That completes one cycle. Continue with a second cycle. Again, make sure you build the backward memory on top of the original memory. Watching a few seconds of the original memory establishes the location. Then, run the backward version again full size.

Take a break. Distract yourself from this exercise by recalling something you did earlier today. After you have taken your mind elsewhere, return to the memory of your bad flight. Note your stress level, zero to ten. Compare it with what it was before the exercise. It is probably a bit lower.

Repeat the exercise again a day or two later, and again after a few days. Test your reaction again, zero to ten. Repeat until the memory of the original flight does not bother you when you recall it.

CHAPTER 15
The Psychological Foundations for Emotional Regulation

When building a house, the electrical wiring is installed early in the construction process. The same is true of our psychological wiring. Much of the cortex, a part of the brain that plays a major role in the regulation of emotion, is constructed during the first year of a child's life. As its construction is actually taking place, the cortex is a beehive of neurological activity. Neurons—or nerve cells—have switches called synapses. In your home, when you flip a switch to turn on the lights, a piece of metal moves to connect the wires running to that switch. The lights stay on until you physically move the metal away from the wires when turning off the switch. In the brain, instead of using metal, these switches use chemicals. When a synapse "fires," it uses chemicals to establish a connection. Unlike the switch on your wall that leaves the light on, the chemicals in the synapse wear out in a few seconds, and the connection goes away

Turning on one synapse doesn't do much. But when thousands of interconnected synapses "fire," significant things happen. Together, these synapses produce thoughts, ideas, feelings, and perceptions in your mind. How do synapses interconnect? When two or more synapse close to each other fire at the same moment, they form knobs that connect the two synaptic switches, perhaps permanently.

When a person feels a certain emotion, it is due to the firing of a large number of synapses. If the person is repeatedly caused to feel that emotion, the synapses involved physically wire together to form a *cell assembly*. Once the cell assembly has formed, the emotion can be triggered more easily, and in more ways. The firing of even one neuron in the cell assembly can cause all the neurons in the cell assembly to fire, and thus produce the emotion.

Establishing the Connections

The phenomenon described above is also involved in the physical construction of circuits that can produce a sequence of feelings. In a child's relationship with its parents, a sequence of events can take place that causes the child to experience a specific sequence of emotions. If the sequence takes place repeatedly, it is transcribed into permanent wiring in the child's brain. A physical connection is established in the brain between the first cell assembly and the second cell assembly, the second with the third, and so on. Ergo, the first emotion tends to produce the second emotion, which in turn produces the third, and on it goes.

Since a baby's primary caregiver is, in most instances, its mother, the infant's psychological wiring is the result of sequences of experiences that are repeated in the child's relationship with her. Ideally, when the child is upset, the mother attunes herself to the child. She immerses herself in the child's feelings so she can discover the child's feelings and give the child a powerful sense that the child is not alone in its experience. If the mother is able to immerse herself in the child's experience, and yet remain calm, she can demonstrate that the feeling—though perhaps intense—can be experienced without damage. The feeling can be "contained." By the mother's sharing and containing the feeling, she teaches the child to contain the feeling rather than be engulfed by it. She needs to make it clear that the feeling, though shared by her, belongs to the child. Clarity about the ownership of a feeling assures the child that, though shared, feelings are not contagious; the child's feelings will not infect, nor cause damage to, the mother. The mother then presents an alternative experience—the relief the child can soon expect—by suggesting that the child imagine feeling better.

For example, the mother comes in to her crying son; his face is scrunched up in pain. She says, "Oh, sweetheart, what's wrong?" He extends his arm. She takes it. She looks at the arm, the hand, and the fingers. She finds a small cut. The mother feels pulled in two directions. She is pulled toward her own reality; the injury is superficial and she knows that her son will be fine. But if she responds to him based solely on her reality and simply reassures him, he will not feel she has connected with *his* reality and *his* distress.

The other pull is toward his reality. This is his first injury. His distress is not unlike that of someone who has lost everything. It is as though he were being swallowed up in an ocean of emotion. Grim as his experience may seem, she enters this dark place with him. By joining him, is she following some primordial instinct? Or is she fortunate enough to have had a relationally gifted mother, simply giving to her child what her mother gave to her?

Just as musicians tune their instruments to each other, she tunes every faculty to her son. Her facial expression is tuned to match his; her body language takes on his. As she speaks, the rhythm and intonation of her speech matches his. By this attunement and matching, mirror neurons in her brain allow her to synthetically duplicate his experience.

Feeling what he feels, as she winces at the pain, their eyes meet in a way that the emotional part of her brain touches his. He, in an experience too profound to explain, knows he is not alone. She holds him, not only physically, but psychologically.

As he clings to her, some mothers would feel dragged down by the undertow of the child's distress. If she is too fearful of drowning in this sea of emotion, she may never again allow herself to feel what her child is feeling. But, let's assume this mother can. She has been there before, for when she was a child, her mother first joined her in her distress, and then accompanied her along a shared pathway to reach emotional safety together.

First, as if they were one, she attunes herself to his emotion. Then she is the mother. She reasserts her separate personhood and in so doing moves her son along a pathway that will soon be carved into his psyche. It is a neurological pathway that will keep him from drowning in a flood of emotion. It will operate implicitly—without his consciously knowing it is there—supporting him emotionally throughout his lifespan.

As she accompanies him to emotional safety, she is in no hurry. Emergency Medical Technicians rush to the site where they will aid a victim. They have been trained that once there, they are to walk— not to run—when about to reach the victim. Though time may indeed be critical, it calms the victim when they act as though there is no emergency. The few seconds taken to reassure the person can be more important in saving their life than to intervene medically a few seconds earlier.

Having joined him in his experience, the mother now can give her son a name for his experience. She says, "Yes, yes. You have a cut there." Then, beginning to point out that she is a psychologically separate person, she adds, "I see. But don't you worry. Mommy's going to get something and we're going to make it all better."

Though she needs a washcloth and a bandage, she does not leave his side. She invites him to come with her. Or, she picks him up and carries him to where these supplies are. She knows that whether the wound is attended to in one minute or one hour, the wound will heal. It is more important that his emotional state be cared for. She cleans the cut and dresses it. "There! You see?" she says with a smile. Then, suggesting that he, too, is a separate person and perfectly capable of functioning independently, she says, "All better! Now you can go outside and play." As he goes off to play, he looks very independent. But, and this is key, his independence is dependent upon something she has given him. Within his mind, he carries—and is powered by—a replica of his mother's face and of the relationship he has with her.

The U-P-S-E-T Sequence

Examining that dialogue, you can see each step of the U-P-S-E-T sequence being played out.

1. **U**pset. When the mother hears her child crying, she responds.

2. **P**roximity. She goes to where her child is.

3. **S**ee. She sees the child's face.

4. **E**motional Attunement and Resonance. She matches the child's body language overtly and physically or mentally in imagination. In this example, she reflexively scrunches her face. By attuning to and resonating with her child's expression, she synthetically creates an experience in herself that matches the experience of the child. Empathically, she says, "Ooaauuwwuhh! It hurts!" By sharing her son's feeling with him, he senses she knows what he is dealing with. At this point, the mother and the child are almost one. By being so emotionally available, she gives the child a deep sense that he is not alone in any way, physically or psychologically.

5. **T**wo-Mindedness. The mother begins a transition to two-mindedness by labeling the experience: for example, "a cut there." This gives the child a term with which to mentally organize his experience. By saying, "Yes, yes, I see," she

begins a transition to two-mindedness, and she has her own separate point of view. She assigns ownership of the experience to the child by following, "You have a cut there," with "That hurts! I'm so sorry," and she indicates the feeling belonging to him. This relieves the child of concern for his mother; by owning the feelings himself, he does not have to take care of her. She continues toward two-mindedness with a shift in her voice and body language.

Why is two-mindedness so important? Though the feeling is shared, it belongs to the child. By making it clear that the feeling belongs to the child, the mother helps the child understand that he has a mind, others have their own minds, and that, while minds are separate and contain different information, they can communicate.

Emotional strength depends on replicas built inside the mind. The child cannot build an adequate replica of himself unless his mother makes it clear that he is a separate individual, physically and mentally. More than anything else, inability to regulate feelings when flying results from inadequate replicas of one's own self and of supportive other persons. Adequate replicas are built only when a child's mother reflects back to the child that he is separate and individual.

Contrast a favorable U-P-S-E-T sequence with the following scene at a playground. An eight-year-old girl slipped and bumped her head. Though the fall was minor, she shrieked as though seriously injured. Her mother ran over. Instead of attuning herself to her daughter or comforting her, the mother shouted accusingly, "What have you done?" When the mother reached for the daughter, the daughter slammed her fists on the mother's chest and shoved her away. The mother yelled, "You don't hit your mother," then turned and walked away in anger. The daughter ran after her. The mother quickened her pace. The daughter gave up and sat down on the grass, sobbing.

A few minutes later, the mother returned. She sat down behind her daughter and applied an ice pack to her head, perhaps in an attempt to repair the misattunement. As mentioned before, Emergency Medical Technicians, of course, carry ice packs and other first-aid items, but they are trained to first tend to the person's psychological needs, then to the person's physical needs.

In another situation, a ten-year-old boy was playing with a Fourth of July sparkler. After it burned out, his finger momentarily touched an area of the sparkler that was still warm. Surprised, he said, "Ow!" His mother reacted as if something terrible had happened. Her frantic reaction caused him to cry. Believing his crying proved he was seriously burned, she asked for directions to a hospital emergency room. When everyone assured her he did not need treatment, she reconsidered. But instead of calming her son, she went to a phone and called a doctor. Not only was she unable to calm her son, her reactions were emotionally destabilizing to him. Responses that destabilize the child are profoundly damaging. Research shows that a child whose mother overreacts has even greater difficulty learning to regulate emotion than a child who—having been orphaned—has no mother at all.

The mother's characteristic response to the child becomes hardwired. Whether calming or destabilizing, how the mother responds becomes a neuronal pathway, one that is physically established in the child's brain. When a mother consistently responds with a stabilizing U-P-S-E-T sequence, feelings of being upset flow toward feelings of calm. When these pathways are not established, the child has little or no way to regulate emotion.

Relationship Molds Capacity

Neuropsychologist Allan Schore has studied how children develop the ability to calm themselves. According to Schore's findings, relationship with the mother (or other primary caregiver) determines not only how emotions flow at the moment, but for years to come. Schore writes, "The child's first relationship, the relationship with the mother . . . permanently molds the individual's capacities." Because it is the period of most rapid brain growth, the emotional sequences a child experiences with its mother during the first year of life become the sequences that will regulate—or dysregulate—emotional states throughout the lifespan. By the mother's sharing and containing emotion, the child gains the capacity to experience emotion fully without feeling threatened or overwhelmed. By attuned and empathic separateness, the mother supports the child's individuality and its ability to reflect on its own mental processes.

Modes of Attachment

The emotional sequences that play out in the relationship between a child and its primary caregiver tend to produce identifiable modes of attachment. A child fortunate enough to have what legendary pediatrician and child psychotherapist Donald Winnicott called the "good enough mother" develops a sense of security in his relationship with her. This is called secure attachment. Other relational styles lead to the development of avoidant attachment or insecure attachment.

Secure Attachment

Initially, emotional security may be due to a sense of unity. When an infant cries, the mother intuitively senses or intellectually determines the cause of the discomfort. Her responsiveness may make it seem to the child that they are one. But at some point, the child realizes they are not one. The child recognizes its mother is a separate person and that she has her own mind. This comes as a shock. Separate mindedness is a threat, for if her mind is separate, she can focus her attention elsewhere. What can keep the child from being abandoned? What is to keep its needs from being unmet?

Unless it is bridged, separateness is traumatic. There are several ways separateness can be bridged: physical touch, intellectual agreement, a merging of identities, and empathic attunement. Of these, only empathic attunement can be represented in the mind in a way that promotes independent regulation of emotion.

If the mother and child share an abundance of face-to-face experiences, a replica of the mother's attuned face is established in the child's mind. Once a replica is established, she is psychologically available at times when she is not physically available. Two more steps are needed for security. One, if the child is to feel secure when she is not present, the child must sense that a replica of its own self resides in the mother's mind. The child's desire for her return is linked to the replica of her in his mind. Two, he needs to sense that the replica of himself in her mind is also linked to a desire to return to him. These replicas and linking feelings are basic to the child's sense of security with regards to any person he is attached to.

Over time, through repeated moments of attunement, another replica is formed: As the child senses himself in the mother's mind, he brings what he believes is his mother's sense of him into his own awareness. This introjection—how he believes his mother regards him—becomes his replica of himself. This process is called "mirroring."

Replicas of the empathic and attuned mother, and of the child's relationship with her, result in what is called secure attachment. Equipped internally with these replicas, the secure child grows up to become a secure adult, one who does not need undue control to feel comfortable. Originally, his mother was his whole world. Security with her, as he discovers a larger world, extends to the larger world. Flying, for such a person, rarely poses a problem.

Avoidant Attachment

Avoidant attachment of a child to its parent develops when, instead of relating with the child through empathic attunement, the parent interacts with the child based on reason. The child's needs are administered to according to the parent's agenda, rather than in response to signals from the child. To an untrained observer, by being kept clean, given toys to play with (alone), and fed on schedule, the child may seem well taken care of. But a young child needs far more. A young child attempts to communicate through eye contact, facial expression, body language, crying, or other vocalization. When attempting to engage the parent, the child needs to find a willing—indeed an eager—partner. Unless the child finds itself mirrored as a gleam in the parent's eyes, it has no place in which to psychologically grow up. Psychologist Harry Guntrip has referred to such circumstances as "the baby in the steel drawer." It could also be the baby in the test tube, or the tiger mother's child, who is to obey.

We adopt our identity. Our physical identity is adopted from what we see reflected in a glass mirror. Our psychological identity is adopted from what we see reflected in another person's face. Just as mirrors at a carnival distort how we look, human mirrors—when warped—distort who we believe we are! Since parents are all-important to a young child, the mirroring a child gets from them is formed by the child into a replica of itself. Later, as an adult, we may realize some of the mirroring we received from parents was warped. A person's replica of self, established by early mirroring, is not easily corrected. Now what? Almost everyone—friends, family, lovers, and enemies—has an agenda. The way they regard you and respond to you is inevitably warped by their own needs. Are there any unwarped mirrors out there? Noted psychiatrist James Masterson, M.D., has said psychotherapy is about finally getting accurate mirroring. He added, "Unfortunately, to get good mirroring, you have to pay for it." In theory, at least, a therapist who has had the benefit of good mirroring when in therapy himself should be able to mirror you without his own agenda getting in the way.

But when a child is building his sense of self, if his primary caregiver—usually the mother—handles him based on her agenda, rather than in response to his signals, the child builds a replica of himself as something invisible. Later, when seeing others, their identity is clear to him, but when attempting to "see" himself, there is not much there; his own identity is vague. Others seem strong and fixed. He seems weak and amorphous. Relating to others is unnerving, for he is concerned that their influence could engulf the tentative sense of self he holds on to.

He desperately needs a substantial identity. As a drowning swimmer grasps any floating object, if his parents offer him a role model to emulate, he seizes it as an opportunity to be someone. Parents generally assign a role model exhibiting approved behavior and eschewing disapproved behavior. When the child's performance is consistent with the role model, the parents reinforce the behavior with positive feedback. Other than approved behavior is either ignored or condemned.

Meanwhile, due to unshared self-awareness, an identity develops based on the child's feelings and desires. This identity, though authentic, is kept private, for whenever the child has attempted to exhibit this authentic self, his parents acted as though it was invisible, or rejected it. Having not been afforded attunement, the child has developed no ability to regulate emotion, nor to contain emotion. Outbursts occur that are truly beyond the child's control. The parents, believing the child can control his behavior, threaten or punish him. This is counterproductive; parental response—positive or negative—is a form of mirroring. Mirroring strengthens sense of identity. In this case, it strengthens an identity the parents wish to squelch! With the aid of negative mirroring, the identity built on feelings and desire grows stronger. Over time, the child develops a substantial identity; one that is oppositional and defiant!

What happens next is crucial. The child's oppositional—but authentic—self may prevail. But if traumatized by threats, punishment, or abandonment, the child can be pushed into serious dissociative pathology. To end his out-of-control behavior and unacceptable emotional outbursts, the child engages in a two-step associative-dissociative process. He identifies with the assigned role model, as "me." He dissociates from the offending authentic self, as "not-me." By identifying with the role model and dissociating from his real self, the child establishes Guntrip's classic master-slave-exile arrangement, with the parents as master, the "me" as their slave, and the "not-me" cast into exile. The "not-me," together with its desires and memories, are hidden away in the child's internal Pandora's Box. This associative-dissociative process takes place consciously, around the age of five or slightly later. Though the decision is made consciously, remembering it undermines the dissociation needed to keep the disavowed "not-me" in exile. To maintain the dissociation, the arrangement is "forgotten."

This arrangement, with "forgetting" as the linchpin holding it together, is fraught with anxiety. To keep the "not-me" identity "forgotten," it and all its associated contents must remain shut away in Pandora's Box, and never see the light of day. Though the child has "forgotten" what is in the box, the child knows what lurks there is something to be afraid of. In every situation, there could be an object, a word, or an emotion associated with *something inside the box. Association could reawaken the memory of something that needs to stay "forgotten."*

Thus, any situation the child does not control or cannot instantly escape from causes anxiety. Remembering could cause the exiled "not-me" to return and, in a flood of emotion, overwhelm "me." Out-of-control behavior could cause the parents to abandon "me." No matter how hard he tries, the child is sure he will ultimately lose control. Something will render him an outcast. He will be imprisoned, or executed. Fear of losing control, of being arrested and imprisoned carries over consciously or unconsciously into adulthood. Here is an example:

> *I'm thirty-five and haven't flown for fifteen years. The anxiety*
> *I felt was unbearable. My life, and that of my family, would*

be greatly enhanced if this fear/anxiety was gone. I know in my heart air travel is safer than most things that I do, but I'm still completely flipped out by it. My hands are sweating right now thinking about it. I don't ever think it can be. I fear also that if I actually board a flight, I'll lose it on the plane, or get arrested, and not be able to make the return flight. Just typing this makes me feel like running somewhere. It's totally nuts and I feel pretty hopeless about ever being reasonable about it.

The child seeks mightily to control himself. He hopes that achievement and perfection will establish the "me" he claims he is. In fantasy, he aspires to be a hero, like the storied Dutch boy who saved his country by using his finger to plug the hole in a leaking dike. In reality, the dike holding back the emotion-filled "not-me" has eleven holes—and with only ten fingers, desire from the exiled "not-me" keeps seeping in, threatening to reveal "me" as the impostor.

Puberty confronts the dissociation-based personality with new threats of collapse. How can the "not-me"—now quickened by sexual desire—be kept sequestered? Panic attacks often begin at puberty when the teenager feels trapped in a body afflicted with feelings that cannot be controlled. Some take refuge in a role that serves as a suit of armor against the disavowed "not-me." If the role is reinforced by "props" (such as a uniform, a book of scripture, tattoos, a wedding ring, ritual, protective gear, special equipment, weaponry, or vehicles), so much the better.

The person doesn't understand why flying is a problem. Everywhere else, everything is under control. He, a self-described "very rational person," is unaware that dissociation underpins his identity. The dissociation he unwittingly relies on holds up if the flight is smooth. But in turbulence, feelings arise that are too hot for dissociation to handle. He experiences what Anna Freud called "signal anxiety." Something connects with its secret contents, and Pandora's Box threatens to open. He must escape to avoid a disclosure that could destroy his adopted identity—the cool, calm, collected, always in control, highly rational "me"—in a tsunami of emotion.

Able to keep emotion at a distance, but otherwise unable to regulate it, relationships are problematic. Others find his facial expressions missing or difficult to read. He finds eye contact uncomfortable; the other person might glimpse the "not-me." Though the "not-me" yearns for relationship, it fears disaster. Desire is approached cautiously, if at all. The fear that desire will lead to disaster is not new. In Greek mythology, Odysseus had himself tied to the mast of his ship to avoid losing control when nearing the seductive Sirens.

By remaining insular, the dissociation-based person can appear strong, independent, and self-reliant, like an Ayn Rand protagonist. With all the renunciation of desire and self-imposed isolation the avoidant personality suffers, one does have to admire the heroic fortitude to keep on going on.

One night, when my daughter was around six, she couldn't sleep because of a panther in the closet. I first tried reassurance, telling her that there was no panther. I then tried reason: We went to the closet and thoroughly examined it, so she could see for herself that there was no panther. Nevertheless, when back in her bed, the panther was back in the closet. Finally, with a flash of intuition, I said, "How would you like to snuggle up with the panther?" She smiled. Together, we pretended she was holding the panther close; she was soon asleep.

Similarly, I have tried every rational approach with clients who are afraid of turbulence. In spite of all assurances that turbulence is not a problem for the plane, the panther remains in the closet. When something threatens us, we push it away. Each thing pushed away increases the force pushing back at us. When we retrieve and embrace what we as children pushed away, like the panther in the closet, we find we no longer need to fear it.

Insecure Attachment

In one trajectory, insecure attachment develops when separateness is not bridged by empathic attunement. The mother is unable to recognize it when her child has a self that is unlike what she believes a child of hers would have. The place in the mother's mind that might have been occupied by an accurate replica of the child is occupied instead by her concept of what her child should be. In public, the mother elevates herself by endorsing her child's perfection. In private, she criticizes the child for failure to meet expectations. From the child's point of view, security is possible only by achieving the impossible. When the child grows up, there is a gnawing need for greater affirmation, applause, or celebrity. When flying, there is anxiety that a public display of out-of-control behavior could shatter his or her self-concept and self-esteem.

In another trajectory, insecure attachment develops when the mother, unable to deal with separation, does not regard her child as separate. In the mother's mind, instead of a replica of herself and a replica of her baby, there is a single replica, one in which she is inseparable with the child. With the child as part of herself, the mother conflates her feelings and her needs with those of the child.

> When I was a kid I was the one that had to take my mother's side and take care of her emotional well being. Now, I try to stay as far out of the family drama as I can. But, that makes me the bitch in my family.

If the mother is forced to be aware that she and the child are separate individuals, emotions may arise that she cannot tolerate. For example, at a time when the mother feels ebullient, if the baby becomes unmistakably distressed, the mother is forced to recognize that her child's experience is not aligned with hers. This may make her feel that her child has abandoned her. Or, she may deny separateness by asserting that the child's distress is not genuine, and tell the child to stop crying or she will give the child something to cry about. She may inflict pain on the child as revenge for having a separate experience, and to reunify their experience.

With needs, identities, and emotions entangled, the child cannot develop an identity of herself as a separate person. The mother's facial expressions that show recognition of the child as separate are associated with aggression or withdrawal. Lacking mirroring as a separate person that is positive, the child does not learn to regulate emotion independently.

To avoid feelings of separateness, the mother maintains undue physical contact with the child. However, when a lover fills the mother's needs, the child is cast aside. Things that go wrong cause a sense of separation; someone must be blamed. Often it is the child who is blamed, and made to pay a price, in some form or other.

Attachment, Replicas, and the Social Engagement System

Remember the job of the amygdalae: to release stress hormones any and every time they sense something non-routine or unexpected. When we are around other people, the amygdalae are almost constantly releasing stress hormones. Some of what they say may be unexpected. What they do is under their control, not ours. This means an almost constant release of stress hormones. If these stress hormones are not somehow counteracted, we would be constantly subjected to an elevated heart rate, increased breathing rate, sweatiness, and tension in the body. Fortunately, the Social Engagement System can prevent this.

It has long been known that stimulation of the vagus nerve slows the heart. This discovery was published in 1921 by Nobel Prize winner Otto Loewi. Neuroscientist Stephen Porges has found that when the Social Engagement System reads another person as trustworthy, it counterbalances the effect of stress hormones by stimulating the vagus nerve. This slows the heart and calms the person. Porges refers to this action as the "vagal brake." When you arrive at a party where there are dozens of strangers, you may notice a wish to leave. In response to the strangers, your amygdalae release stress hormones, activate your Mobilization System, which produces an urge to escape. But your inner CEO, also activated by the stress hormones, overrides this urge. Your CEO starts doing its ABCs. Assessment? "Umm. I don't know. I don't see anyone familiar." Stress hormone release continues.

The host sees you, comes over, and greets you with facial expressions, voice quality, and body language that indicate genuine delight. Your Social Engagement System (SES) sends a signal to the vagus nerve. In spite of the stress hormones, these signals slow your heart rate and provide a general calming influence.

The host introduces you to someone to talk to. As you talk, signals are being sent back and forth between the two of you. The SES, operating completely unconsciously, picks up these signals. Let's assume your SES likes the signals it is receiving and provides even more calming. Meanwhile, your amygdalae continue to notice and react to goings-on in the room they regard as unexpected or as non-routine things. Yet, thanks to signals your SES is picking up from this new acquaintance, you do not feel the effect of the continued release of stress hormones. The desire to leave you felt when walking into the party has disappeared. You are in the midst of a number of people you do not know. Yet, you feel at home.

This is how the Social Engagement System makes it possible for us to interact with each other. Were it not for the ability of the SES to override the effect of stress hormones, we would bolt when seeing a stranger. We might not even go anyplace where we imagine a stranger might be encountered. But just as imagination can trigger the amygdalae, imagination can calm. When you walked into the party, if the host didn't see you come in, your Executive Function might come up with a plan to find someone to talk to. When considering the plan, you would imagine a conversation with someone. What would that imagination be based on? Past encounters, stored in your Internal Replica System. If your past encounters were generally satisfying, imagination of a new encounter can calm you. Your Social Engagement System would respond to the imagined face, slow your heart rate, and produce general calming. If a person has generally benign replicas, the SES can stabilize a person emotionally. The SES, in concert with the IRS, can provide an ongoing calming based on replicas, even while the amygdalae are releasing stress hormones in response to non-routine situations arising in social interactions.

The most important person in a child's life is its mother. The young child builds a replica in his mind of his mother and of their relationship. When the mother has been consistently emotionally available and empathically attuned, a replica of her can cause the SES to apply the vagal brake. As the child grows and interacts with others, the child's SES uses the mother's presence—or a replica of her—to provide calming when non-routine and unexpected things take place. This affords the child a secure environment in which to learn to read faces. When others display emotions, the child's IRS learns the corresponding facial expressions.

But, the converse is also true. What if the child, in his experience with his mother, frequently gets no signals, or even frightening signals, from her? His IRS will store this relationship. When imagining what is likely to happen, the child's replicas give no basis for feeling secure.

When an insecurely attached child becomes an adult, he will carry an Internal Replica System that contains—instead of replicas that stabilize him—replicas of the unpredictable mother-child relationships that destabilize him. As a result of the relationship with his mother, the child is not fluent in reading facial expressions. Or, the meaning of a facial expression can be distorted by an unstable parent-child relationship, and cause the person's Social Engagement System to misread what others mean, and to misunderstand their intent. For example, to a child that is frequently threatened by the mother, eye contact that means relatedness to other children may signal impending aggression to this child. Eye contact that, if read accurately, could reassure and calm a person, causes him to react defensively or aggressively.

If the Social Engagement System is providing a calming effect, and a facial expression changes to absent or to threatening, the system withdraws the braking action; the heart accelerates to the higher rate. As the heart accelerates, the calming effect disappears, and the person's emotional state changes, perhaps dramatically. The same instantaneous loss of calming takes place when a benign facial expression is misread, or when a person who has been providing calming looks away toward another person. Upon losing the braking action, a person can shift instantly from affection to aggression, or from engagement to withdrawal. The person has no way of knowing that his aggression or withdrawal was due to unconscious processes taking place in the SES. Nor does he know that the misreading (or the feeling of abandonment that came when the person looked away) is the result of early experiences, replicas of the relationship with his mother—and others—that have been carved into his psyche. Instead, he believes his response was appropriate; he believes the other person signaled aggression or abandonment. Meanwhile, the other person has no way to understand his inappropriate shift.

Lacking psychologically stabilizing replicas, a person remains dependent upon the physical presence of others for emotional regulation. But, his frequent misreading of facial expressions, tone of voice, body language, or the meaning of certain phraseology causes him to have emotional shifts that frustrate those who attempt to maintain a relationship with him. Relationships tend to break down and leave the person without physical comfort.

For example, a woman may become pregnant in the hope that a child will give her what others have failed to give, the end of aloneness and feelings of abandonment. If, as a mother, she calls on her child to regulate her, the parent-child relationship is turned on its head—just as it was for her when she was a child. This trajectory is passed on from generation to generation. To fly alone, with no one to regulate her, she fears panic. The idea of flying alone causes distress. To actually fly alone seems impossible.

Panic Attacks "Out of the Blue"

In some families, children have no place to express their inner experience. The parents may be mind-blind to inner experience, their own as well as that of their child's. Research by Notre Dame psychology professor Kristin Valentino found that mothers who had experienced childhood trauma exhibit ongoing "traumatic avoidance symptoms" characterized by unwillingness to address their children's thoughts and emotions.* If the parents are unable to tolerate awareness of their own inner experience, unacceptable feelings are triggered when children express feelings. When parents avoid inner experience, they react in a variety of ways. The net effect is that feelings a child should learn to contain, or to regard as informative, come to be thought of as dangerous.

When the child's inner experience is not mirrored, the child does not learn to regulate feelings. Nor does the child develop an accurate sense of identity. Some experts believe most psychological problems result from a lack of empathic attunement, emotional availability, and inaccurate mirroring. Why? Mirroring is the stuff children use to

---

* http://news.nd.edu/news/39767-traumatized-moms-avoid-tough-talks-with-kids-study-shows/

build a sense of self. The replicas produced by mirroring are the construction materials of identity. Without enough material, the child cannot build a sense of self that will stand up under stress.

It's like the story of "The Three Little Pigs." When parents provide accurate mirroring, a child has the materials needed to build a robust self-replica, one that will stand up to stress, like the brick house built by the third little pig. But when the necessary mirroring isn't provided, the child does not have material that is strong enough to build a solid replica of himself. The child can only haphazardly throw together a self-concept that is like a house made of straw, or sticks. So when there is uncertainty, as in the story when the wolf huffs and puffs, the child's "house" is unable to stand up under the stress.

Another unfortunate offshoot of a lack of mirroring is that the child doesn't develop an ability to reflect on what is going on inside. This lack of self-awareness, one's reflection function, means the person does not notice when stress builds up. Instead of finding a way to deal with stress, it builds up until it forces its way into the person's awareness as a panic attack—which seems to have come from "out of the blue."

Does panic brew for some time before it surfaces? Does lava heat up inside the volcano before it erupts? Of course. Research now proves what common sense suggests. In a study that monitored panic sufferers as they went about their daily routines, monitoring picked up signs of an impending attack at least sixty minutes before panic hit. Even as the panic was about to hit, the person was still clueless that it was coming. One of the researchers, Alicia E. Meuret of Southern Methodist University in Dallas, reported the results were "just amazing." She said, "We found that in this hour preceding naturally occurring panic attacks, there was a lot of physiological instability. The changes don't seem to enter the patient's awareness." When the panic finally erupted, the subjects reported "an out-of-the-blue panic attack with a lot of intense physical sensations." The physical sensations reported included shortness of breath, heart racing, dizziness, chest pain, sweating, hot flashes, trembling, choking, nausea, and numbness. Psychologically, subjects reported feelings of unreality, fear of losing control, and fear of dying. Subjects believed something catastrophic was happening, such as having a heart attack, suffocating, or going crazy. Amazingly, the physiological data collected during panic attacks showed nothing catastrophic, or even significant. The physiological measurements taken during the attack were not very different from those taken in the sixty minutes prior to the attack.

What was going on? How could the person be so sure they were about to die or go crazy when all the physiological measurements showed the same heart rate and breathing rate as before the panic attack? The answer is psychic equivalence. In the case of an out-of-the-blue panic attack, although nothing remarkable is going on in the person's body, psychic equivalence causes imagination to be regarded as reality. But what is really going on is this: The person's sense of identity, like the house made of straw, cannot stand up under stress. When stress overwhelms the person, they begin to lose touch with their sense of their identity. When a person's sense of identity falters, the experience registers in the person's mind as almost losing their mind or as almost losing their life.

All this mental processing goes on outside of awareness because, after all, the person never learned how to see what was going on inside. When there is no place to develop an awareness of inner experience as a child, there is little awareness of inner experience as an adult. Thus, a person's psychological self can be under great stress without any awareness of it. Then, when the psychological self collapses, the collapse is expressed in the person's imagination as going crazy or dying. Psychic equivalence causes the person to believe it is true.

Whether built out of bricks or built out of straw, we all have a sense of identity. That is our psychological self. It is produced from the mirroring we took in during our formative years. It is made up out of the bits and pieces of communication we received from our parents about who—according to them—we are.

Panic during Flight

What we see in the SOAR program is this: Whether the client is aware of it or not, there is:

1. Relatively little material with which to construct a robust self-identity (the psychological self);

2. Relatively little development of the ability to look inside to see when stresses start building up (reflective function);

3. Relatively little training in how to regulate intense emotions (Executive Function).

4. Relatively little development of automatic unconscious regulation of emotion (Internal Replica System, Social Engagement System)

As a result, flying is difficult or impossible. The psychological self is weakened:

• When others are in control and there is no way to escape;
• When unable to keep the situation out of mind (perhaps due to turbulence);
• When not physically in contact with the earth;
• When not with someone.

The solutions developed by SOAR help clients strengthen their sense of self by linking the challenges of flight to a moment in which there was real one-to-one connection between their inner world and another person's inner world—exactly the thing that is missing in the early life of so many of us! With our methods, not only is the person's sense of self being strengthened by reconnecting with something that there hasn't been enough of, but in-flight stress is reduced by training the amygdalae not to release stress hormones. As a result, clients who use the Strengthening Exercise to establish links between each challenging moment of flight and a moment of connection in their lives do not come apart during the flight. They are able to fly free of panic.

Replicas and Panic

Good internal replicas can provide the emotional strength necessary to avoid high anxiety and panic when flying. The importance of replicas begins early. A replica of the mother keeps her real to the child when she is away. This first type of replica—a direct replica—is formed in the child's mind by direct experience of its mother. A second type—an indirect replica—is the child's concept of itself. It is formed indirectly as the child takes in the mother's view of him or her. If the mother's view is recognizable to the child as its real self, the indirect replica is a valuable asset that secures the connection between mother and child. The child's sense of being held in the mother's mind and heart means the child is never out of mind when out of sight. This secure relationship with the mother—initially the baby's whole world—expands to become a secure orientation to the world in adulthood.

If the mother's view of the child is not visible, or is not recognizable by the child as its real self, the child feels abandoned. Its emotional development is restricted or even crippled. When it cannot find a recognizable version of itself in residence in the mother's mind, the child struggles to come up with an alternate version of itself, one the mother will take in and reflect back. If that does not work, the child may adopt the orphan version of itself that is in its mother's mind. Or, the child, finding that nothing works, will simply give up.

Sources of Calming

Physical contact, an external source of calming, is not easily internalized. When physical contact ends, the calming it provides fades. After a time, instead of calming, memory of physical contact causes longing. Reliance on external sources leaves the person dependent and clinging.

Even in solitude, internal replicas can replace feelings of isolation with a sense of connection. The replica of an empathic and attuned relationship is a source of lasting, portable, and independent emotional stability. While a companion can offer invaluable comfort in response to distress, internal support can prevent distress. Once established by the Strengthening Exercise, internal links between specific flight situations and a memory of empathic attunement provide targeted calming.

CHAPTER 16
Understanding Arousal

Arousal has to do with how "revved up" a person is. When a car is going sixty mph, the engine is revved up more than when it's going ten mph. How revved up the engine is depends upon how much gas is flowing into the engine. Similarly, a person's arousal is higher when more stress hormones flow into their brain and body. There is some conscious control over it, but most human arousal is regulated unconsciously.

Als's Seven Levels of Arousal

Understanding arousal can help make it less threatening. Neurological researcher Dr. Heidelise Als has classified seven levels of arousal. Understanding these levels can help you be more comfortable with emotion, particularly at higher levels.

Level One—Deep Sleep. Not even dreaming is taking place.

Level Two—Active Sleep. A tiny bit of stress hormone is released by the body clock to increase arousal enough to dream.

Level Three—Drowsy. From Level Two upward, a bit more hormone is released and the person starts to wake up. Or, from Level Four downward, a bit less hormone is released to prepare for sleep.

Level Four—Alert Not Processing. Enough hormones are pumping through the brain and body to keep the person awake, but arousal is not high enough to perform tasks requiring high-level cognition.

Level Five—Alert Processing. Additional stress hormone activates high-level cognition. Executive Function, including reflective function, is available. Links established by practice of the Strengthening Exercise help limit arousal to Level Five.

Let's stick with Level Five for a moment. Let's say you're having a good day. There are no worries standing in the way of focusing on your work. You could say you have 100 percent of your mental capacity available. But that's not quite the case. The mind, like a computer, reserves some of its capacity to maintain basic operations and stay organized. Though your mind has great capacity, you have only part of it at your command. Some capacity is set aside to stay oriented in three ways: to maintain a sense of your identity, to maintain a sense of where you are, and to maintain a sense of time.

Let's say you have one hundred units of mental capacity, and that maintaining sense of self, sense of location, and sense of time takes up ten units. That leaves ninety units to work with. When you're having a good day, and seem to have your mental faculties fully available to you, what you really have at your command are ninety units.

Level Six—Agitation. Emotion enters the picture. It could be a positive emotion such as joy or a negative emotion such as anxiety or anger. Whether positive or negative, emotion takes over some of those ninety units.

If a weak emotion takes over ten units, it leaves you eighty to work with. But if there's a strong emotion that takes over eighty units, only ten units remain at your disposal, leaving your mental capability markedly reduced.

It is in Level Six that reflective function disappears. Executive Function, under the load of agitation, weakens. If the person's Executive Function is not robust, it may disappear. This is the point at which a fearful flier begins to go into a personal movie. Links established by practice of the Strengthening Exercise help Executive Function dismiss false alarms and allow a return to Level Five.

Level Seven—Flooding. Emotion takes over ninety units. Since ten units are in reserve for basic mental activities, there are no units left at your direction. Control of the mind is lost. There is no Executive Function. It has been hijacked by emotion.

This can mean panic—but it doesn't have to. It depends upon whether or not the person is familiar with his or her mind being hijacked by emotion. The person who, as a child, navigated every arousal level accompanied by a caregiver, knows this condition is fleeting. For him or her, flooding is experienced simply as, "Oh, I'm flooded." But, for the person who, as a child, was not accompanied by its caregiver through all arousal levels, flooding may be experienced as an extreme threat. In that case, Level Seven does mean panic. When a parent takes a child to Disney World for the first time, it's their job to accompany the child on rides that are challenging. Similarly, it is the parent's job to accompany their child on the roller-coaster ride through the levels of arousal Als has identified, so the child learns that feelings—even intense ones—are natural and endurable. Most anxious fliers will recognize that their early trips through "Emotional World" were solo. Even as an adult, they equate arousal with fear, and fear with danger. When aroused, they may think, "What if it is too much for me? Will I have a heart attack, or suffocate, or go crazy?

Als doesn't break Level Seven down into different kinds of flooding, but I identify five levels of flooding: A, B, C, D, and E.

Level Seven A—Loss of Control. This is the level at which emotion takes over all ninety units available. Thinking or focus cannot be directed.

Level Seven B—Loss of Location. Emotion takes over, say, ninety-three units. Ten units are required to maintain orientation in person, place, and time. Something's got to give. The first thing to go is the sense of physical orientation. Things seem disconnected, unreal, or surreal. You may see yourself from a vantage point outside your body.

Level Seven C—Loss of Time. Emotion takes over around ninety-six units. Time disappears. Already you are unable to direct your mind's focus. Already you are disoriented or lost. Both become "forever" as sense of time disappears.

Level Seven D—Threat of Loss of Identity. As emotion takes over ninety-nine units and moves toward one hundred, identity cannot be maintained. For the person who has not been accompanied at this level—and psychologically held when here—by a caregiver, the slipping away of identity may be experienced as terror of annihilation.

Level Seven E—Loss of Identity. When emotion takes over one hundred units, identity is no longer produced. Terror of annihilation, if any, ends. There is no time. There is no place. There is no identity. There is no fear. There is only awareness of awareness. Spiritual disciplines refer to this experience by various terms. In Zen Buddhism, it is termed *kensho*, seeing one's nature. When all experience other than awareness has vanished, awareness finds there is nothing to be aware of other than awareness. When all memory, all perception, all thought, and all identification disappears, nothing remains except this one phenomenon: awareness. But when everything other than awareness has been stripped away, what is there to be aware of? Awareness is aware only of awareness. When that occurs, when everything else is stripped away, only one's ultimate identity—the identity we all share—is left.

The person who reaches Level Seven D but not Seven E may be traumatized. In psychic equivalence, what is in the mind is experienced as what is real. The converse is also true. If something does not exist in the mind, it does not exist in reality. Thus failure to produce a sense of self during psychic equivalence is experienced as death. It is this synthetic experience of death that causes panic to be so terrifying. Having been at the edge of annihilation and escaped, the person becomes thereafter vigilant in every moment to avoid annihilation by never again giving up control.

Flooding Is Temporary

During flooding, though there is the fear it will last forever, it can't. Why? When you flip a switch to turn on lights, a piece of metal physically connects the wires attached to the switch. And as long as the switch stays in that position, the connection remains. But in the mind, connections are made not by metal but by chemicals. Connections made by chemicals last only a few seconds. Level Seven experience can be the result of a huge number of connections, all of which are being made chemically. The Level Seven experience is temporary because the chemicals wear off in a few seconds.

When the connections wear off, you go from Level Seven to Level Six, from panic to high anxiety. The conditions that pushed you into Level Seven may still be present and may push you back up again. This explains why panic may seem to come in waves. The distinction between high anxiety and panic can be lost, causing you to believe you have been in a state of panic for hours when actually you've been shuttling between Levels Six and Seven.

Understanding Als's Seven Levels of Arousal can sharpen your ability to distinguish between Level Seven and Level Six. Recognizing a level and knowing it is temporary can help you accept that level without fear.

Positive Flooding

It's possible for flooding to be a positive experience. Orgasm is a perfect example. There are different levels there, too. In Level Seven A, ninety units of mental capacity are filled with pleasure. That's nice. But in a Level Seven B orgasm, you lose awareness of where you are.

In Level Seven C, time disappears, transporting you into a state of eternity. In Level Seven D, identity disappears. Freed of identity, all sense of separation vanishes.

How does the person deal with fear of Level Seven D annihilation during the sexual experience? Research suggests that orgasm is possible only when oxytocin has shut down the fear system. Without this shutting down of the fear system, entry into orgasm—with its loss of person, place, and time—may not be possible. When in the experience, orgasm—like panic—seems timeless. In a state of panic, there is fear it will never end. But it does end. With panic—as with orgasm—the chemical connections wear out. The experience of timelessness yields as a sense of time returns. The experience of oneness is lost as identity reappears. It is important to hold onto knowing that whether the flooding is panic or orgasm, you always come back.

Neutral Flooding

Neutral flooding is caused not by rising emotion but by rising concentration. In some sports, neutral flooding—the mind filled with concentration on the game—is called being "in the zone." In automobile racing, it is called "driving 11/10ths." Let's say the maximum speed a car can go around a certain curve is 100 mph. Going around a 100-mph curve at 100 mph is called "driving 10/10ths." In a long race where peak concentration can't be maintained, you go around it at 90. This is called "driving 9/10ths."

There is a special case in which a driver goes around a 100-mph curve at 110: that's "driving 11/10ths," being in the zone. How is that possible? Under the stress of competition, the demand for extra performance sometimes presses the 10 units of mental capacity reserved for basic orientation into service to drive the car. In this extraordinary state of mind, not just 90 units but all 100 units become available, and the 100-mph curve in an ordinary state of mind is a 110-mph curve in this extraordinary state of mind. This phenomenon is discussed at length in a book by Hungarian-born psychology professor Mihaly Csikszentmihalyi entitled *Flow: The Psychology of Optimal Experience.* The flow state, as Csikszentmihalyi describes it, is an optimal state of intrinsic motivation, where the person is fully immersed in what he or she is doing.

When this state occurs during racing, the driver, the car, the track, and the world are all one. During a race in Rouen, France, approaching a 90-degree turn at 140 mph, I had the experience that I was watching from a few feet above the car. I did not know who was driving the car. Actually, I was not sure anyone was driving, for it seemed as though the car and the track were part of a reality that was simply unfolding.

During what Csikszentmihalyi calls flow, immersed in the game, the player's sense of identity is gone. Though every ounce of the person's being is engaged in the action, there is no sense that she is playing any role at all in what is happening. The player experiences the game as though what is happening is unwinding, like string from a spool. This occurs in all sorts of activities, from sports to mathematics to the arts—in performance, on the page, and on the canvas.

• • •

Panic is sometimes called flooding. More accurately, panic is fear of flooding. Flooding, though unusual, is normal. It is a state in which identity begins to disappear (does disappear in Level Seven E) because the mental capacity that ordinarily produces identity is all but used up by intense mental activity or pleasure, or all but overtaken by emotion. If it is understood simply as what it is, fear of it can subside. It helps to understand that flooding—which can be negative, neutral, or positive—is temporary, and that identity always comes back.

PART TWO

AVIATION

CHAPTER 17
How Flying Works

To feel emotionally safe, you need to feel physically safe. Though flying is one of the safest things you can do, statistics are not enough. You need to become a mini-expert. You need to know, for example, that the wings are far too strong to break. You need to know that things that could break are backed up. You need to know what the backups are, and what pilots do to take care of problems.

Stability
What keeps the plane from flipping over?

Some of the things anxious fliers worry about simply can't happen. As you become a mini-expert, you will be able to rule out some of these fears. One concern is that the plane will flip over. Perhaps it's from Hollywood movies. Perhaps it's from media hype. Perhaps it's from your own imagination. But the plane is not on the verge of going out of control at every moment. An airliner, like any vehicle, has built-in dynamic stability. Dynamic stability is the tendency of a vehicle to move straight ahead unless it is forced to do otherwise.

You can try out dynamic stability by taking your car to an empty parking lot. Turn the steering wheel to start making a circle. It takes effort. You have to hold some pressure on the wheel. If it were not for the power steering on your car, it might take a lot of effort. If you let go of the pressure, the steering wheel centers itself and the car travels straight ahead. The same dynamic stability is build into an airliner. If the pilot turns the wheel to start making a circle, it takes effort. The pilot has to hold pressure on the wheel. If the pilot lets go of the pressure, the wheel centers itself and the plane glides straight ahead.

This tendency to move straight ahead is caused in a car by the way the front wheels are attached, and in a plane by the way the wings are attached. Did you make paper airplanes when you were a kid? To make it fly straight, you bent the wings upward into a V shape. This upward angle of the wings is called dihedral. You didn't have to be an aeronautical engineer to use dihedral to give your paper airplane stability. You found out by trial and error, or an older kid showed you.

Next time you look at an airliner, notice that, as you look from the fuselage outward toward the tip of the wing, the wing rises slightly. That's dihedral. (In case you didn't know it, the fuselage is the central body of the plane to which the wings and tail assembly are attached.)

How a Plane Changes Direction
It's scary when a plane dips and turns. What's happening?
When a bicycle or motorcycle turns, it leans into the turn. So do speedboats and planes. Pilots call it banking. When a plane starts to bank, it's tempting to think the angle might increase enough to turn the plane upside down. That's because, as a passenger, you're not aware of the effort required to make banking happen. For a car to turn, pressure must be applied to the steering wheel. Similarly, for a plane to bank, pressure must be applied to the control wheel. It takes some pressure to bank the plane a little. It takes more pressure to bank more. The plane never banks more than the pilot causes it to because dihedral is always trying to return the wings to level.

Like an arrow, the plane goes where it's pointed unless caused to do otherwise by the pilot. To point the plane in a different direction, the pilot has to turn the plane by banking it. For example, to turn left, the plane needs to bank to the left, tilting the left wing down and the right wing up. To do that, the pilot applies pressure on the control wheel to move it to the left (counter-clockwise) and hold it there. The control wheel is attached to ailerons, horizontal panels on the rear of each wing. Normally, the ailerons are in a neutral position and have no effect on the wing. But to turn left, the ailerons on the left wing are moved up against the airflow, to tilt the left wing down, while the ailerons on the right wing are moved down against the airflow, to tilt the right wing up.

By maintaining pressure on the control wheel, the pilot keeps the ailerons deflected against the airflow until the plane has turned to point in the desired direction. Once this has been achieved, the pilot relaxes the pressure. The ailerons return to their neutral positions. The wings return to level. The plane stops turning and again flies straight ahead.

Unlike Hollywood movies in which pilots hold onto the controls for dear life, pilots do not need to touch the controls unless they want to point the plane in a different direction or to climb or descend. Airliners plummet—or plunge, or dive—only in Hollywood movies, or in "movies" you create in your own imagination. If you see an airliner plummet in a movie, know it is fantasy. Planes do not uncontrollably plummet or plunge. In a steep descent, as the plane's speed increases, the wings produce more lift. The increased lift stops the plane from going down so rapidly. When a plane is at cruise altitude, if there is a problem with the pressurization system that cannot be corrected, the pilots do an "emergency descent." In an emergency descent, the throttles are brought back to idle, the speed brakes are extended, and the landing gear is extended. This keeps the plane from picking up excessive speed when the nose is lowered. And if you "see" an airliner plummet in your own mind, know that it, too, is fantasy.

Climbing and Descending
When I feel the plane go down, I'm afraid it's falling.

Though a pilot could begin a climb or descent so smoothly you wouldn't even notice it, there are reasons why it isn't done. First, most pilots don't know that even routine movements of the plane can make a passenger feel anxious. Second, pilots like to feel the plane respond when they move the controls. Third, Air Traffic Control expects altitude changes to be made more quickly than a gentle climb or descent would allow.

Your amygdalae may tend to react to these changes, but by using the Strengthening Exercise, you can train them not to.

A plane can be made to climb in two ways. One way is simply to increase the power. As the speed starts to increase, the nose gently rises to maintain the same speed. Likewise, to descend, simply decreasing the power will cause the nose to gently lower to maintain the same speed. The other way to climb is to point the nose higher by pulling back on the control wheel. This causes the elevator—a panel on the rear of the horizontal tail surface—to deflect upward against the air stream, which causes the rear of the plane to lower and the nose to rise. Power must be increased if speed is to be maintained. To descend, pushing forward on the control wheel causes the elevator to deflect downward against the air stream, which causes the rear of the plane to rise and the nose to lower. Power must be reduced if speed is to be maintained.

Rudder
How do you keep the plane going straight in strong winds?

It's no more difficult than what you do in your car when you're driving in a crosswind. During takeoff, we steer the plane down the middle of the runway with the rudder. We use a little pressure on the rudder to compensate for the crosswind.

We also can compensate for the crosswind by slightly turning the nose wheel (that's the front wheel, beneath the pilot's cabin). Generally, we steer with the nose wheel during taxi and on takeoff until the air is moving fast enough past the rudder for it to be effective.

The rudder is also needed for a crosswind landing when the wind—instead of being lined up with the runway—is blowing across the runway.

Airliners have two or more engines. As you may know, an airliner can fly on just one. But if the engine on the left wing is working and the one on the right wing is not working, doesn't it push the airplane sideways? Yes, it does. That's why planes have a rudder. If there is more thrust on one side than the other, the rudder can compensate. It isn't difficult. On a car, if a tire goes flat, the car pulls to the side. The driver uses the wheel to compensate. With the airplane, if one engine is pushing more than the other, pilots use the rudder to compensate.

Engines

I'm afraid that if the engines quit, the plane is just going to fall.

Many believe the airplane is held in the air by the engines, and that if the engines quit, the plane will fall like a rock. Not so. The plane is basically a glider. Though power from the engines is needed to push the plane forward through the air when climbing and when cruising, going downhill is effortless. No power is needed at all. The plane just glides down. Even though it's heavy, the plane is so perfectly shaped that, for well more than a hundred miles, it glides down from cruise altitude with no need for engines at all before leveling off in the airport's traffic pattern to get into position for landing.

Adventurous people leap off cliffs and glide down on hang gliders. Even though a jetliner is heavy, its aerodynamic shape is so well designed that its glide performance is twice that of a hang glider! Consider another glider: the space shuttle. It's blasted into space by a rocket. The rocket falls away. Momentum carries the shuttle into orbit. When it comes back to land, it just glides down. Every landing is done completely without engine power. Your airliner has much bigger wings than the space shuttle; it glides far better than the space shuttle does. So next time the thought of "what happens if the engines quit?" hits you, remember the many times you have seen the space shuttle descend without any engines and touch down perfectly on the runway.

People who believe the engines hold up the plane sit on pins and needles, expecting the plane to fall at any moment. If the initiation of a normal descent doesn't cause you terror, there's no reason to expect terror if engines were to fail. Why? Because the glide with engines inoperative is indistinguishable from the glide of a normal descent. In either case, the nose needs to be lowered only two to three degrees below the horizon for gravity to maintain the speed necessary for flight. From cruise altitude the plane can glide for twenty to thirty minutes, plenty of time for the pilots to correct any problem with an engine or, like the space shuttle, to glide down to a runway and land.

Nonetheless, to ensure reliability, jet engines are constantly monitored. Sensors transmit data to a computer that tracks engine performance. Any abnormality in operation is detected long before it becomes a problem. In addition, a periscopelike device regularly inspects the interior of the engine. If it is not operating properly, the captain may elect to shut down the engine. A three- or four-engine plane may continue the flight, but regulations require that a two-engine plane land as soon as practical. To understand how rare engine problems are, consider that initial certification of the twin-engine 767 for trans-Atlantic flight required two million hours of domestic flying without any engine problem. Two million hours! In spite of that figure, it's easy for an anxious flier to think, "What if they both quit?" Have you ever seen two lightbulbs in your house burn out at the same time? Incandescent bulbs last from 800 to 1500 hours. Fluorescent bulbs last about 10,000, one two-hundredth as long as the engines showed they could go without failure. I've never seen two bulbs burn out at the same time. I doubt that anyone has. From that point of view, the idea of jet engines burning out at the same time becomes almost unthinkable.

In spite of how rare engine failures are, every takeoff is planned so that an engine failure can occur without creating an unsafe condition. When planning the takeoff, the pilots calculate three speeds: V-1, V-R, and V-2 (V stands for "velocity"). Each V-speed is a checkpoint during takeoff. Before reaching V-1, the takeoff will be aborted if an engine fails. If an engine fails after reaching V-1, the takeoff will be continued. Since the plane can fly on one engine, it is safer to continue the takeoff—and then to land using the full length of the runway to stop—than to stop with limited runway remaining. V-R is the speed at which the nose is lifted off the runway. V-2 is the speed at which the plane initially climbs following an engine failure. A slightly higher initial climb speed is used with all engines operating.

Though rare, planes do sometimes collide with birds. In my thirty-eight years of flying, I collided with a bird only once. There was no damage whatsoever to the plane. But if the bird happens to be in just the wrong spot, it can be ingested into the engine. Engines are built to be able to ingest birds and still run. But a large bird may bend fan blades enough to cause vibration inside the engine. Since jet engines came into use in the 1950s, only one airliner has been forced to land due to bird ingestion. In that instance, a flock of birds caused both engines to lose power. The plane did not fall out of the sky: It glided down for a landing in the Hudson River where, due to buoyancy of the fuel tanks, it floated.

Primary, Secondary, Backup, and Emergency Systems

In my car, if something goes wrong, I can pull over to the side of the road. But if something happens to a plane, I'm dead.

A person unfamiliar with aeronautical engineering might think that if anything goes wrong, the flight is doomed. It just isn't that way. Imagine your car had two engines. If one quit, you could keep going with power provided by the other engine. Same thing with powerboats; a lot of them have two engines. With an airliner, safety requires redundancy. We have two, three, even four of everything needed for normal operation.

Each system is tested before flight and is monitored during flight. The primary systems are used when flight begins. As the flight progresses, if any primary system begins to operate outside of normal parameters, the plane automatically switches to an identical secondary system. If the secondary system restores normal operation, the pilots are not even informed until the plane is parked, so that the primary system problem will be reported to maintenance.

If the secondary system doesn't restore normal operation, the instrument panel displays a message informing the pilots. Using prescribed steps on a checklist, the pilots switch to a backup system. Backup systems are less complex. By removing some of the sophistication built into the primary and secondary systems, the backup system is usually able to restore normal operation. If the backup system doesn't restore normal operation, the pilots—using the checklist—switch to the even more basic emergency system.

As an example, consider the braking system. To allow heavy braking without damage to the tires, airliners have sophisticated anti-skid systems. In a typical design, if a fault develops in the primary braking system, the system automatically switches to a secondary system. If the secondary system does not isolate the fault and restore proper braking, a light comes on, and the captain switches to a third system. Should the third system not work perfectly, it automatically switches to a fourth system. And if the fourth system does not perform properly, a light comes on telling the captain to manually switch to the emergency system. The emergency system bypasses the anti-skid system and sends hydraulic pressure to the wheel brakes according to the amount of force the pilot applies to the brake pedals. With the anti-skid system bypassed, the pilots need to brake judiciously to avoid damaging the tires, just as you would if driving an automobile not equipped with anti-skid brakes.

Even though there are redundant systems, each system is designed for a high degree of reliability. In years of flying airliners with the braking systems described above, not once did I have to use even the secondary braking system!

Traffic Collision Avoidance System (TCAS)

What if another plane gets in your way? What keeps you from hitting other planes?

It may be helpful to understand that pilots can be as obsessed with control as an anxious passenger might be. Pilots are comfortable only when they know they have everything under control and can keep it that way. Obsession with control led to the development of TCAS, the Traffic Collision Avoidance System. Pilots knew they could depend on Air Traffic Control (ATC) to maintain separation between them and other planes at 18,000 feet and above. But below 18,000 feet, small planes are sometimes not controlled by ATC. Small planes are hard to spot when flying toward the sun, or in hazy conditions. Feeling vulnerable, pilots wanted better control.

Research to develop a collision avoidance system pilots could use in the cockpit began all the way back in the 1950s. When the Airline Pilots Association began lobbying Congress to have TCAS installed, airline management and air traffic controllers opposed the device. Some argued that the money spent developing and deploying such a system would be better spent elsewhere. Wanting more control of collision risk, pilots continued their efforts. As a result, it finally became law that every U.S. Airliner had to have TCAS installed by December 1991. Other countries soon followed.

In the cockpit, the TCAS displays other aircraft at or near the same altitude. A computer determines whether any of them could pose a collision threat. If the computer finds any possibility of a threat, it alerts the pilots. If the threat shifts from possible to actual, the computer directs the pilots to climb or descend. Pilots follow instructions from the TCAS and immediately advise Air Traffic Control of the change in altitude.

Ground Proximity Warning System (GPWS)

Most accidents are caused by pilot error. I'm worried that the pilot may make a mistake.

Airline flying is remarkably safe for numerous reasons. One of the many is that, following any accident, investigators make recommendations to prevent that type of accident from happening again. As a result, airliners are now equipped with devices that prevent pilot error. An example is GPWS, the Ground Proximity Warning System. For years, one type of accident, tabbed Controlled Flight Into Terrain (CFIT), had continued to occur in spite of changes in cockpit procedure intended to prevent such accidents. Controlled Flight Into Terrain means a perfectly functioning plane was flown unknowingly into the ground.

In 1969, Don Bateman, the Chief Avionics Engineer for Honeywell, began developing a system to prevent CFIT. Bateman's system used a radar signal from the plane to determine the distance between the plane and the ground. If the system saw the plane closing in on the ground, it automatically checked the position of the landing gear and flaps. If they were not in the proper position for landing, the system assumed the pilot was heading toward the ground—not intentionally for landing but unintentionally and unknowingly. This triggered flashing lights and a voice command—"Pull Up, Pull Up"—that continued until the pilot regained a safe altitude.

Ralph Waldo Emerson said, "Build a better mousetrap and the world will beat a path to your door." Maybe that applies to a ninety-nine-cent item, but Bateman's device was expensive. Though this device was the solution to the CFIT problem, the airlines did not beat a path to his door. Nor did the FAA, the Federal Aviation Administration, in its wisdom, see fit to require airlines to purchase it. But something changed all that.

Normally, when Air Traffic Control issues a descent clearance, the altitude specified is higher than any obstruction on the ground. But on December 1, 1974, a Trans World Airlines 727 heading into Washington's Dulles Airport was given a descent clearance with rarely used phraseology that did not ensure terrain clearance. The pilots, believing ATC was still responsible for terrain clearance, descended into hills twenty-five miles northwest of the airport. This CFIT accident at an airport used by members of Congress resulted in legislation that required every U.S. airliner be equipped with a Ground Proximity Warning System (GPWS). The FAA inaugurated it two weeks later—December 18!

Bateman's GPWS device put an end to accidents in which planes unknowingly flew into the ground, at least in the United States. Foreign airlines were slow to adopt GPWS technology but did so after an Avianca 747 was unintentionally flown into the ground as it approached the Madrid airport in darkness on November 27, 1983.

Since its invention, GPWS has been improved through Global Positioning System (GPS) technology. Instead of relying only on a radar signal bounced off the ground, the Enhanced Ground Proximity Warning System (EGPWS) employs GPS terrain-height information.

Automatic Landing
Can the plane land itself?

Crashes due to pilot error in bad weather have largely been ruled out by advanced autopilot systems that lock onto signals from the runway and land the plane automatically. The most advanced systems offer such precision that landing is possible when visibility and ceiling are near zero. Special equipment is required both at the runway and on the airplane as well as simulator training for pilots certified to conduct these landings.

What Can Cause an Accident?
With all these safety systems, how can a crash happen?

When you consider all the redundancy built into the plane, all the safety systems, all the simulator training of the pilots, the flight planning and flight following by the dispatchers, the checks and balances in maintenance and inspection, the constant monitoring of engines, the navigation systems that allow automatic landing, it's hard to imagine how an accident is possible at all.

Accidents and terrorism are, as most anxious fliers look at it, different things. Most say terrorism can happen anywhere. But those who still worry about terrorists can gain some help by knowing that before 9/11, domestic security was a farce. It was put into place because of an epidemic in the 1960s of "Take me to Cuba" hijackings. Screeners were paid minimum wage and training was minimal. Though those of us in the industry knew weapons could easily get through this screening, it discouraged most would-be hijackers. After a few years of no hijackings, Senator Teddy Kennedy proposed screening be discontinued as an unneeded nuisance.

At the same time, terrorist activity was on the increase in the UK, Europe, and the Middle East. Well thought out measures were put into place. Security was still not taken seriously. Though there was no increased security on a domestic flight, inspection on flights leaving the United States for Europe matched the security in place in Europe.

That all changed after 9/11. In the United States, public interest in terrorism went from nil to obsessive. Measures that should have been in place all along were suddenly implemented. Inspection on domestic flights was dramatically improved. For years airline pilots had been asking the FAA to require secure cockpit doors. The FAA's response was that we really didn't want such doors because if we crashed, they might jam and trap us in the cockpit. But 9/11 changed all that. In a few weeks, the secure doors we should have had all along were authorized. Had we had such doors earlier, the terrorist operation that took place on 9/11 could not have been carried out.

Some say, "Well, if flying is so safe, why are there still accidents?" The question seems to imply that safety should be absolute. Or, that when we point out how safe flying is, we are either engaged in deception, or not looking at the problem as realistically as they are. I think some self-examination is called for. Why does air safety need to be absolute while road safety can be—literally—"hit or miss?" Why the double standard? The double standard is due to psychology. When driving, a person can control their emotions; they can't when flying. And, rather than recognize where the problem lies, it is less damaging to the ego to assign the problem elsewhere.

Whether by land, sea, or air, as long as transportation takes place, there will sometimes be mishaps. As my Air Force squadron commander once said, "The only way to make planes completely safe is to park them in freshly poured concrete."

Levity aside, safety is taken seriously in aviation. It is considered a near miss if planes pass each other with three hundred or four hundred feet of separation. On a two-lane highway, we think nothing of zipping past oncoming traffic with a separation of only three or four feet. Though Air Traffic Control tracks air traffic on radar—and every airliner has TCAS in the cockpit as a backup—an anxious passenger obsesses about the possibility of a midair collision in spite of all the measures taken and systems in place that make such an incident a remote possibility.

Ask an airline pilot whether he or she feels safer in the cockpit of an airliner or behind the wheel of their car. You will always be told the cockpit. Why? Because the pilot has far more control and many more backups in the air than he does on the ground. Also, the pilot feels safer in the air where only professionals are encountered and the space in which these professionals operate is vast, not to mention carefully monitored by ATC.

Flying, though not absolutely safe, is remarkably safe. There is good reason to be intellectually in a state of peace about security when in the air. But there is an equally good reason to be emotionally unsettled. The reason lies simply in how we are mentally wired. When the amygdalae release stress hormones, our inner CEO needs to do its ABCs. At the moment of commitment, the CEO's office, the orbitofrontal cortex, resets the amygdalae. It is far easier for the CEO to do its ABCs when behind the wheel of a car than when seated in the passenger cabin. It is not always easy to assess the significance of a noise or a motion the plane makes. Without an assessment, one cannot build a plan of action. With no plan of action, there can be no commitment. With no commitment, the amygdalae continue producing stress hormones.

Since your inner CEO finds it easier to do its ABCs in a car than in a plane, the car *feels* safer in spite of incontrovertible evidence that the plane is far safer. But since your inner CEO can recognize flying is safer, it can wisely choose to train the amygdalae not to react to the noises and motions when flying.

We've been flying planes for more than a hundred years. When there has been an accident, the cause has been determined and a fix put into the system to keep that from happening again. This means, for an accident to happen today, in most cases it is something that has never happened before—something that has not happened even once in the previous hundred years.

CHAPTER 18

Weather

Good weather? Bad weather? What does it mean? How do I know it's safe? A captain may announce that the weather at the destination airport is good or bad. This oversimplification, for public consumption, can lead to misunderstanding and completely unnecessary concern. Whenever there's an accident, reporters can be counted on to say weather may have been the cause. Disregard what they say. Reporters know very little about the relationship between weather and safety. With a more sophisticated understanding, every concern you have about the relationship between weather and safety can be allayed.

Bad Weather

I'm afraid of bad weather and I start checking it days before my flight.

If you were to overhear a conversation about weather between pilots, dispatchers, and weathermen, you might never hear the term "bad weather." Instead, you would hear them say the weather is above minimums (legal to takeoff or land) or below minimums (not legal to takeoff or land). Take a tip from pilots. Forget about good and bad weather. If it's legal to fly, it's safe to fly. Bumpy? That's safe, too. Bumps just make it harder to keep the flight out of mind.

How do you know if weather is above or below legal minimums? It is simply a matter of measurement. Weather is measured every few minutes at every airport. The measurements are published immediately and are available within seconds to the dispatchers who plan the flights, to the pilots who confirm the planning of the flight, and to pilots in the air. To take off or to land, the measurements must meet or exceed the criteria legally required by the FAA (or the equivalent authority in other countries).

A licensed dispatcher plans the flight. The captain reviews the plan with the dispatcher. To determine whether the flight can legally be flown, they study the weather at the departure airport, en route, and at the arrival airport. If it is possible for the ceiling or visibility at the destination airport to be lower than legally required for landing, one or more alternate airports at which the weather will be unquestionably satisfactory must be specified in the flight-planning documents. Of course, if the flight is landing in an hour or two, these forecasts are pretty reliable. But if the flight is landing in eighteen hours, well, everyone knows, weather is changeable. That's why alternate airports are plotted into the flight plan.

These planning documents are signed and attested to both by the captain and the dispatcher. Both must certify that the planning is complete and that the flight can be conducted safely. Adequate fuel must be loaded on the plane to fly to the destination airport: This includes 10 percent extra to compensate for greater than forecast headwinds, plus fuel for an approach to the runway, plus fuel to then divert to an alternate airport, plus fuel to stay in a holding pattern, if that is called for, for a minimum of a half hour, plus fuel for landing.

For takeoff, visibility—the distance the pilot can see ahead of the plane—must be adequate for steering the plane down the runway. Most runways have lights at the edges and a white line down the middle of the runway, as well as centerline lights. Centerline lights are a row of lights imbedded in the runway on the white line to guide the plane down the runway in fog. The visibility required for takeoff depends upon whether or not the runway has these features. Transmissometers installed alongside the runway measure the visibility. Takeoff is not permitted if visibility is less than required or if water or snow on the runway is in excess of specified limits.

For landing, there must be sufficient visibility and ceiling. Ceiling is the distance between the runway and the clouds above it. Typically, the visibility must be one-quarter mile or more (that's more than 1,300 feet), and the ceiling two hundred feet or greater. However, with advanced equipment, landings can be made when visibility and ceiling are lower.

Measurements of wind speed and direction are constantly available. Headwind helps a plane take off or land by reducing the length of runway needed. Except in extreme weather, high wind velocity is not restrictive if landings or takeoffs can be made directly into the wind. Whatever wind Mother Nature provides is that much less speed that needs to be produced by the engines. At any point during the flight, the pilots can use a device in the cockpit to obtain, within seconds, current weather information for any airport in the world. Legal limits are always more conservative than safety limits. If the weather is legal for flight, the weather is safe for flight.

When driving your car, if the speed limit is fifty-five mph, you know you can drive faster than that and still be safe. But in airline operations, the limit, whatever it may be, is the limit—period! Limits are not exceeded in the slightest. Though a pilot could exceed the legal limits somewhat without compromising safety, doing so could mean revocation of the pilot's license.

Storms
I'm afraid a storm will break something on the plane or make the pilots lose control.

Your airliner is built the same as the planes that fly smack into hurricanes to measure their intensity and track their movement. Anything Mother Nature can dish out, your airliner can handle.

The dispatcher plans the flight taking into consideration all factors, including the possibility of en route storms. While en route, the pilots use radar to scan the area ahead. Storm clouds are shown as green, yellow, or red: green indicates slightly bumpy, yellow moderately bumpy, and red very bumpy. Though the plane could handle even the areas that appear red, passengers would find the ride uncomfortable.

Lightning
Can lightning make a plane crash?

Lightning is not a problem for the plane. You are safe from lightning in your car because you are enclosed in metal and are insulated from the ground by the rubber tires. You are safe in a plane because you are enclosed and insulated from the ground by air.

Static electricity that builds up when walking on a rug can discharge with a pop and a slight shock. In the dark, a flash may be observed. Similarly, static electricity accumulates on the surface of a plane when flying through clouds. The plane is equipped with devices to prevent static electricity buildup. Occasionally, in spite of these devices, static electricity builds up and discharges with a flash and a bang indistinguishable from lightning. Though dramatic, neither a static discharge nor lightning cause damage to the plane other than, in the case of lightning, a superficial mark, usually on a wing tip. It is only by inspecting the plane after landing and finding such a mark that the pilots can tell if the plane had a static discharge or a lightning encounter. When flying at night, lightning miles away can light up the cloud you are in, giving the impression that the lightning is nearby. Unless there is sound accompanying the light, the lightning is not nearby.

• • •

Images of airliners falling are based on imagination—your imagination, some reporter's imagination, some passenger's imagination
reported in the media, or Hollywood's imagination—not reality.
Whatever imagination you have of airliners falling needs to be
erased or filed away as fantasy.

CHAPTER 19

Turbulence

For most anxious fliers, nothing is worse than turbulence. Pilots find this incomprehensible. Knowing that it is not a problem for the plane, pilots can't understand why it is such a huge problem for so many passengers. We need to address this issue both emotionally and intellectually. First, consider the facts.

Types of Turbulence

One type of turbulence is caused when the sun heats the surface of the earth. Differences in temperature cause upward and downward movement of air. A passenger in a slow-moving hot-air balloon would experience flight through such air as a gentle ascent or descent. But due to the speed of a plane, a gentle ascent becomes an abrupt bump upward, and a gentle descent becomes an abrupt bump downward. This type of turbulence is often found in desert airports such as Phoenix and Las Vegas.

Still another type of turbulence is found in clouds. Again, differences in temperature cause upward and downward movement of air. The impression in the cabin is that the plane is in violent air. Nothing could be further from the truth. It is not the air that is violent. It is speed—the high speed of the plane—that turns gently moving air into dreaded bumps. The movements that result may seem large. Yet, in most instances of turbulence, the actual distance the plane moves up or down is only a fraction of an inch and cannot be read on the plane's altimeter.

Another kind of turbulence is caused by strong surface winds. Hills, trees, and buildings that cause upward, downward, and sideward movement of air, as it scrubs against the surface of the earth, disturb wind. As a plane flies through such air, the path of the plane is altered only slightly. Nevertheless, an anxious passenger may imagine a dangerously large deviation and worry that a wing will touch the ground, or that the plane might be driven into the ground. This is impossible for two reasons: 1) The plane has moved such a small amount that an observer on the ground would be unable to detect any deviation from the ideal path to the runway; and 2) the various slight deviations simply average out.

Clear Air Turbulence (CAT)

Turbulence can be caused by clear air turbulence (CAT) as faster moving air scrubs against slower moving air. During CAT, autopilots on large airplanes use a "turb" mode. What do you think the autopilot does when in "turb" mode? Do you think it's more aggressive, or less aggressive? It's less aggressive. In fact, it's downright sluggish. There is no reason to have the autopilot correct for every bump because bumps tend to cancel each other out.

What causes CAT? As the earth spins, it produces centrifugal force that slings air away from the earth, outward toward space. This effect is greatest at the equator. Since the earth is about 25,000 miles in circumference at the equator and makes one rotation every 24 hours, the surface of the earth at the equator is moving eastward a bit faster than 1,000 mph. Even as centrifugal force spins air away from the earth, gravity seeks to pull it back. But, because air is constantly flowing up, the air has no place to go other than north or south, away from the equator.

Now, imagine you can see that air slung off from the equator again, after it has had time to migrate north or south. Because the circumference of the earth is less at any point north or south of the equator, the surface moves at a slower speed than at the equator. The equator-speed air—called the jet stream—is moving faster than the earth below. Flying from San Francisco to New York, the eastward-moving jet stream helps you get to New York faster. But when going from New York to San Francisco, you have to go against the jet stream. Staying in or out of the jet stream is easier said than done because the position of the jet stream is constantly in flux.

The Jet Stream

The jet stream is like a train that zips around the earth at the altitudes jet airliners use. Regardless of the speed of a train, the air inside is not turbulent. But just outside the train, the speed of its passage causes turbulence. At a train station, a person standing on the boarding platform has trouble reading their newspaper when a train passes by. That's how it is with the jet stream. Inside the jet stream where all the air is moving at the same speed, the air is smooth. But where the fast-moving air meets air that is moving slower, there is turbulence.

To understand how simple and mechanical jet stream turbulence is, place a pencil on a table. Put your palm on top of the pencil. Now, push your hand forward. This causes the pencil to roll. Your hand represents the jet stream moving forward. The table represents air that is standing still. The pencil represents air that, because it is rolling as it moves forward, is turbulent. Because it is fluid, air is free to shape itself, and it shapes itself into roller bearings that allow the faster moving jet stream air higher up (represented by the hand) to ride on roller bearings of air.

Now, pick up the pencil. Using both hands, hold one tip of the pencil with the fingers of your left hand and the other with the fingers of your right hand. Hold the pencil horizontal at eye level, and rotate it with your fingertips so the side nearest you is rotating upward. That means the other side of the pencil, though you can't see it, is rotating downward. Think of the pencil as a roller bearing that is rotating due to being sandwiched between the fast-moving jet stream air on top and the slower air underneath. When a plane enters the front edge of the rotating air, it bumps up. The distance from the front side of the roller to the back might be the size of a football field, so in half a second, as the plane reaches the back edge (that is rotating down), it bumps down as it exits. Then the plane flies right into the next roller; it again bumps up and down, and goes into the next roller, and so on. Since the plane spends only a fraction of a second bumping up or down, the distance the plane ascends or descends is no more than a fraction of an inch.

By monitoring the radio, pilots usually know if there is CAT ahead on the route. Still, CAT can be encountered unexpectedly. An area on your route that had been smooth for hours can become rough just as your plane reaches it. Areas of turbulence are usually too wide to try flying around. But since turbulence is limited vertically, climbing or descending can often eliminate it. Your captain will ask the Air Traffic Control if there are any altitudes that are reportedly smoother. If a smooth altitude is both practical and available—not in use by other planes—the captain will climb or descend to it. Keep in mind that there are limits to how high a plane can fly. The higher you go, the thinner the air, and the less power the engines produce. If a descent below the turbulence means cruising several thousand feet lower, it may be impractical due to greater fuel consumption resulting from the thicker air.

Other Turbulence at Cruising Altitude

Planes can navigate around scattered thunderstorms that extend to cruise altitude. Though the plane can fly through thunderstorms, they are avoided, both for passenger comfort and because they may contain hailstones. Running into hailstones at five hundred mph pockmarks the leading edge of the wing. These pockmarks are expensive to repair, and, if not repaired, slightly increase fuel consumption. When thunderstorms form a line, pilots use radar to find the least turbulent area.

Turbulence and Wind Shear

Wind shear is an abrupt change in the velocity of wind horizontally. Since turbulence is caused by changes vertically, turbulence does not necessarily mean wind shear. Wind shear with a velocity change great enough to pose a problem is rare, so rare that for many years the presence of wind shear during takeoff or landing was addressed by a slight speed increase. After it became known that wind shear could pose a risk in exceptional situations, pilots were trained to recognize and avoid those situations. Then, Doppler radar was developed to detect it. If Doppler radar shows wind shear approaching the cautionary range, the entire airport is shut down until the velocity of the wind shear returns to a normal range.

Turbulence during Descent and Landing

Routes increasingly narrow as traffic funnels toward the airport. To obtain the best inbound routing, pilots rely on cockpit radar, reports from pilots ahead, and Air Traffic Control. If a severe storm moves directly over the runway, landing is halted due to the possibility of wind shear. Depending on fuel remaining, planes hold until the storm moves away from the airport or divert to an alternate airport where weather is not a factor.

The Seat Belt Sign Does Not Mean Danger

First, turbulence is not a danger for the plane. Second, passengers wearing a seat belt never get hurt due to turbulence. Third, in some cases the seat belt sign is turned on at the request of the flight attendants if passengers in the aisles are making drink and food service difficult. The seat belt sign is often put on early to aid the flight attendants as they secure the galley before it gets rough. Even when it is safe to walk around, a flight attendant can get hurt wrestling a heavy serving cart back into its narrow stowage slot in the aft galley, the part of the plane that moves around most in turbulence.

As to what is happening in the cockpit, that Hollywood movie stuff of pilots holding onto the controls for dear life is just Hollywood hooey. What do pilots really do during turbulence? They let the autopilot fly the plane as they sip their coffee or eat a snack. From a pilot's point of view, the greatest risk during turbulence is getting coffee stains on a shirt.

Pilots Using the Lavatory

When the door of the lavatory is locked, a light illuminates in the cabin to inform passengers the lavatory is occupied. There is also a light in the cockpit so the pilots will know when it is unavailable. If a pilot needs to use the lavatory, it means waiting until the light goes out, then unhooking the headset, sliding the seat back, unbuckling the seat belt and shoulder harness, getting up to go back to the cockpit door, opening it, and stepping out of the cockpit. More often than not, by the time a pilot can get unhooked and ready to use the lavatory, the light is on again, signaling that a passenger beat the pilot to the lavatory.

I received an e-mail from a client who wrote, "When there was turbulence the pilots happened to take a trip to the lavatory. I was nervous of course, but then they waved at me while they were shifting from the cockpit to the lavatory. I was put so much at ease. I thought, 'If they can go to the bathroom while we're shaking, then it must be okay.' On my return trip the same thing happened. The turbulence was very heavy around the Midwest and I was nervous, but again the pilots came out to go the restroom." I replied to her that use of the toilet during turbulence is standard procedure for pilots.

When the seat belt sign is on because of turbulence, passengers are supposed to remain seated. That means the lavatory is free. Typically, pilots use this time to visit the lavatory, even if the trip isn't urgent. In all the years using this strategy, I never had the least trouble using the lavatory during turbulence. Just in case we hit a bump, I held a hand on the ceiling to brace myself. But in all my trips to the lavatory during turbulence, I never needed to use any effort to avoid the ceiling—or any other part of the lav, for that matter.

So though you might think turbulence is in some way a danger, pilots don't feel that way at all—for them it's an opportunity to use the lav. Remember, of course, this is the lavatory in the front of the plane. In turbulence, the back of the plane moves around more than the front. Though I had no trouble using the front lavatory, I wouldn't have tried to use the rear lavatory during turbulence—no one should.

Knowing Turbulence Is Safe Is Not Enough

When I was a 747 copilot, I flew many trips between New York and Tokyo. On a fourteen-hour flight, there is plenty of time to talk, and on one flight, a captain who knew I was working with fearful fliers asked me, "Well, what are people afraid of anyway?" His use of the word "anyway" shows, I think, how puzzled pilots are that anyone would think flying is something to be feared. So when I told him "turbulence," he was dumbfounded. He said, "What! Why?" I tried to explain, but nothing I said made any sense to him. Exasperated, he said, "Well, I can fix that."

He went on to tell me that when he came to work at the airline, being at the very bottom of the copilot seniority list, he was assigned the flying that was left over after everyone else had had their pick. That meant he was stuck with flying cargo through Central America in the middle of the night on piston-powered propeller-driven Douglas DC-6s. Since there were no passengers on the flight, the airline saw no reason to equip the planes with radar. So the pilots had no way to know where the thunderstorms were, and Central America has some of the worst thunderstorms in the world. In light of that, the captain said, they just wore their seat belts and their shoulder harnesses and put the plane on autopilot and drove straight ahead. If they missed the storms, fine, but if they hit one, the plane would "buck and snort and moan and groan," as he put it.

On his first few flights he wasn't sure that the plane would stay together. But taking a cue from the seasoned pilots he was flying with, who seemed completely bored when charging through the storms, he decided not to exhibit any concern. He told me, "I never got to the point that I liked it, but I did get to the point that I realized the plane could handle anything! Tell people that," he said, "and that will cure them."

Though I've told many people that story, and though they may have finally been convinced the plane can handle anything, there is another issue when it comes to turbulence. It's not just a question of whether the plane can handle it physically. It's a question of whether an anxious passenger can handle it psychologically.

Even after a person understands that turbulence is safe, it continues to be identified—misidentified, that is—as a thing to be feared. It would be more accurate to say that turbulence defeats a common strategy for keeping fear at bay. For many people, emotional safety depends upon control. Without control, escape is required. Since flying offers neither physical control nor physical escape, emotion can be controlled only by psychological escape. Keeping the mind off the flight may work if the flight is smooth. But when turbulence intrudes, psychological escape is impossible. The person's only remaining strategy is defeated. Turbulence is feared because it renders them powerless to control emotion.

What can be done? In addition to the Strengthening Exercise, which works automatically, Chapters 9 and 22 offer several techniques you can employ consciously to deal with turbulence.

CHAPTER 20

A Complete Flight

To regulate anxiety, Executive Function needs a balanced perspective of the situation. Flying needs to be viewed in proper context. You rightfully feel better by knowing everything about a flight is carefully thought out. Let's consider a flight from beginning to end.

Planning and Preparation

A licensed flight dispatcher plans the flight and certifies, by signing an official document called the dispatch release, that all factors—weather, maintenance, airspace restrictions, alternate airports, and so on—have been considered and that the flight can be conducted safely. The captain reviews the plan and, by cosigning the dispatch release, certifies that he or she has done a complete review and that the flight can be conducted safely.

The copilot thoroughly checks the exterior of the plane. In the cockpit, the captain checks the interior and the maintenance logbook. If either finds a discrepancy, they notify maintenance. If maintenance can clear the discrepancy before the scheduled departure time, no announcement is made to the passengers. If they need more time, passengers are notified of a maintenance delay. This announcement can strike fear in the heart of the anxious flier who thinks,

"There's something wrong with the plane." I see it a different way. It is important to understand that it's rare for a plane not to need maintenance of some kind between flights. The announcement only means the maintenance cannot be completed before the scheduled departure time. It may mean nothing more than the mechanics need to replace one of the radios on the plane, and the new one has to be brought over from the other side of the airport. In most cases the problem is something that was discovered during the inbound flight. The plane flew in fine with that slight deficiency. And, though the plane could be flown out without fixing it, the airline is not going to do that. Rather than cause you concern, a maintenance delay should reassure you. It shows you the system is working.

While in flight, if a primary, secondary, backup, or emergency system is found to have a fault, in most cases the plane continues flying to its destination. But once it lands, the plane will not be flown again until the fault has been corrected. Though the plane could fly fine without the fault corrected, the discipline that ensures safety requires every primary, secondary, backup, and emergency system to be operational before beginning a flight. The plane is accepted only when everything is right. It is only after the captain is fully satisfied that he or she signs the logbook, accepting the plane, and certifying that it is fully airworthy.

One of the pilots checks the switches and circuit breakers that cannot be reached while seated at the controls. Once seated, each pilot follows a prescribed pattern to check every switch and instrument. Think of shopping in a supermarket. Though you have a shopping list, you save that for later use as a backup. You cover every aisle, going down one, and up the next, until you have shopped the entire store. Then you get out your shopping list and make sure every item on your list is in the cart.

Just so, in the cockpit, the captain goes down one row and up the next to check the setting of every switch (or dial) on the left side of the cockpit. The copilot does the same on the right side of the cockpit. Then, to be certain every switch is in the correct position, the checklist is used. Unlike shopping at the supermarket, where usually only one person checks the list, both pilots are involved. One pilot reads the checklist; the other pilot, touching the instrument, states its setting. The pilot reading the checklist confirms that the stated setting matches what the checklist calls for. If the setting varies from flight to flight, both pilots must agree that the setting is correct. Each item on the checklist is addressed in this fashion until the checklist has been completed. Then, the pilots contact Air Traffic Control (ATC) to confirm the route filed by the dispatcher is approved with or without modifications. ATC assigns a "transponder code," a set of numbers to be set into a device that will cause the flight number to show up on ATC radar screens.

After the doors are closed and the flight attendants confirm the passengers are seated, the pilots obtain pushback clearance. When cleared, the plane is shoved back from the terminal by a tug. Most airliners are equipped with an auxiliary power unit (APU), a small jet engine that provides power for starting. The APU also provides electrical power and air-conditioning when the engines are not running.

As the engines are started, it is not unusual for the cabin lights to go out. So the APU can operate unattended, it's equipped with a protective system to shut itself down if operation is not within certain parameters. The protective system is sensitive and may shut down the APU unnecessarily when an additional load is put on it, as is the case when using power for the APU to start the engines. If the APU shuts down, the plane is without electrical power until the APU can be restarted or a long, heavy-duty extension cord is plugged into the plane. When there is difficulty getting the engines started, it is generally due to APU problems, not an engine problem. APU problems can be a nuisance, but there is no safety problem because the APU is not needed during flight.

On the Runway

After engines start, the pilots contact ground control by radio and request taxi instructions. Ground control issues a taxi clearance with specific routing to reach the runway being used for takeoff. When approaching the runway, ground control instructs the pilots to switch to the control tower radio frequency. The tower controller will, when traffic permits, clear the flight onto the runway. On the runway, if there are clouds in the area, the pilots use radar to check the departure route for thunderstorms. If any storms lie along the departure route, the pilots obtain clearance to route around them before taking off. Once tower has confirmed that the runway is unoccupied and the airspace on the initial departure route is free of traffic, the plane is cleared for takeoff.

To begin the takeoff, the pilot making the takeoff (the captain and copilot take turns) pushes the throttles forward about halfway to partially rev up the engines, and then, pushing the throttles full forward, says, "Set takeoff thrust." The pilot making the takeoff looks outside to guide the plane down the runway while the other pilot, using the engine instruments, adjusts the throttles and announces, "Takeoff thrust set." The pilot making the takeoff has one hand on the control wheel and one hand on the throttles. During the take-off roll, the pilot who is not making the takeoff calls out, "Eighty knots," when that speed is reached. About 15 percent longer than a statute mile (5,280 feet), a "knot" is a nautical mile: 6,076 feet. So at eighty knots the plane is going about ninety-two mph. The pilot making the takeoff crosschecks for the same reading. If the reading is the same, the takeoff is continued. If the reading is not the same, the takeoff is aborted.

Why is this crosscheck of airspeed indicators done? Years ago, there was an incident in which a blockage in the tube leading to one of the airspeed indicators, due to an insect nest in the tubing, caused an erroneous speed indication. Though it is unlikely that an insect would again cause such a blockage, we do this speed check on every takeoff because in aviation, nothing is left to chance.

The next callout is "V-1": At that point, the pilot making the takeoff, by moving the hand from the throttles to the control wheel, shifts from the "stop if an engine fails mode" to the "fly if an engine fails mode." The next callout is "V-R": The pilot making the takeoff begins pulling back on the wheel so as to bring the nose wheel off the runway, and then continues pulling back on the control wheel until the nose of the plane is elevated ten to eleven degrees.

Climb and Cruise

Once the plane is off the runway, the pilot pulls back a bit more so that the nose is elevated up to approximately eighteen degrees. The pilot not making the takeoff calls out, "Positive climb." In response, the pilot making the takeoff calls, "Gear up." The other pilot moves the gear handle to the up position. (An automatic safety device prevents the gear handle from being moved when the plane is on the ground.) Because the wheels are spinning, there may be a rumbling noise—or a vibration—when the landing gear is brought up into the "wheel wells"—the area inside the fuselage and wing where the gear is stowed. On most planes, doors close over the retracted gear to streamline the plane.

The plane climbs at an angle of about eighteen degrees until 1,000 feet above the runway; at that altitude the "noise abatement" procedure is initiated. Power is reduced to lessen noise near the airport. As engine speed and power are reduced, the nose is lowered to approximately fourteen degrees to keep the plane moving forward at the same speed. There may be a feeling of light-headedness for about two seconds as the nose is lowered from eighteen to seventeen to sixteen to fifteen to fourteen degrees. An elevator causes that feeling when it reduces its rate of climb to stop at a selected floor. Though the physical sensation is similar to falling, neither the plane nor the elevator is falling. The feeling doesn't bother you in an elevator because you *know* what's going on: You know the elevator is not falling; it's just slowing its ascent. Now that you know what's going on in the airplane, the feeling won't bother you on board, either.

As speed increases, the flaps (which make the wing bigger and more curved to fly at slower speeds) used for takeoff are no longer needed, so they are retracted. You may feel some vibration during flap retraction. Speed is limited to 250 mph until reaching 10,000 feet, then increased to 300. As the plane climbs, if there is conflicting traffic, ATC, to avoid the traffic, will either have the flight turn or level off briefly. If the flight needs to level off, as the plane starts reducing its rate of ascent, you can expect to again feel momentarily light-headed. Light-headedness does not mean falling.

Just as you press the button of the floor you want the elevator to go to, when ATC instructs the pilots to climb to a certain altitude, the pilots dial that altitude into the autopilot. When the airplane approaches its selected altitude, the autopilot slows the plane's ascent; it stops climbing at the selected altitude.

In addition to feeling light-headed as the plane levels off, you will hear the engines slow down. This does not mean the *plane* is slowing down. In a car, the engine is mechanically connected to the wheels. When the engine slows down, the car slows down. This is not the case in an airplane. There is no mechanical connection. The engines push the plane with a force called "thrust." When a plane that has been climbing levels off, less thrust is needed than when ascending. The pilots reduce thrust, which is done by slowing the engine speed. When the plane resumes its climb, you feel a momentary heaviness—just as you do when an elevator resumes its ascent. You hear the engines speed up to produce the additional thrust needed to climb. It may help you to think of this as "stair-stepping"; the plane leaves the ground and climbs to the first step, pauses there until traffic is out of the way, then climbs to the second step and pauses again until traffic clears. Depending upon traffic, this might happen several times—or not at all.

Throughout the flight, a licensed flight dispatcher monitors the flight on a computer screen. The dispatcher has other screens showing weather conditions en route, at the destination, and at alternate airports. If any change occurs, the dispatcher contacts the pilots with the updated information. The dispatcher even has a doctor on standby to provide medical advice to the pilots by radio. A medical supply kit is made available to any doctor who may be on board. If a passenger needs to be taken to a hospital, the dispatcher advises the crew as to the best diversion airport, and arranges for an ambulance and medics to be waiting. En route, the dispatcher and the pilots monitor weather at the destination and alternate airports. If weather deteriorates, the dispatcher and the pilots discuss strategies, such as whether to hold and wait for the weather to improve, or to land elsewhere, refuel, and then continue.

Descent

Prior to descent, pilots learn which runway and what type of navigation is being used for landing. On a sunny day, pilots may be expected to navigate to the runway visually. On cloudy days, pilots are guided by radar and by signals that can be followed to the touchdown spot on the runway. If cruising at 30,000 feet, descent begins approximately 120 miles from the airport. The plane glides down at idle power. Traffic may make it necessary to do some "stair-stepping" on the way down. If so, at each leveling off, you will feel a bit heavy in your seat. Engine power is increased to maintain speed while temporarily level. When the descent resumes, power is reduced again to idle. Glide continues until between 2,000 and 6,000 feet. ATC, using radar, assigns a direction and speed to fly so that planes inbound to the runway are spaced about five miles behind each other. This spacing provides protection from wake turbulence and time for exiting the runway after landing.

In preparation for landing, flaps are extended to accommodate the slower speed. Flaps make the plane less streamlined. Additional power is applied to compensate for the additional wind resistance (called "drag"). Engine speed may be changed several times due to gear extension and changes in flap setting.

Every change is potentially unsettling to a passenger. Though these changes are routine and do not mean trouble of any kind, an anxious flier may think the plane is speeding up or slowing down, or that the pilot can't get the right speed. Prepare yourself by expecting a number of changes. As the plane approaches the runway, expect abrupt changes of engine speed as the pilot nails down the exact landing speed and landing spot.

Wind, even a strong wind, is rarely a problem. A headwind aligned with the runway reduces the plane's forward speed, reducing the length of runway needed for stopping. If the wind is not aligned with the runway, the pilot uses techniques to compensate.

If the plane is still in the thick of clouds when reaching the minimum legal altitude, the "missed approach" procedure spelled out on the runway chart is initiated. Since no further descent is allowed, the pilot must abruptly stop the descent and initiate climb. The nose of the plane is raised quickly and almost full power is applied. This is the standard "missed approach" procedure. This unexpected dynamic change catches passengers off guard, and can—naturally— be frightening. Just when passengers are counting on the flight being over, the plane ascends again. To compound the distress, it may be a minute or two before the pilots make an announcement.

It may be helpful to entertain the possibility of a missed approach. When the gear is extended, check your watch. From the point where the gear is extended, it takes approximately 120 seconds to reach "minimums." If you cannot see the ground as you approach 120 seconds, anticipate the possibility of a missed approach. If, however, you reach 120 seconds and cannot see the ground, don't worry that a missed approach has not been initiated. Most runways are equipped with an array of powerful lights that penetrate fog. The pilots are allowed to continue and land if the lights are in view, even when the runway and the ground are obscured by fog. After a missed approach, another approach may be made, perhaps to a different runway with lower minimums. Otherwise, the flight will divert to an airport where weather is not a factor.

Occasionally, a missed approach is made because the preceding plane failed to exit the runway expeditiously. Although the preceding plane may be far down the runway, regulations do not allow the tower to issue a landing clearance until the runway is vacant. In case the preceding plane may be able to exit the runway, pilots hold off initiating the missed approach as long as possible. Because the pilot has absolute control of the plane, a missed approach initiated when the plane is only a foot or two from the runway is not in any way unsafe.

Though there may be no visual connection with the ground, there is always electronic connection. From the time you leave the ground until you return to the ground, your plane is tuned to and guided by radio signals from the ground. The place the signal comes from is shown on maps. These signals from the ground are also used to produce a GPS-like display in the cockpit.

Landing

Power (on jets it's called "thrust") is produced by the engines. During flight, air is forced out of the rear of the engines to push the plane forward. But after landing, the direction of the thrust is reversed to help slow the plane down. To reverse the direction of thrust, the pilot deploys devices at the rear of the engine that deflect the engine exhaust air forward.

Wheel brakes and spoilers are also used to slow the plane. Wheel brakes are the same in principle as disc brakes on a car. The tires need good contact with the runway for the brakes to be effective. If lift continued to be produced by the wing after landing, contact between the tires and the runway would be reduced. The lifting action of the wing depends upon smooth flow of air across and underneath the wing. So, to eliminate lift, spoilers—panels on the surface of the wings—are raised to "spoil" the otherwise smooth flow of air across the wing.

If seated aft of the wing, a passenger may be able to see the reverse thrust deflectors deploy at the rear of the engine. If able to see the wing, a passenger can see the spoilers pop up vertically from the surface of the wing. Both help the plane slow down so the plane can exit the runway and taxi to the terminal.

PART THREE
STRATEGY

CHAPTER 21

Planning and Starting Your Flight

Just planning a flight can cause anxiety. The amygdalae respond whenever anything non-routine comes to mind. Since you don't routinely fly, each planning issue you consider properly triggers the release of stress hormones. You may prefer to keep planning out of mind. It seems that the more attention you pay to planning, the more anxious you become. That may be true—but only up to a point. There is an anxiety peak. After that, you start gliding downhill. Each time you, as the CEO, decide what to do about an issue and commit to a plan of action, your assistant Amy is signaled to get her fingers off the intercom and leave you alone, at least about that issue. Once you start making decisions and commitments, you are over the hump. It gets easier. When your planning is done, you will feel better. You know what you are doing, and what to expect.

Choosing an Airline

Not all airlines are the same. When choosing an airline, there are several factors to consider, the fare being just one. Though all airlines must comply with government regulations, these are minimum standards. Some regulations are archaic and do not adequately protect the public. New airlines and low-fare airlines rarely exceed these minimum standards. Established airlines generally have higher standards. Ask yourself these questions:

1. *Does the airline have its own mechanics and maintenance facilities, or does it outsource maintenance?* When an airline has its own maintenance, their mechanics get passes to fly on the airline. The mechanics know that the planes they and their families fly on are planes they have worked on. Self-preservation is a powerful incentive to do the job right. Up-to-date information on the amount of outsourcing by an airline can be found by going to the U.S. Department of Transportation website at www.rita.dot.gov/bts/ and typing the phrase "airline maintenance outsourcing" in the search window.

2. *Does the airline have a pilots' union?* Management always says safety is the number one priority. But safety costs money. Management must answer investors whose money is riding on the airline while they remain on the ground. Though FAA regulations require the captain to certify that an airliner is airworthy before accepting it for flight, the FAA cannot be counted on to back up a pilot who is fired or "disciplined" for refusing to accept an airliner. By acting as a group, pilots can demand quality maintenance. Backed by a group, an individual pilot can refuse a plane that needs maintenance without having to worry about being fired. You can see whether the pilots of an airline have a union by searching the Internet using the airline's name plus the words "pilots union."

3. *Does the airline have a statistically significant track record?* Anxious fliers tend to make the mistake of choosing relatively new airlines that have had no accidents. An

accident-free record may comfort the anxious flier, but a sta-tistically savvy person is not impressed. An accident rate of one per five million to fifteen million flights is a better indi-cator of safety than being accident-free for a million flights or less. It is possible, but I believe unlikely, for a new airline to be as safe as an established airline. When airlines with fewer than five years of operation are assessed as a group, their fatal accident rate per passenger miles flown is higher than that of established airlines. There's good reason for this. Established airlines have had time to develop their flight planning, flight monitoring, maintenance program, and training curriculum, and to build a dedicated staff of profes-sional mechanics, pilots, dispatchers, and flight attendants.

Look at www.airsafe.com for accident rate statistics. Compare the statistics. If the airline is not listed, it has not flown enough flights to produce meaningful statistics.

4. *What about foreign airlines?* Major European, Japanese, Canadian, and Australian airlines have accident rates similar to major airlines in the United States. Travel by air is less safe in some developing countries, but always safer than driving. The EU has blacklisted some airlines. To see an up-to-date list, search the Internet using the term "EU airline blacklist."

Some anxious fliers feel more confident when they've done due diligence by executing this research. Most, though, find it unsettling to consider safety issues at all. If this is so for you, just know that any airline you pick is far safer than travel by automobile. Spending a day flying is safer than spending a day following your usual routine, if your routine involves driving. How can you be sure of that? Research by Michael Sivak and Michael J. Flannagan, both from the Univer-sity of Michigan Transportation Research Institute, has shown that driving just 10.8 miles on an interstate highway, or approximately five miles of urban driving, has the same risk of fatality as taking a flight all the way across the country or even to another continent.

About Business Aviation

Though the safety record of business aviation does not match that of the airlines, travel on a private jet is far safer than driving. That said, there are ways to avoid the problems that have led to the higher accident rate. If you are the person in charge when flying on a business jet, leave the decision about whether to delay or cancel the flight completely up to the pilots. The pilots know what they *should* do. But executives with important business to negotiate have been known to throw a pilot's judgment off balance, without knowing they are doing so. The pilots are in a difficult position. If they take a stand, you may move your business elsewhere, and the pilot could be in trouble with his company for losing your business. So my recommendation is that you say not one word to the pilots about how important the flight is. If the pilots say they may need to delay or cancel the flight, the next words from you—even if you are the CEO of a major corporation—should be, "You're the boss."

If you are not the person in charge, keep an eye on the person who is. If you sense he or she is influencing the pilots, talk to the pilots privately.

Thinking, Fast and Slow

Nobel Prize winner Daniel Kahneman has written a book titled *Thinking, Fast and Slow*. There are an amazing number of insights in the book about how the mind works. He reveals that there are two different mental systems: One is quick, and one is slow. They both are useful. For example, we need intuition (thinking fast). In some cases it is accurate; in others, it is way off base. How good fast thinking is depends upon experience and training. He writes, "We have all heard such stories of expert intuition: the chess master who walks past a street game and announces, 'White mates in three' without stopping, or the physician who makes a complex diagnosis after a single glance at a patient." Most of us, he says—excluding chess masters and brilliant physicians—have to work at thinking; we have to use slow deliberate thinking to obtain the right answers.

I think this applies to fear of flying. Most people have limited experience about how flying works. But they have a lot of experience reading about crashes or seeing what claim to be documentaries about crashes on television (most documentaries are grossly misleading). Unless one is a frequent flier, most of our experience with flying comes from the media, and most of that is about crashing. This means our fast thinking—based on our television-viewing experience—tells us flying is quite dangerous. But the fast thinking of pilots—based on real experience with flying—tells them that flying is remarkably safe.

Is there a way your fast thinking can accurately reflect flight safety? Imagine you are a reporter, and your job is to gather information on every flight that takes off and lands in the United States. You are going to spend one minute gathering information on each and every flight. Let's figure you work a forty-hour week, fifty weeks a year, for forty years. You study sixty flights an hour, for eight hours a day; that's 480 flights a day, 2,400 a week, and thus 120,000 flights a year. If you do that for forty years, you study 4,800,000 flights. At that point, you turn the job over to a new reporter who does the same thing for forty years. At the end of the second reporter's career, there is still less than a 50/50 chance that either you or he gathered information on a crash. Both you and your successor, when using your fast thinking to answer the question, "Is flying safe?" would most likely say, "Yes, in my experience, it is absolutely safe." Your experience in this case would overestimate safety. Only after a third reporter had spent forty years doing the same thing would the 50/50 mark be reached. There is a 50/50 chance the third reporter would answer, "Well, flying isn't *absolutely* safe, but it is awfully safe because in all the time I reported on flying, there was just one crash." But, since there is a 50/50 chance this third reporter would not run into a crash, he might still say, as the first two did, "Yes, in my experience, it is absolutely safe." (By the way, these numbers are based on findings by MIT professor Arnold Barnett, who says that, based on airline flying in the United States from 2000 through 2008, the chance of fatality when boarding a random flight was one in twenty-three million.)

Your experience allows a more accurate assessment of driving. In the same way the reporter is aware of every flight (not just flights that crash), you are aware of every car trip you take. You know the result of each. And since you rarely have an accident, your fast thinking gives you the feeling that driving is—at least if you are in control—absolutely safe. Even so, if your slow thinking thoroughly studied road accidents, it would recognize driving—even with you in control—is not absolutely safe. What, then, happens when your fast thinking about driving and your slow thinking about driving collide? You think, "Yes, accidents *can* happen, but I'm a safe driver, and even if I have an accident, I will be able to walk away from it." It is very hard indeed to accept that your own driving could result in your demise.

That, again, is a bias error. Why? Fast thinking—based on personal experience—contains a bias error because you have never been killed in an accident. Therefore, you fully expect, when you drive, to get to your destination just fine.

When you consider taking a flight, your fast thinking about flying based on media exposure (it's dangerous) slams into your fast thinking about driving (it's safe). What would it take to give up your fast thinking, which is, Kahneman says, lazy thinking, and dig into the matter? It's not even necessary for you to do the work. Why? It's been done for you.

Since 95 percent of airline accidents occur during takeoff and landing, risk of flying depends almost entirely on the number of flights involved in the trip. The length of the trip is not significant; a long flight has pretty much the same risk as a short flight. But with a car, as Sivak and Flannagan pointed out above, the risk of fatality depends upon how many miles are driven.

In terms of time, at fifty-five mph, eleven minutes forty-seven seconds of driving equals the risk of taking a flight. Since the average airline trip is 694 miles and takes about an hour and a half, eleven minutes forty-seven seconds of driving has the same risk of fatality as the average airline flight. But it also means that eleven minutes forty-seven seconds of driving equals flying eight hours to Europe or flying fourteen hours to Asia.

If stats don't reassure, my personal experience may help. I flew with the airlines for thirty-one years at a time when planes were not nearly as good as they are today. I know literally hundreds of pilots and hundreds of flight attendants who flew year in and year out, all over the world. Each spent an entire career in the air. And yet, I do not know one single pilot or one single flight attendant who was ever harmed in an accident.

Preboarding Strategy: Meeting Your Captain

The only thing that was an absolute must for me was meeting the pilots. It helped tremendously. I worried at first that they wouldn't understand, or would think I was weird. Just the opposite; they always were very understanding. Most said they had family members who didn't like to fly. But, the pilots are always great. When they pulled out photos of their kids, that did it. Knowing they were going to make sure they made it back home to their children was all it took for me. Having met them on so many flights, I don't feel like I need to do that anymore. I just settle back in my belief/knowledge/experience that they know what they are doing and do it extremely well.

To facilitate meeting the captain, prepare two letters (see samples in Appendix B). One is for the passenger service agent in the boarding area. It asks that you be allowed to board early. The other is for the captain, explaining you are an anxious flier and are working on overcoming difficulty with flying. It asks that you be allowed to visit the cockpit when you board. While the plane is on the ground and sitting at the terminal, this shouldn't pose a problem and is still allowed. You have to board early so the flight attendants have time to run the letter up to the cockpit or tell you there isn't time for you to meet the captain.

Get to the boarding area early. Present the first note, or simply tell the gate agent that you are an anxious flier, you're working on overcoming flight anxiety, and you've been told it makes a big difference if you can meet the captain, and you need to board early so there's time once onboard to do that. Don't expect the gate agent to give you permission to meet the captain. That can come only from the captain. What you need from the gate agent is permission to board early. If the gate agent agrees to board you early, ask if you should stay close by or stand by the entry point. If the gate agent is not cooperative, just go and stand as close to the entry point as possible. Listen for the first boarding announcement. It usually goes like this: "We would like to invite our first-class passengers (or passengers in a certain zone) to board at this time." This is followed by "people with children, and anyone who needs extra time." Extra time? That's you. It doesn't matter where your seat assignment is, if you qualify as needing additional time, you can board ahead of your row number. But don't wait to hear that. As soon as you recognize the beginning of the boarding announcement, get on the plane. Don't wait for the announcement to end. Boarding early is important. The flight attendants take your letter up to the captain only if you are on the plane at the beginning of the boarding process.

From a chat room discussion at www.fearofflying.com:
Captain Tom: Jennifer, once you meet the captain, you will get a good feeling about him or her. All captains have to go through the same training. If they can get through a check ride in the simulator and a check ride with a flight check captain in the plane, they're fine.

Captain Steve: Hi, Jennifer. That's right. That's why I ride as a passenger with no worries whatsoever.

Captain Tom: No simulator instructor or flight check captain is going to turn someone loose with an airplane that they do not have 100 percent confidence in.

Jennifer: Thanks! That is reassuring!

If You Can't Meet the Captain
On some foreign airlines, flight crew members don't know about fear-of-flying courses. If you receive a blank look when you ask them to let you meet the captain, that may be the reason. When the plane is under way, you will be all right even if you don't meet the captain. Though it would help you feel better about letting go of control. A client posted the following on the SOAR message board:

> Letting go of control doesn't mean you're at one with the universe. Letting go doesn't mean you are prepared for the inevitable

doom that is chasing you down and will only catch you on that damn plane. Letting go just means that you realize you're going to be just fine and that worrying, fretting, or being anxious won't affect the reality of the situation.

So, whether you meet the captain or not, once the plane has departed, that is a closed issue. You will stop worrying about your decision. The Strengthening Exercise will "kick in" and take care of you.

Onboard Strategy

A flight attendant will ask for your boarding pass and point you toward your seat. Instead of going to your seat, find a flight attendant who is not tied up at that moment. A good place to look is in the galley. Ask the flight attendant to take the note to the captain while you wait. Say, "I'm an anxious flier, and I'm working on it with someone, and he says it's really important for me to meet the captain. I understand about security so I don't want to go up to the cockpit unannounced. Please take this letter up to the captain for me." Place the letter in the flight attendant's hand like you are serving a summons. Then say, "I'll wait right here while you check with the captain."

Two things can go wrong, so be prepared:

- The flight attendant says, "Give me your seat number and if the captain says it's okay, I'll come and get you." That's a brush-off! Do not accept it! Instead, say, "I have to find out about this right now. I'll wait right here while you check."
- The flight attendant says, "Because of security, you can't do that anymore." That's not true. So just say, "I understand, but please

take the letter up anyway. Maybe the captain, or the copilot, has a moment to come out and speak with me here."

Do not approach the cockpit on your own; just have the letter carried there. If the captain receives the letter, he or she will likely meet with you. Approach the cockpit only if accompanied by a flight attendant. If the captain or flight attendant signals from inside the cockpit to come up, don't. A sky marshal might not be able to see the signal. Wait to be accompanied. Captains are usually more than happy to help anxious fliers. Don't worry about interrupting any-thing. The pilots finish their initial checks before passengers board. Ask the captain about expected turbulence and the destination weather. Let the captain know it will help if he or she makes extra announcements about what's going on. Also, about twenty to thirty seconds after leaving the runway, the noise-abatement procedure calls for engine power to be reduced and the nose lowered (which causes a feeling of light-headedness). The noise-abatement proce-dure is more noticeable on some takeoffs than on others. Ask the captain if the change will be significant enough for you to notice it.

Why Does Meeting the Captain Help So Much?

If you could fly in the cockpit, you would have a great flight. Instead of imagining what might be going on, you could see competent pilots in complete control. Since you can't do that, the next best thing is meeting the pilots who are going to be in control.

When you take your seat, picture the cockpit. Picture the pilots in complete control. Picture them in control of takeoff. Picture them in control during cruise. Picture them in control during land-ing. If you hear a noise or feel some unexpected motion, picture the captain's confident face, realizing that he or she knows how to deal with anything that could possibly happen. Each year, he or she practices everything that could go wrong in the simulator.

Everyone knows about Captain Sullenberger's landing in the Hudson River. And, most probably, if you knew you were flying with him, much of your concern about your flight would vanish. Your confidence would come from knowing he was severely tested and that he passed the test. You should also know that what every airline pilot goes through yearly in the flight simulator is far more of a test. What Captain Sullenberger did is what every airline pilot can do. The pilots you will be flying with could do what he did just as well as he did.

Medication

I am a former extremely fearful flier. I flew and loved it until I was twenty-five. My dad was an airline pilot, so I flew a lot. Then—out of the blue—I developed a big fear. I flew anyway, hating every second of it for the next ten years, using diazepam, booze, you name it. The shakes, the anticipation, the terror, it all increased until I just stopped. I couldn't do it anymore. Even thinking about it had me in a cold sweat. The drugs don't work. I started on one 5 mg diazepam—and felt more relaxed BUT then needed two, until I was popping five 10 mg pills per flight to try to stop myself from feeling the fear. They are no match for the fear. They mask it, make it worse, and stop you from getting rid of it. I understand why my doctor prescribed the diazepam, but he was lazy and ill-informed to do it. It prolonged my fear and stopped me from looking into real, long-term solutions. By taking a pill you are telling yourself you can't cope. Every time you take a pill you are acknowledging the fear—setting off down a superfast highway of faulty thinking—and letting it win! By taking a pill you are saying this is a lifelong condition about which I can do nothing, over which I have no control. And it's not true. I have flown nine times in the last year and I can tell you I now enjoy it. No drugs. No booze. I have stopped feeding the fear. I now trust myself and my brain to calm me.

If you've been using, or are considering using medication for flight anxiety, in light of research that shows serious drawbacks, you should reevaluate the decision with your physician. Anti-anxiety medications entail significant risks in flight, and they provide little if any benefit. In fact, they stand in the way of desensitization; by increasing the anxious flier's sensitivity to flying, they complicate future treatment.

The World Health Organization has warned that sedatives should not be used for flight anxiety due to risk of venous thromboembolism (VTE). When sedated in a seated position, as is the case except in business class or first class, blood stagnates in the legs; that can cause clots that may travel to the lungs. Symptoms of VTE are chest pain and breathing difficulty. Death can result if not treated. Among healthy individuals, four hours of seated immobility doubles the risk of VTE, to one in six thousand.* The same risk may apply to sleeping medications as well.

Though benzodiazepines such as alprazolam (Xanax), lorazepam (Ativan), clonazepam (Klonopin), and diazepam (Valium) may reduce anxiety prior to flight, these medications can cause sharply increased difficulty if used during the flight itself. Control of panic depends upon the ability to distinguish imagination from reality. During flight, when mental acuity is needed, the use of such medications reduces reflective function and opens the door to psychic equivalence and terror. The same is true of alcohol.

In addition, use of anti-anxiety medication has been shown in research by F. H. Wilhelm and W. T. Roth at the Stanford University School of Medicine to cause two additional problems:

* See WHO Research Into Global Hazards of Travel (WRIGHT) project on air tavel and venous thromboembolismat http://www.who.int/cardiovascular_diseases/wright_project/en/

1. Benzodiazepines make the person more sensitive to flying (more likely to panic on future flights if not sufficiently medicated); and

2. Benzodiazepines block the process of desensitization that would otherwise naturally take place. They make it impossible for the person to become accustomed to flying.

The medical research involved two flights. On the first flight, half of the anxious fliers were given alprazolam and half were given a placebo. On the second flight, no medication was administered. Results:

1. Placebo Group: Though 43 percent of those given a placebo instead of active medication experienced panic on the first flight, some desensitization took place, and only 29 percent experienced panic on the second—also unmedicated—flight.

2. Active Medication Group: On the first flight, physical measurements of arousal—heart rate and breathing rate—were significantly higher than in the placebo group (114 versus 105 beats/min, and 22.7 versus 18.3 breaths/min). Medication, however, blocked awareness of this elevated arousal and only 7 percent reported panic. On the second flight, their first unmedicated flight, 71 percent experienced panic! The high physiological arousal on the first flight sharply increased their sensitivity to flight, as shown by the high number of previously medicated subjects who panicked when unmedicated on the second flight.*

---

* The Stamford University School of Medicine research report is available at http://www.ncbi.nlm.nih.gov/pubmed/9299803

Since medication makes it increasingly more difficult to fly, the amount needed to control anxiety increases. When the medication loses its effectiveness, some passengers become desperate and, in a state of panic, may imbibe alcoholic beverages, even though they know the combination is dangerous. When taken together, benzodiazepine and alcohol reduce the breathing rate, possibly to unacceptably low levels, and can cause unconsciousness or death.

By reducing reflective function, anti-anxiety medication can cause the person to believe what they most fear is actually taking place. For example, in routine turbulence, the medicated passenger can believe the plane is plunging out of the sky. After the flight, instead of recognizing the problem was imagination, they continue to believe the plane fell thousands of feet. They credit medication for making it possible for them to endure the near-death experience. Further medicated flying causes additional experiences of terror, until the person can no longer fly at all.

The same is true of alcohol, depending upon how much alcohol is used. Anti-depressant medications that have a mild anti-anxiety effect on the ground are, anecdotally, ineffective in flight. Natural tranquilizers, such as valerian root or chamomile, except for a placebo effect that can be significant when a person believes in a product, offer little if any relief.

In the short term, the effectiveness of medication in reducing either anxiety or panic varies from individual to individual. In the long term, benzodiazepines appear to cause the person's ability to fly to deteriorate. Most anti-anxiety medications expose the user to several serious risks, including that of dependence. Even the occasional use of alprazolam at the recommended dosage has been known to cause seizure. When anti-anxiety medications do successfully sedate the fearful flier, they increase the VTE risk. Because it's so problematic, some psychiatrists will not prescribe benzodiazepines under any circumstances. Therefore, the use of anti-anxiety medication for flight anxiety can rarely be justified.

. . .

The toughest part of your flight—now that you have learned and practiced the Strengthening Exercise—is in the boarding area. Once you meet the captain, anticipatory anxiety falls away. Anticipatory anxiety is mostly about giving up control. Once you meet the pilots, it feels right for them to be in control. They care about themselves. They care about their families. And now they care about you. At this point, all your tools and skills and practice will kick in. But until you meet the captain, use the 5-4-3-2-1 Exercise whenever you notice anxiety.

CHAPTER 22

Anticipatory Anxiety

My anticipatory anxiety has always been the worst part of flying for me. But it's getting better, slowly, in large part because now I absolutely know that I won't be afraid on the flight. I try to counter the "what if" thoughts—what if I panic; what if I have to leave and can't—with telling myself it is normal that I'm nervous before a flight, and it doesn't mean anything about how my experience on the plane is going to be. I practice deep breathing as well as the Strengthening Exercise, and I also try to hit the gym. It does wonders for burning up that extra adrenaline. Also, I cut my coffee intake to one cup a day. I try to keep busy. I try— and this is the hardest part—to accept the anticipatory anxiety as just there, that I don't have to analyze it or pay it heed.

Why is anticipatory anxiety so different from flight anxiety? In the case of anticipatory anxiety, a person is trying to imagine what it will be like when something in the future is taking place. In flight anxiety, the event actually *is* taking place and the amygdalae decides whether or not to react. To prevent stress hormone release and therefore anxiety during flight, we train the amygdalae not to react. So, as the flight takes place and the raw data is examined by the amygdalae, we can keep it from releasing stress hormones. But in anticipatory anxiety, you are not dealing with raw data or incoming data. Instead you are dealing with imagination. After you imagine

what may happen—including how awful it may be—the amygdalae is not in a position to make a determination about whether or
not to react because your point of view that it is awful is integrated
into the imagination, and it is presented to the amygdalae as a fully
developed image of disaster.

When a securely oriented person considers a flight, what the
person expects is based on what happens in the overwhelming number of cases. Crashes happen so rarely that Executive Function dis-
misses the risk. The person expects to arrive safely at the destination.

However, the imagination of a person with insecure orientation
is not based on what happens in the overwhelming number of cases,
but on the exception: what *could* happen. With insecure orientation, Executive Function is unable to dismiss risk that cannot be
completely ruled out. Anticipatory anxiety takes place when imagination merges with reality. Allowing what *could* happen to remain
active in the mind causes stress hormones to build up. If anxiety
rises high enough, reflective function falters and psychic equivalence takes place. The person believes the crash they imagine will
take place if they get on the plane. Just as psychic equivalence needs
to be avoided during flight, it needs to be avoided on the ground,
too. Measures need to be taken to control anxiety prior to flight.

The Anticipatory Anxiety Exercise

Anxiety is produced in areas of the brain that are visual in their orientation. When uncertain, we can be reassured by what we see on
another person's face. The Anticipatory Anxiety Exercise is based on
social-referencing research. "Visual Cliff" research has shown that
the face of a person who is important to us can be powerfully reassuring. In a fascinating, safely conducted experiment reported in *Developmental Psychology*, children between six and twelve months of age
were put on a table fitted with a transparent Plexiglas extension. The

babies would crawl quite happily on the table itself. But when reaching the transparent extension, they balked. Even when tempted by a toy at the far end, not one baby ventured out onto the Plexiglas. But if the child's mother stood smiling at the far end, most of the children crawled out confidently. However, if the mother simulated a fearful expression, none of the children ventured out.

The experiment showed that when uncertain about safety, young children are powerfully influenced by their mother's facial expression. Visual reassurance remains important to us, even as adults. So, for the exercise, think of a person you know well who is comfortable with flying. It helps if you respect that person's opinions, too.

You can do the exercise either with the person or by using your imagination. Start with the person sitting at a table across from you. Rather than listening to what he or she may say, you're going to be watching the person's face. After all, in some cases, people tell us what they think we want to hear. In other cases, they might offer reassurance that they, themselves, don't believe. If you focus on their eyes, you are likely to discover their real feelings. As you do this exercise constantly focus on their eyes and the part of the face just below the eyes, where what is genuine is so often evident.

- Without letting your eyes leave the person's face, pull out a photograph. Hold it up in front of you so the imaginary or real person can see the photograph and you can see the face as he or she looks at the picture. You, of course, can see only the back of the photo. The photo is one of you seated on a plane with your tray table open. On the tray, there's something for you to eat and something to drink. As the person sees the picture of you eating on the plane, what does his or her face convey? Does seeing you eating a meal on the plane give the person some pleasure? Hopefully, he or she sees nothing in the photo of you on the plane that causes any concern.

- Try another picture: Use a photo of you seated on the plane with the tray table closed and with the seat belt sign on. Again, as the person sees the photograph, does any concern register on his or her face? Or, does the expression communicate that everything is all right? If the person's face exhibits concern about your feelings, that's fine, but hopefully there's no concern for your safety. Knowing that he or she sees this situation as benign can be reassuring.
- Try another picture: Use a photo of you seated as the plane is taking off. Again, notice the face of the friend. Hopefully, the expression will reveal that he or she is not concerned about your situation, and, if there is any concern, it's about how you're feeling in that moment during takeoff. It's helpful to know the person cares about your feelings, and still know that everything is all right. Perhaps you can see how similar this is to the "visual cliff" situation, in which the mother knew—though the child may have had doubts—that it was fine to crawl out on the transparent Plexiglas. Knowing about safety in an emotional way makes doing something much easier.
- Present a picture of you seated on the plane as the plane lands. Again, notice the other person's face, how he or she feels about the situation, and about your having completed the flight.

Increased emotional strength depends upon links between moments of uncertainty and a moment in which another person was attuned to you. You do not need an ideal moment or an ideal person. Any attuned moment can be used, even one from a fleeting relationship. Moments of connection don't last. Neither do most relationships. Few of us would have emotional strength if it depended entirely on people still in our lives. Whatever moments you have had are real. You have a right to draw strength from any moment you recall.

Anticipatory Anxiety and Control

After meeting the captain, the Strengthening Exercise kicked in. My flight went quite uneventfully. I was so happy I did it!

Boarding an airliner violates the basic rule of security: Don't give up control. But the rule is more sophisticated than that. It is actually, "Don't give up control except to someone you know and trust." Many people with whom I've worked have said they would have no anxiety if I were flying the plane. That isn't because they know my flying skills; it's because of trust. Others may not be as interested in your welfare as you are. When you shop for a used car, the salesperson may be more concerned with his or her commission than your welfare. But flying is unique. The interests of the person in control are the same as yours. The pilot can't get back safely on the ground without also taking care of you. Pilots want to return to family, just as you do. Knowing that, you need only to determine that the captain can do the job. How can you know?

First, consider your gut feeling. I believe when you meet your captain, you will feel confident he or she can do the job.

Second, testing of airline captains is unlike any other profession. If a doctor makes a serious mistake, the patient may not survive. Yet, the doctor continues to practice. If a lawyer makes a serious mistake, the client may spend time in jail while the lawyer continues to practice. It takes action by a professional board to stop an incompetent doctor or lawyer. Such action is not dependable. Doctors and lawyers are not *physically* linked to their mistakes. Pilots are. You can depend on gravity. One big screwup and gravity does more than revoke the pilot's license.

If you want to know whether a doctor or a lawyer is good or not, you check out his or her reputation. You don't have to do that with pilots. If you can see the pilot, you know he or she is a good one. The ones who weren't good aren't visible; they're six feet under. The issue isn't lack of flying skill that gets young pilots into trouble;

it's judgment. Judgment, to be good, needs some seasoning: That's the thinking behind the saying, "There are old pilots, and there are bold pilots, but there are no old, bold pilots."

Fortunately, today with flight simulators, the boldness of a young pilot can be sobered very quickly by simulated experience. Because the simulator is safe—except to the pilot's ego—instructors lead young pilots into scenarios where they will make mistakes that would be fatal in a real airplane. This allows the young pilot to safely make all the mistakes there are to be made, and to learn from them. In addition to years of flight experience and several levels of licenses, pilots are well tested by gravity before any airline will hire them.

Third, since the invention of the flight simulator, even a young pilot can have more experience dealing with flight challenges than the oldest pilot did years ago. The first year of employment at an airline is a probationary period. In the simulator, an instructor certified by the FAA throws every possible problem at the pilot. After the probationary period, retesting is done at least yearly throughout the pilot's career.

A flight is like an arranged marriage. You don't choose the person who holds your fate. But you can refuse the arrangement. Board early. Meet the captain. See how you feel about the captain the airline has paired you with. If marriages were arranged with the degree of care that airlines take before turning a $100,000,000 airliner over to a pilot, maybe an arranged marriage would be an equally safe bet.

Anticipatory anxiety will end when you meet the captain. Count on it. Until then, use the 5-4-3-2-1 Exercise when you feel anxiety. You can lower your anticipatory anxiety more by reclaiming control. Give yourself the option to meet the captain and then decide. If you don't feel good about the captain, get off. Though this sounds impractical, I believe the captain will gain your full confidence every time. Even after you have boarded the plane, you are free to walk off the plane for any reason.

Anxiety about Panic

Don't let the anticipatory anxiety throw you off— it doesn't mean that you will fall apart on the plane.

The other main part of anticipatory anxiety is worry about how much anxiety you will experience during flight. High anxiety and panic are due to psychic equivalence. If you have completed six to eight sessions of the Strengthening Exercise, the amygdalae are reprogrammed to avoid releasing stress hormones that weaken reflective function and allow psychic equivalence to take place. Even though you may feel anxiety now, it is in no way an indication that you will not be protected when flying. When flying, protection from anxiety is provided in five ways.

1. Thought Redirection: Flying thoughts are directed not to another anxiety-producing thought but to a non-flying moment.

2. Thought Spacing: Redirecting each "what if" thought away from flying to something else extends the time between anxiety-producing thoughts so that anxiety can dissipate rather than accumulate.

3. Oxytocin Production: The Strengthening Exercise establishes links between flight and empathic connection. During flight, incoming data associated with empathic connection triggers the release of oxytocin, which inhibits the release of stress hormones.

4. Security Linking: The Strengthening Exercise establishes links between flight and emotional security. Thus, during flight, incoming data associated with security will not trigger the release of stress hormones.

5. Knowledge: Information about the safety systems and backup systems that make flying remarkably safe coupled with an understanding of the training pilots undergo can reduce anxiety about physical safety.

Since the amygdalae function at an unconscious level, there is no way to test amygdalae response to flying without taking a flight. This leads to anxiety about how well unconscious control will do its job, particularly after having relied on deliberate and conscious control. If concern persists, consider taking a short flight to test the effectiveness of Systematic Inhibition.

Anticipatory Anxiety That Becomes Panic

I was just going about my day and all of a sudden I was feeling heart palpitations about my flight.

Anticipatory panic can result when strategies to keep the flight out of mind suddenly fail. Blocking and distancing strategies can be used for years with no awareness that they are the only way you deal with feelings—until they let you down. Once blocking and distancing strategies fail, they cannot be reestablished unless bolstered by the use of alcohol, drugs, or other destructive behavior. There may appear to be no other option. Long-established use of these strategies can render a person clueless as to what reflective function is or how to use it. The only answer is a 180-degree turnaround. There are four elements:

- Let feelings in. Notice feelings at their lowest perceivable level.
- Disentangle them. When separated one from another, feelings are easier to manage.
- Put feelings accurately into words. Words allow feelings to be contained inside.

- Share what you feel with someone so you both can experience the feeling.

Anxiety That Confidence Will Tempt Fate

Every time I feel more relaxed about flying, my subconscious imposes on me that I just have to be scared. I feel that not being scared is abnormal for me.

It's interesting how fear of not being fearful develops. It begins with the first trauma in your life. Until your first trauma, you didn't know such a horrible thing could happen, since it happened unexpectedly, out of the blue. How can you go on when something unexpected could happen again? What can you do? You begin to expect it. By expecting it, you're sort of braced for it. You're anxious at every moment, expecting a bolt out of the blue. If nothing awful happens for a while, you may begin to believe that by expecting bad things to happen you're keeping them from happening. In some situations, being hypervigilant makes sense. For example, if a parent is sometimes violent, being hypervigilant may help the child know when he or she needs to avoid the parent. Fast-forward to adulthood. You learn more about what makes flying so amazingly safe. You learn about simulator training, backup systems, and so on. You realize, as your flight approaches, that you are not anxious. Will letting your guard down cause something awful to happen? Even as an informed adult, it's difficult to give up those childhood strategies learned as a protective device.

Anxiety about Greater Anxiety

If I have this much anxiety now, I'm afraid I'll have more on the flight!

When conscious efforts have failed to control flight anxiety, it's hard to believe unconscious control can work. This doubt leads to anticipatory anxiety. You worry that you'll have even worse feelings during the flight. But anticipatory anxiety and flight anxiety are different. Anxiety about a flight comes from a different source than anxiety during a flight.

To understand the difference, think of the amygdalae as having a front door and a back door. Sensory information enters the amygdalae through the front door: Your eyes, ears, and body sense what is going on around you. Imagination is different. Imagination is not from outside; it is produced inside. It's presented to the amygdalae not by your physical eye or any of your senses, but by your mind's eye—through the back door.

Information is raw data for the amygdalae to process and make a determination about. Imagination is fully formed imagery, the meaning of which is already determined. This makes a huge difference to the amygdalae. When the amygdalae process information, they determine whether what is going on around you is routine or non-routine. But when the amygdalae process information coming from the mind's eye, via the back door, they are not free to make that determination. If you've decided the information is threatening, the amygdalae have no choice: They must react by releasing stress hormones.

The anxiety you feel before a flight is caused by imaginative data you input to the amygdalae through the back door. During the flight, the amygdalae will be free to make their own determination. They will ignore what they have been trained to ignore. Regardless of how much anxiety you feel now, your amygdalae will, as they have been trained, respond to what actually goes on around you during the flight.

A more accurate test can be done if you plan ahead. Before you begin practicing the Strengthening Exercise, view some video of flight. (In-flight video can be viewed online at www.flightlevel350 .com and other sites.) Using a scale of zero to ten, note your anxiety level as you view the video. After doing six to eight sessions of the

Strengthening Exercise, using the same video, once again note your anxiety level.

Once you have completed six to eight sessions, even if you stumbled through, the Strengthening Exercise is ready to protect you during flight. There is nothing more you need to do until you board the plane and meet the captain. It has been my experience that no one panics once they have learned and properly practiced the Strengthening Exercise.

Anxiety When Forecasting Feelings

I just feel as though I'm going to get on the plane and freak out. I feel like I will start yelling, "Let me out!" That's the part that worries me the most, my mind flipping out.

Trying to imagine what you will feel about an upcoming flight is just another attempt to maintain control. Will your feelings be tolerable? Or, will the feelings be too much to bear? You know you can't change your mind about the flight once it takes off, so you try to forecast your feelings. Anxiety develops because when you try to imagine what you will feel, you inevitably overestimate the distress that will be experienced during the flight. Why?

First, in an actual flight, concerns are spread out over the entire length of the flight. But when forecasting feelings, the concerns are concentrated into a moment of anticipation. This causes forecast feelings to be grossly exaggerated.

Second, you have only the distress of past flights on which to base expectations. That causes you to overestimate.

Third, you've never flown with the powerful protective effect of the Strengthening Exercise. Research has shown that nothing is as emotionally potent as the human face. Facial expression of empathic attunement inhibits the amygdalae. Empathic attunement, when linked to specific moments of the flight experience, overrides other factors in determining amygdalae response.

When you feel anticipatory anxiety, ask yourself if you're forecasting your feelings. If so, take a 5-4-3-2-1 Exercise break. If thoughts keep pestering you, try something invented by therapist Jerilyn Ross: Wear a rubber band on your wrist. The moment you notice an anticipatory anxiety thought, snap the rubber band hard. After a few times, anticipation of the sting may help inhibit anticipation of your flight.

Anxiety about Having No Way Out

When the door closes, I'm trapped. There's no way out. There are so many things that can go wrong with the plane. If anything goes wrong, if one little screw comes loose, we're dead.

During the dolphin show at the aquarium in Mystic, Connecticut, the trainer explains that it's easy to get dolphins to jump over a stick but difficult to get them to jump through a hula hoop. Dolphins are air-breathing mammals. They can't swim backward. If encircled by a space too tight to turn around in, a dolphin can drown. The dolphin's brain is genetically wired to avoid being encircled. To jump through the hoop, the dolphin has to develop enough trust in the trainer to overcome instinctive fear.

We humans look at the door of a plane the same way dolphins look at a hula hoop—a life-threatening trap. So why don't the pilots feel that way? Pilots know there are many ways out that you can't see and may not even know about: engineering ways out. For everything needed on the plane, there is a primary system, a standby system, a backup system, and an emergency system. Since you can't see these ways out with your eye, use your "mind's eye." Imagine the door of the plane. Pretend that you go over to the door and do a bit of graffiti with a marker, writing, "primary, standby, backup, and emergency." If a primary system fails, it automatically switches to the standby. If the standby doesn't restore proper operation, the pilots get out the manual and use a checklist to switch to the backup.

And, if needed, they can switch to an even more basic system, the emergency system. The engineering ways out are in the manual. We have been flying airplanes for more than a hundred years. Whenever there's been an accident, the cause has been determined, and a way out of that problem has been developed. To run out of ways out, we would have to run into something that hasn't happened in a hundred years. That's why accidents are so incredibly rare. It's because we have engineering ways out.

Anxiety That Anxiety Will Continue

I know how terrible anticipatory anxiety can be. I almost didn't get on the plane. However, as soon as I started walking toward the plane, calm came over me and I started to relax. Sometimes it takes getting on the plane for everything you've learned to kick in!

Anticipatory anxiety ends when the biggest thing causing anticipatory anxiety ends—anxiety about turning over control to another person. We're wired up at birth to trust. Distrust is something we learn; perhaps overlearn. Mark Twain wrote, "We should be careful to get out of an experience only the wisdom that is in it—and stop there; lest we be like the cat that sits down on a hot stove-lid. She will never sit down on a hot stove-lid again—and that is well; but also she will never sit down on a cold one any more."

Just as the dolphin needs trust in the trainer to counter its fear of the hula hoop, you need trust in the captain to counter your fear of giving up control and allowing the door to close you inside. Board early. Meet the captain. When you do, issues of trust and control are resolved. Since the captain cannot get the cockpit on the ground safely without getting the cabin on the ground safely, all you need to know is that the captain is alert, intelligent, and confident. Expect anticipatory anxiety to peak as you wait in the boarding area. You will be tempted to bail out. Don't. If you do, though you may feel a few moments of relief, that relief will be replaced with disappointment and dissatisfaction with yourself. Push through the feelings and meet the captain. As soon as you meet the captain, anticipatory anxiety will disappear. You will find the anxiety is replaced—not with the shame of bailing out—but with satisfaction and pride.

Anxiety When "Going into Your Own Future"

One thing that I do have a hard time getting over is that it could be my flight is the one that crashes. Since there are no guarantees, it's hard for me to get past that feeling. If I knew that I would get there safely, it would be so much easier for me! Do you have any suggestions?

Anxiety can lead you to imagine what a future flight will be like. Trying to imagine the flight will not help. No matter how many times you attempt to peer into the future, your imagination will not accurately reveal the future to you. It might seem harmless to use your imagination like this, but it quickly brings trouble. Before you know it, you can lose track that the future you picture is imaginary. Initially, it's no problem. You know the things you picture are imaginary. But, if you continue, the pictures you imagine become memorized. Once memorized, the images come to mind unbidden. They no longer seem like imagination. They take on a life of their own. It becomes hard to keep them out of the mind. Finally, they feel like something that's really going to happen. Don't go into your own future. Don't allow imagination of what might happen become memorized. Be vigilant. Notice it the moment you start doing it. Don't cause yourself higher and higher levels of anxiety. Immediately use the 5-4-3-2-1 Exercise to burn off the stress hormones and return to balanced thinking.

Anxiety about Making the Right Decision

I made a reservation with them because they're the only airline with a non-stop flight. But then I started thinking that their planes are old. So

I called and made a reservation on an airline that has newer planes. But then I started thinking about how that meant taking two flights. And I wondered which was more dangerous, one flight on an older plane or two flights on a newer plane. So I decided to go back to the first airline. But the prices had changed. Now I don't know what to do. I think I want to take the non-stop flight, but I don't want to spend more money. I shouldn't have changed my mind in the first place and now I'm really angry at myself.

Gather the best travel information you can get, make your decision based on that, and commit to it. If you've been thorough and done your best to make a sensible decision, no further thinking can improve upon it. Secure orientation is associated with the best decision that can be made with the information at hand. Insecure orientation is associated with absolute categories such as "right" and "wrong," or "safe" and "unsafe." Oversimplified categorical thinking creates an emotional trap because anything not absolutely safe is deemed unsafe. Categorical thinking causes anxiety because it's impossible to know in advance that the "right" decision has been made. Give yourself a break from categorical thinking. Recognize you've made the best decision you can with the information at hand. Once the decision is made, you can spend the time before the flight in one of two places: the frying pan or the fire.

- The Frying Pan: anxiety that you don't know the outcome. Accept not knowing. It is impossible to know in advance. The outcome does not determine what the right decision is. Even if things don't turn out right, if your decision was made based on the best information you had at the time, you made the best decision.
- The Fire: belief that you do know the outcome. If anxiety forces you to repeatedly imagine disaster, your imagination will become memorized. Psychic equivalence takes place in which the disastrous outcome is experienced as inevitable.

The first condition, frying pan anxiety, is difficult. But failure to accept anxiety produces the far more difficult second condition, psychic equivalence, which sends the message that disaster is certain.

The skipper of an ocean racing yacht told his crew, "I'll listen to anything anyone has to say—once!" He wanted everyone's input. It would be fully considered. But once fully considered, he would hear nothing more of it. This is how a good executive works and how your Executive Function needs to work. It needs to give full consideration to any non-routine matter brought to its attention—once.

Worry, if done masterfully, is good strategy. Worry, if done continuously, is useless.

A client, never free of anxiety due to childhood trauma, was obsessed with the idea that her flight was doomed. She'd worried for weeks about hijackers and bombs. In the boarding area, she saw two men whispering. She said to her boyfriend, "They're the hijackers." Her boyfriend summoned a security supervisor who explained to her, "It's okay. They're a gay couple." Instead of saying, "Oh, I see," she replied, "Good cover!" Instead of accepting the explanation, she used it to reinforce her preconception. When they were onboard, she saw a man dialing his cell phone. She said to her boyfriend, "He's programming the bomb!" A flight attendant was called and asked the man to put away his cell phone. My client then said, "It's too late; he already has it programmed!"

Normally, when there's anxiety, we search for the cause of the anxiety so we may find a way to relieve it. But when anxiety is caused by something in the past, placing its cause in the present only increases the distress. Knowing this woman's history, I told her, "Look, you have generalized anxiety. You have it for a reason and you're never going to get away from a certain basic level of it. Whenever you attempt to get rid of it, you try to figure out what's causing it. But that doesn't work because things from years ago have caused your anxiety. By identifying something going on now as the cause of your anxiety, and then by fleshing it out, all you do is increase the intensity of feelings you don't want." I told her how, on a trip to Africa, I fell asleep on the beach and got terribly sunburned. The next day my skin itched so badly, despite all my willpower, I couldn't keep my hands off it. Every time I touched it, it got worse. Finally, I took off all my clothes so nothing touched my skin and—literally—sat on my hands until the itch calmed down enough that I could resist touching it. I asked my client to accept, on her next flight, a certain amount of anxiety as normal for her, and to "sit on her hands" to keep it from getting worse. She did much better.

Use the 5-4-3-2-1 Exercise to dispose of built-up stress hormones. If you have generalized anxiety, this will return you to your basic anxiety level. Note this level. Rate it on a scale of zero to ten. Accept this level as basic. Acceptance helps you avoid the problems that develop when you attempt to rid yourself of basic anxiety. Give your concerns one full and complete hearing. Make the hearing thorough so that further consideration is not called for.

Anxiety about Feelings of Abandonment

I know we all have to die. It's just that dying in an airplane is the worst way in the world to die.

The emotions experienced of being abandoned, even in very early childhood, are indelible. Years later, a trigger can toss us back to those feelings of being alone and helpless. But onboard, you have someone with you inside, built up by the Strengthening Exercise; and you have someone with you outside, the captain, who is "in the same boat" with you and knows how to get both of you safely to your destination. If you wish, you can have someone with you on the ground, too. Ask someone you trust to track your flight from the ground by computer. Knowing you are in someone's thoughts and feelings helps keep you from feeling alone.

How Reframing Can Reduce Anticipatory Anxiety

As the plane flies, the imagined event takes place in reality. Imagination of what your flight might be like is replaced by the reality of how your flight actually is. And, since the Strengthening Exercise has established protective links between the reality of flight and a moment that causes you to produce oxytocin (which shuts down the fear system), the flight is fine.

But, if you don't get to that point, if you don't get on the plane, you don't find out that it will be fine. So what can we do about anticipatory anxiety? One promising possibility is termed "reframing." During reframing, you craft a comprehensive set of responses to your fears to weaken the effect of the troublesome thought.

For example, suppose the thought is, "What if there is a terrorist on the plane?" One reframe is, "What if there is a terrorist off the plane? Where are terrorists most likely to be? On your plane or somewhere else? Obviously, the most likely place for a terrorist is somewhere else. That being the case, you don't want to be somewhere else; you want to be on the plane where there is no terrorist."

Now, does that make sense? It is really a play on words that involves messy logic. Nevertheless, as the mind starts to untangle the logic, it gets mired down and the emotional impact of the original thought tends to weaken. Reframing was invented by Virginia Satir and Milton Erickson. My first exposure to reframing was in a workshop in which participants were invited to think of something they didn't like and put it into a statement. One statement offered was, "I don't like being in New York because the air is so bad." The person conducting the workshop responded with, "New York has such an air about it." The meanings of the word "air" in the two statements are so different that the mind has trouble holding onto the meanings of both statements at the same time. As the mind shuttles between the two meanings, the impact of the negative statement is lessened.

So if you think, "What if there is turbulence?" A reframe would be, "The best place to be when there is turbulence is in the plane, because the wall of the plane keeps the turbulent air from coming inside." This reframe causes confusion with mental sleight of hand. It shifts the person's focus on the plane as the threat to the implication that the turbulent air is a threat and the plane is protective. Again, the confusion defuses the original thought. A reframe that could be used during a period of turbulence is to think of the path from where you are to your destination as containing a specific number of bumps. Though you don't know how many there are, the number of bumps is already established by Mother Nature. So, instead of hating it when you feel the plane bump, count them. Each one you count proves the plane is getting that much closer to its airport for landing. Each bump gets you closer to where you want to be.

"What if I have a panic attack?" A reframe might be, "Attack panic. Get out your sword and charge at it." The person imagines charging forward with a drawn sword, and then has trouble finding anything to imagine sticking the sword into. As a result, when the target can't be found, even in imagination, the threat—at least for the moment—is burst like a bubble.

"When the door closes, I feel trapped." A reframe might be, when you are on the plane, think of five places you are glad you are not. Though being on the plane is not your ideal place to be, it is a lot better than being at the North Pole without a parka, up to your chin in quicksand, in the ocean where you see lots of shark fins sticking up, in an elevator falling from the top of the Empire State Building, or being held up at gunpoint on the street. But don't use mine; come up with your own. Coming up with your own makes this particular reframe useful.

"I'm so anxious about my flight. What if it is really awful?" Or, "What if the flight is really turbulent?" A reframe may be, "My previous flight was a good one, so I figured it wasn't the Strengthening Exercise working; it was just that the flight was an easy one. I need to have a challenging flight this time to positively prove the Strengthening Exercise will work every time, no matter what. That way I'll know, and I will never have to have this fear ever again."

Reframing is a mind game, yes, but one that can have a significant effect on the power of thoughts to cause persistent distress.

The Abstract Point of No Return (APNR): Making It Your Choice

I make a commitment that I'll be on the plane no matter what. So far it's been successful beyond my wildest dreams.

Flying, like anything the amygdalae recognize as non-routine, will release stress hormones to activate Executive Function. Whenever there is a stress hormone release, it's Executive Function's job to make an assessment and to determine what—if any—action is needed. The next step is commitment. Commitment ends stress hormone release.

Risk is ever-present when driving. Yet, most anxious fliers do not feel anxious when their own hands are on the wheel. This leads to the misconception that being in control inhibits anxiety. It is not control, but commitment, that moderates anxiety. Your inner CEO can assess the situation and build a plan of action to take, but it isn't until commitment to the course of action—or inaction—that a signal is sent to the amygdalae to discontinue the release of stress hormones. Without commitment, Amy will keep pushing that intercom. Once you do your ABCs, relief will come.

Since commitment resolves anxiety, what steps can resolve anticipatory anxiety through commitment? First, imagine the extreme possibilities: the best a flight could be, and the worst a flight could be. First, the worst: At check-in, hundreds of people are in line ahead of you. Security mistakes you for someone on a list of suspicious characters. The plane is delayed for hours, first at the terminal, and then on the taxiway. Finally, you take off and climb up to cruise altitude. Though, as a pilot, I can't imagine how it would happen, I'm sure you can imagine the plane plunging. You endure the most extreme terror, knowing you are doomed, with people screaming, and things flying around, and then . . . it's over. You're dead. Then what? Nothing. Notice that it is not being dead that is so awful—it's getting dead, a state of terror before dying.

Most fearful fliers wish a doctor could "knock them out" before the flight and wake them when it's over. Being "knocked out" has no effect on whether or not the plane crashes. It only means that a plane crash doesn't cause you terror. As Woody Allen said, "It's not that I'm afraid of dying. I just don't want to be there when it happens." Notice that on the worst flight possible, once you're dead, you're—sort of—safe, emotionally.

Now, imagine also the best flight possible. There's no line at check-in. You go through security without a hitch. At the boarding area, they move you up to first class. You're seated next to your favorite movie star, who finds you fascinating and spends the flight talking with you. The food and wine are superb. The air is perfectly smooth. When you land, your luggage is the first off the belt. Your new friend wants to take you out for the evening. Realistic? Of course not. But neither flight is. Your flight will be neither the worst nor the best, but somewhere in between.

On your flight, once the door closes, physical escape becomes impossible. But you can control whether or not you play the victim or the agent of the situation. Think of this: Imagine you're in a room with a group of people where there's a huge sheet of steel and a sledgehammer. Someone picks up the sledgehammer and slams it into the sheet of steel. The noise frazzles everyone in the room—except the one swinging the sledgehammer. There's a huge difference between a noise caused by someone else and a noise you yourself cause. When someone else causes an awful noise, you are the victim of what happens. When you cause the noise, you're the agent of what happens.

Instead of being a victim, forced past the point of no return when "they" close the door, you can be the agent of what happens. Of course, that doesn't mean closing the door yourself; that's someone else's role. Your role—if you are to avoid being the victim—has three parts.

1. Recognize that the door is going to be closed.

2. Decide which side of the door you're going to be on when it is closed.

3. Commit to your decision, *no matter what—even if it kills you.*

A person with good Executive Function knows—because of commitment—that he or she will be on the plane when the door closes. But for a person with impaired Executive Function, commitment is difficult. Whether the chance of fatality is one in a thousand, one in a million, or one in a billion, he or she is unprepared to commit unless the desired result is certain.

It might seem that balking at a commitment that could (though rarely) be fatal is self-preservation. But excessive need for certainty is self-destructive. On the one hand, it can lead to indecisiveness. Since the results of any course of action are rarely certain, the person who requires certainty avoids commitment. On the other hand, the need for certainty can lead to ineffective decisions based on magical thinking, false guarantees, superstition, or illusion of control. It is an illusion, for example, to believe that control of a car's steering wheel, accelerator pedal, and brake pedal makes safe arrival certain.

Noted psychiatrist James Masterson, M.D. said that a person with impaired Executive Function is like a sailor who, instead of steering his boat, allows the wind and tide to determine where it goes. When ending up someplace he doesn't want to be, he regards himself as the victim of circumstances.

If you commit to being inside when the door is closed, then you are the agent—not the victim—of the situation. The same is true if you commit to being outside when the door is closed; you are the author in that situation as well. But if you cannot commit at all, you're like the sailor who allows prevailing conditions to determine where you end up: if you're on the plane when the door closes, you could feel victimized by being trapped; if you're not on the plane when the door closes, you may feel victimized that you can no longer get on.

ABCs & APNR

Assess. Is the flight an opportunity, irrelevant, or a risk? It is an opportunity to do something you want or need to do? The risk of flying is less than the risk of staying home; the flight exposes you to considerably less risk than routine driving.

Build a plan. You have considered the best and worst flights possible. Good Executive Function rejects those extremely unlikely possibilities and builds a plan of action based on what is most likely. Without question, the most likely result is safe arrival at your destination.

Commit. Instead of waiting and finding out which side prevailing conditions place you on when the door closes, determine now where you will be.

Sitting on a fence isn't comfortable. The only way you can eliminate anxiety is by making a commitment—and it doesn't matter what that commitment is. You can commit to being outside when the door closes, you can commit to never fly again, or you can commit to being on the inside when the door closes. If the latter, not only will you be rid of anxiety, you will have the self-satisfaction of setting a course, maintaining it, and arriving at your desired destination. There is great satisfaction in being where you want to be.

If you want that satisfaction, mentally advance to the point of no return from the present moment to a time in the future. Establish once and for all your placement on one side of the door or the other. Make the commitment absolute: Absolute commitment means it's just as certain where you will be when the door is closed as if the event had already taken place.

Thinking needs to shift from "what if" your flight is the one plane in twenty million that crashes to "even if" yours might be the one that crashes, you are making the commitment anyway. Commitment requires a shift from thinking "what if I panic" to I'm flying "even if I panic." In other words, you are following through with your plan even though the final result might be a crash or a panic attack. It means commitment no matter what, even if it kills you. Confront what happens in one flight in several million and commit anyway. Allow nothing to stop you from being on the side of the door you have committed to being on when it closes. Take it to the bank. Carve it in stone. It's a done deal. When commitment is absolute, Executive Function signals the amygdalae to stop the release of stress hormones. Anxiety disappears.

As the flight gets closer, if commitment lapses, anxiety will return. As you attempt to make the commitment again, remember this paradox: If you commit primarily to get relief, it may not work. Commitment needs to be done primarily for self-satisfaction, and only secondarily to escape anxiety. Search in advance for the hidden strategies that would let you sneak out of the commitment such as, "Yes, I'll do it no matter what, but if I don't sleep well the night before, then I don't know." Or, "The weather doesn't look good." Or, "There was a crash on the news." Or, "If I don't feel well." Or, "If I don't feel like I can do it."

It is, I think, worth knowing how the Abstract Point of No Return was discovered. Some years ago, I bought a race car, a

Formula 3 Lola. It weighed 880 pounds. The engine was behind the driver. There was nothing in front of the driver but some tubing and a fiberglass shell. When I first saw how little protection there was for the driver, it gave me pause. The cockpit was form-fitted to my body. Sliding into the cockpit feet first was like slipping fingers into a glove. Once in, it wasn't easy to get out. As I worked my body into the cockpit, I felt physically committed to the car and what I was planning to do with it. At the same time, the thought went through my mind, "You shouldn't be doing this."

Notice the word "you." All of us have multiple facets of self. This statement was coming from a protective, hesitant facet of myself; it was directed toward a more adventurous and bolder facet of myself. I felt anxious as these two parts struggled to be dominant. Suddenly, the conflict disappeared. Though what happened did not involve words, if there had been words, they would have gone something like this: "Well, you shouldn't be doing this, but I can see you are committed, and nothing is going to change your mind. So if I tell you that you shouldn't be doing this when you're going around a curve at ninety mph, we're both going to get killed. Though I object to what you're doing, I'm going to disappear." At that juncture, that facet of myself vanished and a state of total calm came over me. The matter was resolved. I was committed. I was going to do it no matter what, even if it killed me.

In his book *The Right Stuff*, Tom Wolfe wrote about test pilots and astronauts who were able to face formidable risks and maintain good Executive Function. The right stuff is the ability to determine a course of action and commit to it, even in the face of significant risk. One of the test pilots Wolfe wrote about was Air Force Captain Charles "Chuck" Yeager, who made the first supersonic flight on October 14, 1947, in the Bell X-1. While variations of the X-1 continued to explore supersonic flight, the Air Force contracted with North American Aviation to develop a supersonic fighter. This plane, the F-100, went into production in 1953. Since the technology of supersonic flight was still in its infancy, the plane had major design deficiencies. As a result, during the twenty years the F-100 was flown by the USAF, one out of three crashed. I clearly recall walking toward my F-100, parachute over one shoulder and helmet in hand, knowing it was not safe. But knowing I was going to do it, no matter what, the closest thing to anxiety was a feeling of determination to stay keenly focused.

* * *

The French philosopher Descartes famously wrote, "I think, therefore I am." The anxious flier could say, "I consider, therefore I am anxious." Outcomes are often uncertain. Consideration, short of commitment, sustains anxiety. In such cases, the only certainty available is that which can be produced by commitment. After prospective courses of action—or inaction—are assessed, reality-based living calls for decision and commitment even though safety is not absolute. Though commitment can be based on an illusion of certainty, pretending properly belongs to childhood, where it's done to prepare for adult reality-based living. When committed to fly no matter what, Executive Function signals the amygdalae to discontinue stress hormone release.

"I am committed, therefore calm." Such is the power of commitment to limit anxiety. The purpose of this book is not to turn the reader into a test pilot or astronaut, but to develop enough of the right stuff to embrace living without certainty, and to commit to the extraordinarily small risk of flying on a modern jetliner.

CHAPTER 23

Ten Supportive Strategies

The Strengthening Exercise teaches the amygdalae to ignore specific non-routine situations detected by, for example, the eye. But imagination presented to the amygdalae by the mind's eye is different; the amygdalae have no choice but to release stress hormones when the anxious flier imagines something is threatening. This is where supportive strategies based on Cognitive Behavioral Therapy (CBT) play a role. The following strategies support good Executive Function. They will help you avoid thinking that leads to unnecessary emotional distress, which is the mental equivalent of shooting one's self in the foot.

Strategy 1—Neutralize Memorized Imagination

It's a given that an anxious flier will entertain the possibility of crashing whenever a flight is coming up. Initially, of course, such thoughts are recognized as imagination because they are brought to mind intentionally. But if imagination of crashing is repeatedly brought to mind, eventually it becomes memorized. It then comes to mind unintentionally and masquerades as fact. When memorized imagination of crashing shows up in a dream, it seems like an omen.

Imagination made factual by memorization not only sets the stage for psychic equivalence during the flight, it causes extreme anxiety before the flight. It can make a person "just know" that if he or she gets on the plane, it will crash. Like the dog chasing its tail because it doesn't know it's its own, anxious fliers suffer because they don't know the omen is their own creation. If a dog figures out the tail is its own, it ends the chase. But, psychic equivalence is so powerful that fearful fliers who are told the "tale" is their own creation still chase it.

Obviously, being decisive, as discussed in the previous chapter, heads off the memorization problem. But if the damage is done, creating and memorizing versions of the flight that compete with the existing memorized imagination can neutralize the memorized disaster. Use the best and worst possible flight scenarios from the previous chapter. Vividly imagine each of them. Then, make up a third scenario, a flight somewhere in the middle. Vividly imagine every detail of it. A sense of the disaster omen will remain because your repeated imagination of it has become memorized. But by repeatedly imagining the worst flight, the best flight, and the middle flight, they, too, will be memorized. When multiple versions of your upcoming flight have been carved into memory, psychic equivalence breaks apart.

Strategy 2—Shift from "What If" to "What Is"

No one would—or could—voluntarily become a schizophrenic, unable to distinguish between imagination and reality. Yet, when you repeatedly imagine "what if" this and "what if" that, you damage your mental ability to experience reality. Increase your ability to experience reality through the practice of experiencing "what is." Focus on what is real—not imaginary—right where you are, at this moment in time and no other. Though it's useful to use one's imagination to plan ahead, it is also useful to develop your ability to experience "what is" so that, when enough planning has been done, there is a return to the richest moment there is: The one you are living right now.

Strategy 3—Be Your Own Reassuring Expert

If you went to a movie about a doomed airliner with a pilot, while you sat on the edge of your seat scared to death, he or she would probably fall asleep bored to death. The pilot's imagination about aviation is limited by the reality of years of experiencing flight as it really is. Since your imagination is not limited by experience, you need to give it some limits by becoming a mini-expert on how flying works. By becoming a mini-expert on flying, you can lecture yourself when you begin to imagine things that are far-fetched. You, as a mini-expert, can reassure yourself about what is going on.

Try going back and forth between playing the role of anxious flier, asking "What's that?" and pretending you are an expert answering the question. If you don't have an answer, don't let that stop you. Make something up! The very act of making something up keeps you from locking onto a single reality that might lead to psychic equivalence. Re-read Part Two to become more informed about how flying works.

Strategy 4—Avoid Media Presentations of Flight Disasters

Avoid television programs about flight disasters. If you do view one, do not accept the presentation as fact. Though these shows may appear to present accurate information, they distort facts to enhance entertainment value. They leave out information that the problem has been corrected, for to do so would render the program out of date.

News about flight disasters is rarely accurate. Reporters often present speculation, sometimes by so-called experts, as fact. In particular, avoid imagining what people on a flight must have felt. Speculation about what people felt is based on your own worst fears. It leads you to tie the very worst experience you can imagine to the event. Since the event happened, you easily fall into the trap of believing the worst experience you can imagine also happened. This is highly—and unnecessarily—traumatizing.

After 9/11, I worked with clients who viewed the tragedy on television. I also worked with some clients who were in the World Trade Center when it was attacked. Clients who viewed television and imagined what people in the buildings were experiencing were far more traumatized than clients who were actually in the buildings. Clients in the buildings, rather than engaging in imagination, were focused on finding a way out. All were successfully treated and returned to flying without distress. Those traumatized by imagining what people felt were much more difficult to treat.

Strategy 5—Resolve to Keep Reflective Function Active

When anxiety arises, determined effort is required to construct an accurate mental representation inside the mind of what exists outside the mind.

Pilots are trained to question everything they do. When one pilot makes a statement about the position of a switch, the other pilot must cross-check to make sure the statement is correct. In addition to cross-checks by another pilot, a good pilot constantly questions himself or herself. Do what pilots are trained to do. Do not accept what you have in mind as correct. Question yourself. Cross-check: Talk to your seat mate. Compare your version of reality with that of others.

Strategy 6—Maintain Reflective Function to Avoid Target Fixation

In training, fighter pilots learn to shoot the plane's guns. They shoot at a 20 foot by 20 foot sheet of canvas suspended vertically from poles in the ground. Approaching the target in a shallow dive, the pilot must fire at the target, then pull up before reaching a "foul line," marked on the ground 1,600 feet back from the target. There have been instances of "target fixation": Focusing only on the target, the fighter pilot stopped reflecting on the overall situation and "forgot" about pulling up before reaching the foul line. So it wasn't only the bullets that hit the target—the plane hit the target, too! The pilot can avoid target fixation only by keeping all the elements of the task actively in mind.

As a passenger, target fixation may mean focusing on being 30,000 feet above the ground with nothing under you (nothing you can see, that is) instead of reflecting that the plane is secure in gelatin-like air. Or target fixation may mean focusing on something that could break and cause disaster, instead of remembering that if one element breaks, standby, backup, and emergency elements take over to guarantee uninterrupted service.

When emotions arise, stress hormones push reflective function aside and move you toward target fixation. You can maintain active awareness of your thoughts and feelings by writing them down, or by keeping a conversation going with another person not only about your thoughts and feelings but also—and this is important—the other person's thoughts and feelings about the same situation, which may be quite different.

Strategy 7—Anchor Your Imagination to Fact

Every day, for a full week before your flight, track the flight you will be taking on a computer. Several websites are available. Just search the term "airline flight tracking." As it takes off, know that in one week you will be taking off just as the flight you are tracking is taking off. As it cruises, you will know that in one week you will be cruising at the same spot. When it lands, know that in one week you will be landing where this flight is landing. Seeing your flight operate routinely day in and day out will help you anchor to reality, rather than what you imagine.

Strategy 8—Relaxation Techniques: The 5-4-3-2-1 Exercise and Other Techniques

The 5-4-3-2-1 Exercise is nothing more than a focusing exercise to fully occupy your mind, allowing stress hormones to burn off. It's a great backup during flight and works for anticipatory anxiety as well. Remember, stress hormones can cause your reflective function to shut down; when that happens, quality control of thinking is lost, and your CEO becomes ineffective. Because the 5-4-3-2-1 Exercise requires intense concentration on non-threatening things, the stress hormones are used up without being replaced, helping your CEO get it together again.

Another technique is "square breathing." To perform "square breathing," inhale for a count of four. Hold your breath for a count of four. Exhale for a count of four. Hold the exhale for a count of four. Repeat. You may find that square breathing allows you to resume your activities with a sense of balanced attention and mental poise.

Another technique, one that helps you hold your focus, involves maintaining slight tension in the diaphragm. Using a pencil or pen, carefully draw the straightest line you can on a sheet of paper. Did you hold your breath while drawing it? If you don't know, try it again and see if you instinctively held your breath when concentrating. Try drawing a straight line first holding your breath, then while breathing normally. Which line is straighter? You may find that slight tension in the diaphragm helps you concentrate. Concentrating on something that is non-threatening can reduce anxiety, so if a slight tension in the diaphragm helps you to concentrate, there are simple techniques to aid you in doing so. One way is to breathe through a drinking straw. Another is to breathe through pursed lips. Experiment to see if these techniques are helpful to produce calming results.

Strategy 9—Have Someone Track Your Flight

Insecure relationships early in life may have led you to feel that when you're out of sight, you're out of mind. Ask someone you trust to track your flight on his or her computer. Give them information about an Internet flight-tracking site and your flight itinerary.

Strategy 10—Keep a Journal

Another strategy for maintaining connection is recording a running commentary of your flight experience. In advance, ask a friend if they will read your in-flight journal. Write down what you experience moment by moment during the flight, aware that, very shortly, your friend will be reading and sharing your experience. Focus on accurate expression. When an emotion is put accurately into words, some of its intensity is stripped away. For example, rather than writing, "I'm feeling nervous," you might write, "My heart is beating too fast and there are beads of perspiration on my upper lip and forehead. I keep taking huge gulps of air." You will discover that writing down your emotions as they are experienced helps move feelings outside, reducing buildup inside.

• • •

Different people need different strategies. When they actually try out a strategy, anxious fliers are sometimes surprised at what works and what doesn't work. Try each of them. See which work best for you.

As described in this book, inhibiting the release of stress hormones is a practical and effective way to protect the operation of Executive Function and allow it to better regulate emotion when flying or when facing other challenges.

Properly regulated, arousal serves us well. Arousal brings potentially important issues to mind. Like the skipper of the ocean racing yacht, give the issue your full consideration, Then, having done so, make a commitment to act on the matter or to drop the matter. Upon this commitment, a signal is sent to the amygdalae to stop the release of stress hormone, thereby regulating anxiety.

Remember: You are smarter than your amygdalae. As an airline passenger, when stress hormones arise, it is nothing more than a call for your Executive Function to assess some situation your amygdalae regard as non-routine. For a passenger, a number of things will happen on any flight that the amygdalae regard as non-routine. Though control of the flight is not in your hands, control is in the hands of an experienced expert who maintains continuous Executive Function. Your job is to dismiss each non-routine alert as a false alarm. The pilot's commitment is to get you to your destination safely. The commitment I am inviting you to make is to experience the flight as it is, adding nothing, and subtracting nothing.

Acknowledgments

Much of what is presented in this book was developed during studies with James F. Masterson, M.D., Ralph Klein, M.D., Judith Pearson, Ph.D., authorities on psychological theory and clinical practice, and with Allan Schore, Ph.D., whose work has increased our understanding of the regulation of emotion. Mentalization concepts developed by Peter Fonagy and associates are essential to understanding the psychodynamics of flight phobia. Strengthening Exercise improvements were made possible due to Social Engagement System research by Stephen W. Porges, Ph.D.

I am grateful for the generous support of two talented aviation experts, David Blatner, author of *The Flying Book*, and airline pilot Patrick Smith, author of *Ask The Pilot* and *Cockpit Confidential,* who read the manuscript and offered advice.

Suzi Tucker, Mary Kay Culpepper, Tami Riggle, and Walter Figiel were of special help with editing and revision. The work Elaine Partnow did to help refine, edit, and finalize the manuscript was invaluable.

Mentors Cynthia P. Deutsch, Ph.D., Elaine Rapp, ATR, and Glen Boles, Ph.D., encouraged the professional studies that made this book possible.

The book took shape during long discussions with my wife, Marie. Her insights into anxiety and her skill as an editor were invaluable.

Appendix A: Flight Checklist

An excellent strategy is to create various checklists for yourself, which help with reassurance and commitment.

Consideration Checklist
- List your options: to fly, to drive, to take the train, or to stay home.
- Organize each option as a set; list the desirable and the undesirable features of each option.
- List the best and the worst result that could happen with each option.
- List the best and the worst feelings that could happen with each option.
- Make a tentative commitment to the option that is in your best interest.

Tentative Commitment Checklist
- Are you willing to risk encountering every feeling?
- Are you willing to risk encountering every result?
- If so, consider yourself tentatively committed.

Absolute Commitment Checklist
- List your secret "ways out": What could occur that could melt your resolve? (Options might include not sleeping the night before, news of an accident, weather you may mistakenly think is risky, or worry about turbulence.)
- Are you doing this no matter what—even if it kills you?
- Is your commitment so absolute that being on that flight is as

certain as if you were already on board with the door closed?

- When you notice anxiety disappear, you have moved into the APNR (Abstract Point of No Return).
- Expect to have to repeat this. Even seemingly absolute commitment may vanish and need to be reestablished.

Non-Absolute Commitment Checklist

- Anticipatory anxiety comes from giving up control to a person with whom you have, as yet, no caring and responsive relationship.
- Anticipatory anxiety vanishes upon meeting, and becoming confident in, your captain.
- Your commitment to fly is tentative and is to be firmed up one way or the other only after boarding and meeting the captain.
- Your commitment is to board and to meet the captain—not to fly.

Day of Flight Checklist

- Wake up according to your plan. Tension? Do the 5-4-3-2-1 Exercise, if needed.
- Monitor continuously for first indications of tension. Use the 5-4-3-2-1 Exercise.
- Before leaving home, satisfy yourself that preparations are complete.
- Leave early to allow a leisurely drive. Notice scenery during drive.

Take with You Checklist

- Magazines, puzzles, computer game, copies of letter of introduction.

- Stay occupied visually with the real ("what is") rather than the imaginary ("what if").
- Paper and pen for writing down your feelings and listing everything that causes anxiety so you can add that thing (or things) to your next Strengthening Exercise practice session.
- A sticky note saying, "If I can read this, it is not yet time to worry about turbulence" to stick on the seat in front of you.
- Luggage, carry-on items, money, credit cards, identification, passport.
- Ticket or e-ticket information, phone numbers of people who will offer emotional support.
- A visual program or app to coach you through the flight. Available at www.fearofflying.com.

Airport Checklist
- Check in early. Check baggage. Carry on only essential items.
- Stop in one spot to experience the sounds, sights, and/or smells of the airport.
- Focus just on what you see. Identify each thing you see. Then view these as shapes, forms, and colors in an abstract painting.
- Focus just on what you hear. Identify each thing you hear. Then hear it as merely vibrations or music.
- Note a possible lowering of your tension level.

Boarding Checklist
- Ask gate agent if you can board early by presenting letter of introduction.
- Observe from boarding lounge window. Memorize what you see.
- Later, when in the passenger boarding bridge, which has no windows, use what you have memorized to picture what is outside.

- Notice whether the passenger boarding bridge is uphill, downhill, or level, so you will know whether to expect things to feel "off" when inside it.
- This is the worst part of the flight because everything is ahead of you and the Strengthening Exercise has not yet kicked in.
- Strategy: Tell yourself that if you "bail out," you will do it after meeting the captain if you don't feel better by then.
- Use the 5-4-3-2-1 Exercise.
- If the gate agent will not board you first, stand at the Jetway entry. Go on immediately at the start of the first boarding announcement.
- Touch the side of the plane. See how strong and firm it is.
- Find a flight attendant not directing passengers to their seats. Ask that your letter be taken to the captain while you wait there.

Seated in Cabin Checklist

- Monitor your experience. Scan your body for physical sensations and tension. If you notice any, use the 5-4-3-2-1 Exercise.
- Avoid psychically distancing. Focus on what you see, hear, smell, and physically feel.
- Feelings are not your enemy. Feelings result from your thoughts. Embrace your feelings. Check thoughts for accuracy. Demand evidence. No evidence? Drop the thought and notice what you see and hear.

Door Closure Checklist

- Prepare yourself for the door closing: visualize you—yourself—closing the door. Describe the scene to yourself. Write down your feelings.

Takeoff Checklist

- Accept that when the engine revs up, it will stir a response, just as a crescendo in music stirs a response.
- Accept acceleration. Acceleration presses you back in your seat, just as it does in your car when going from zero to 60, but in a plane it lasts twice as long because you're going from zero to 120, or so. The greater the acceleration, the more runway remains in reserve. Track the increase in speed by wiggling your toes more rapidly as speed increases. Watch outside and attempt to predict when the nose will rise. When the nose rises, you are past V-1. You have it made. Relax and listen for a thump followed by less wind noise as the gear doors close.
- Notice power reduction and corresponding lightness at noise abatement.
- Notice lightness when leveling off at an altitude.
- Notice power increase and heaviness as climb is reestablished.
- Accept that turns are required, and that dihedral keeps the plane from banking more than the pilots can cause through force on the controls.
- Flip through magazine ads, if needed, to maintain non-threatening visual activity.

Turbulence Checklist

- Turbulence is natural, routine, and not a problem for the plane.
- Think about the gelatin-like air.
- Post a note on the seat back in front of you: "If I can read this, it is not yet time to worry (about turbulence)."

Descent and Landing Checklist

- Accept that there may be stair stepping during descent.

- Accept that large power changes are required to change speed and accommodate gear and flap extension.
- A noise similar to a blender is associated with flap extension.
- An increase in wind noise—and possibly a thump—is associated with gear extension. You might hear a sound like water flowing through pipes, which is hydraulic fluid going through pipes to move the gear.
- Feel a vibration? The speed brakes are being used, the flap setting is being changed, or the flaps are at the maximum extension for landing.
- Landing guidance is electronic. The plane can be landed automatically.
- For everything needed on the plane, there is a main system, a standby system, a backup system, and an emergency system.
- Warning systems are active to warn the pilots of any possible mistake.
- You are safer on a modern jetliner than sleeping in your own bed at night.
- Enjoy your flight.

Appendix B: Sample Letters

Letter of Introduction to the Passenger Service Agent at the Boarding Area

Dear Passenger Service Agent:

I have been working on overcoming fear of flying by reading a book on the SOAR program by licensed therapist and airline captain Tom Bunn, LCSW. He says meeting the captain is the single most important thing we can do to deal with flight anxiety.

To facilitate this, please allow me to board either ahead of the other passengers, or in the first group of passengers.

Yours truly,
(Your name)

Letter of Introduction to the Captain

Dear Captain,

I have been working on overcoming fear of flying by reading a book on the SOAR program by licensed therapist and airline captain Tom Bunn, LCSW. He says meeting the captain is the single most important thing we can do to deal with flight anxiety.

If possible, I would like permission to visit with you briefly before the flight.

Yours truly,
(Your name)

Glossary of Terms

Aileron: An aerodynamic panel at the rear of the wing that regulates banking.

Amygdalae: Two complex almond-shaped brain structures responsible for the release of stress hormones.

Attunement: Communication by the imaginary or the physical matching of another's activity, body language, facial expression, and prosody.

Avoidant Attachment: Characterized by a pervasive pattern of social inhibition, feelings of inadequacy, extreme sensitivity to negative evaluation, and avoidance of social interaction.

Benzodiazepines: A class of sedative medication.

Cognitive Behavioral Therapy (CBT): An approach that seeks to reduce anxiety by replacing irrational or unrealistic thoughts with rational ones.

Dihedral: The upward angle at which the wing is attached to the fuselage.

Dysregulate: Impairment of a physiological regulatory mechanism.

Executive Function: High-level cognition; makes assessments, builds plans, and commits to actions.

Fuselage: The central body of the aircraft to which the wings and tail are attached.

Homeostasis: A state of internal equilibrium.

Orbitofrontal Cortex: Located in the frontal lobes, it is involved in the cognitive process of decision making.

Oxytocin: An anti-stress neuropeptide that inhibits stress hormone release.

Phobia: A disorder in which emotion is not well-regulated, causing fear of emotional overwhelm, or fear disproportional to risk.

Prefrontal Cortex: The region of the brain responsible for Executive Function; the CEO of the brain.

Processing: That which takes place below consciousness.

Psychic Equivalence: When what is in the mind or imagination and what is real are experienced as the same.

Reflective Function: The ability to critique and correct one's own mental processes, as well as to mentally simulate the mind of another person.

Satisfices: A term that suggests less-than-absolute certainty suffices and satisfies.

Synapses; Synaptic: The point at which electrical or chemical connections take place in the brain.

Venous Thromboembolism (VTE): The blocking of blood flow in a vein.

References

Carter, Sue, and Stephen W. Porges. "The Biochemistry of Love: An Oxytocin Hypothesis." *EMBO Reports* 14 (2012): 12-16.

Csikszentmihalyi, Mihaly. *Flow: The Psychology of Optimal Experience.* New York: Harper & Row, 1990.

Fonagy, Peter, György Gergely, Elliot L. Jurist, and Mary Target. *Affect Regulation, Mentalization, and the Development of the Self.* New York: Other Press, 2005, 8, 348.

Guntrip, Harry. *Psychoanalytic Theory, Therapy, and the Self.* New York: Basic Books, 1971, 157.

Hebb, Donald O. *The Organization of Behavior: A Neuropsychological Theory.* New York: Wiley, 1949.

Kagan, Jerome. *Galen's Prophecy: Temperament in Human Nature.* New York: Basic Books, 1994.

LeDoux, Joseph E. "Insights from Other Animals." In *The Human Amygdala,* edited by Paul J. Whalen and Elizabeth A. Phelps, 43–60. New York: Guilford Press, 2009.

Loewenstein, George, and Jennifer S. Lerner. "The Role of Affect in Decision Making." In *Handbook of Affective Science,* edited by Richard J. Davidson, Klaus R Scherer, and H. Hill Goldsmith, 642–91. Oxford: Oxford University Press, 2003.

Masterson, James. F. *From Borderline Adolescent to Functioning Adult.* New York: Brunner/Mazel, 1980.

Nagasawa, Miho, Takefumi Kikusui, Tatsushi Onaka, and Mitsuaki Ohta. "Dog's Gaze at Its Owner Increases Owner's Urinary Oxytocin during Social Interaction." *Hormones and Behavior* 55 (2009): 434–41.

Porges, Stephen W. "The Polyvagal Theory: Phylogenetic Substrates of a Social Nervous System." *International Journal of Psychophysiology* 42 (2001):123–46.

Porges, Stephen W., Jane A. Doussard-Roosevelt, and Ajit K. Maiti. "Vagal Tone and the Physiological Regulation of Emotion." *Monographs of the Society for Research in Child Development* 59 (1994): 164–86.

Schore, Allan. N. *Affect Regulation and the Origin of the Self.* Mahwah, NJ: Lawrence Erlbaum Associates, Inc., 1994, 75.

_____. "Attachment Trauma and the Developing Right Brain: Origins of Pathological Dissociation." In *Dissociation and the Dissociative Disorders: DSM-V and Beyond,* edited by Paul F. Dell and John A. O'Neil. New York: Routledge, 2009.

_____. "Relational Trauma and the Developing Right Brain: An Interface of Psychoanalytic Self Psychology and Neuroscience." *Annals of the New York Academy of Sciences* 1159 (2009): 200.

_____. Synopsis. *In The Impact of Early Life Trauma on Health and Disease: The Hidden Epidemic,* edited by Ruth A. Lanius, Eric Vermetten, and Clare Pain. New York: Cambridge University Press, 2010.

Sivak, Michael, and Michael J. Flannagan. "Flying and Driving after the September 11 Attacks." *American Scientist* 89 (2003): 6–8.

Sorce, James F., Robert N. Emde, Joseph J. Campos, and Mary D. Kinnert. "Maternal Emotional Signaling: Its Effect on the Visual Cliff Behavior of 1-Year-Olds." *Developmental Psychology* 21 (1985): 195–200.

Souter, David. "Text of Justice David Souter's Speech." *News.harvard.edu/ gazette* (2010). http://news.harvard.edu/gazette/story/2010/05/ text-of-justice-david-souters-speech/.

Sparks, Erin A., Joyce Ehrlinger, and Richard P. Eibach. "Failing to Commit:

Maximizers Avoid Commitment in a Way That Contributes to Reduced Satisfaction." *Personality and Individual Differences* 52 (2012): 72–77.

Twain, Mark. *Following the Equator.* Hartford, CT: The American Publishing Company, 1898, Chapter XI.

Uvnäs Moberg, Kerstin. *The Oxytocin Factor.* Cambridge, MA: Perseus Books, 2003, 66, 96.

Wilhelm, Frank H., and Walton. T. Roth. "Acute and Delayed Effects of Alprazolam on Flight Phobics during Exposure." *Behavior Research and Therapy* 35 (1997): 831–41.

Wolfe, Tom. *The Right Stuff.* New York: Farrar, Straus and Giroux, 1979.

Index

About the Author

Captain Tom Bunn, MSW, LCSW, has flown many different airplanes for the Air Force and commercial companies, has developed a safety device for the F-100, worked on the first Fear of Flying program at Pan Am, and founded SOAR in 1982. He has a master's degree from Fordham University and did postgraduate study at Gestalt Center of Long Island, the New York Training Institute for Neurologic Programming, and The Masterson Institute. He is a licensed therapist.

He has appeared on *Good Morning America* and *Live! With Regis and Kathie Lee.* News shows at CNN, FOX, and MSNBC have covered the SOAR program. The *New York Times,* the *Boston Globe,* the *Wall Street Journal, USA Today,* and other publications have published articles on SOAR. A *Newsweek* magazine cover story on phobia featured SOAR. The SOAR program has been offered as part of continuing education programs at CUNY in New York City and at Fairfield University in Connecticut.

He lives with his wife, Marie, in Easton, Connecticut. Visit him at www.fearofflying.com.